Voting Rights under Fire

The Continuing Struggle for People of Color

DONATHAN L. BROWN AND
MICHAEL L. CLEMONS

Racism in American Institutions
Brian D. Behnken, Series Editor

 PRAEGER™

An Imprint of ABC-CLIO, LLC
Santa Barbara, California • Denver, Colorado

Library of Congress Cataloging-in-Publication Data

Brown, Donathan L.
  Voting rights under fire : the continuing struggle for people of color / Donathan L. Brown and Michael L. Clemons.
       pages cm. — (Racism in american institutions)
  Includes bibliographical references and index.
  ISBN 978-1-4408-3247-5 (hardback) — ISBN 978-1-4408-3248-2 (ebook)
1. Suffrage—United States—History.   2. Election law—United States—
History.   3. African Americans—Civil rights.   4. Civil rights—United States.
5. Racism—United States—History—20th century.   6. United States—
Race relations.   I. Title.
  JK1846.B76   2015
  324.6'208900973—dc23   2015005531

ISBN: 978-1-4408-3247-5
EISBN: 978-1-4408-3248-2

19 18 17 16 15   1 2 3 4 5

This book is also available on the World Wide Web as an eBook.
Visit www.abc-clio.com for details.

Praeger
An Imprint of ABC-CLIO, LLC

ABC-CLIO, LLC
130 Cremona Drive, P.O. Box 1911
Santa Barbara, California 93116-1911

This book is printed on acid-free paper ∞

Manufactured in the United States of America

Contents

Series Foreword

Voting Rights under Fire is a timely addition to Praeger's series Racism in American Institutions (RAI). With continued debate over existing and proposed voter ID laws and a host of other measures that seem designed to impede the ability of people of color to vote, racism as an institutional factor in U.S. voting and politics is clear. The RAI series examines the ways in which racism has become a part of the fabric of many American institutions. For example, while the United States may have done away with overtly racist policies such as Jim Crow segregation, racism still affects many of the United States' established institutions from public schools to corporate offices. Similarly, schools may not be legally segregated, and yet many districts are not integrated. Voter ID laws have targeted perceived voter fraud, but there is no real fraud to speak of and hence these anti-voting measures serve to take us back to the period before the advent of the Voting Rights Act when people of color, especially black people, could not vote. These laws do not protect voting rights, they ensure disfranchisement. This open-ended series examines the problem of racism in established American institutions. Each book traces the prevalence of racism within that institution throughout the history of the United States and explores the problem in that institution today, looking at ways in which the institution has attempted to rectify racism, but also the ways in which it has not.

Voting Rights under Fire deals with a significant aspect of racism in an American institution, but one fraught with misunderstanding. It is that misunderstanding, among other important issues, that authors Donathan L. Brown and Michael L. Clemons seek to address. Both authors are well-suited to this task, having published and taught on issues of discrimination and public policy for many years. They contend that where anti-voting measures are concerned, race and racism are in numerous instances the common denominator that explains why states pass such laws. They take a longue duree approach to these issues, explaining the long history of disfranchisement in the United States as well as the overall importance of the passage of the Voting Rights Act. Most importantly, they show how the past informs the present, how numerous politicians have worked to undermine the effects of the Voting Rights Act, and how the effects of these two forces have continued to guide anti-voting measures like voting ID laws.

Donathan Brown is a recognized expert on the intersection of race and public policy. His methodology is multifaceted and cross-disciplinary, and much of that methodology guides *Voting Rights under Fire*. Michael Clemons is an authority on U.S. political traditions and political science, especially as it pertains to communities of color. Both authors have tackled an immense subject. Voting is the paramount way in which most Americans exercise their civil rights and participate in the U.S. democracy. Abridging voting rights in any way should be anathema to the American people, and yet anti-voting measures pass with relative ease. Understanding why that is the case may help to re-secure voting as our most cherished and treasured civil right.

Brian D. Behnken
Iowa State University
Ames, Iowa

Acknowledgments

The success of this book involved the input and contributions of many individuals. As to be expected, we will inevitably, but inadvertently, omit someone, so please accept our apologies ahead of time. It was only after the publication of *When Race and Policy Collide* that the idea to investigate and dedicate a project toward analyzing the role race plays within past and present laws pertaining to voting rights was born. For this, much gratitude is owed to our gracious senior acquisitions editor, Kim Kennedy-White. Here at Ithaca College, much appreciation is in order for my truly exceptional undergraduate advisee, Holly Athas. Holly's work began early within the research and writing stages. She provided fantastic editing throughout the lifespan of this project. Appreciation is extended also to Old Dominion University's Department of Political Science and Geography, the College of Arts and Letters, and the Consortium for Research on Race, Diversity, and Policy, which provided support for this project. We are particularly appreciative of the constructive feedback of the reviewers, which helped to improve the overall quality of the manuscript. Last but not least, we extend a hearty "thank you" to our "better halves," as well as our families who demonstrated on our behalf the loving qualities and character of patience and support while this project was in progress.

Introduction: Voter Identification Laws Then and Now

Claims over the existence and influence of in-person voter fraud continue to fuel much debate throughout the country. Following the aftermath of the 2000 presidential election between George W. Bush and Albert Gore, especially the fiasco surrounding the Florida recount that resulted in Bush carrying the state by less than 600 votes, lawmakers and electors alike became more receptive to new voting measures. Passed by both chambers of Congress and signed into law by President Bush, the Help America Vote Act (HAVA) of 2002 promised sweeping reform to the nation's voting process. While much of the law's key provisions pertained to previously discovered shortcomings, there was a new twist added to the act. To begin, these key provisions included the following authorizations:

- HAVA authorizes federal funding for states to upgrade voting machines. States that accept this funding must eliminate and replace all punch card and lever voting machines, unless the machines can be adapted to meet heightened standards to ensure reliability, improved access for voters with disabilities and limited English proficiency, and other new federal requirements.
- Voting machines must provide voters with an opportunity to privately and independently verify, change, or correct the ballot before it is cast and counted.
- States must ensure that at least one voting machine at every polling place meets enhanced requirements for accessibility for voters with disabilities.
- Voting systems must produce a permanent paper record for purposes of manual recounts and audits.
- States must provide ballots in multiple languages and jurisdictions covered by Section 203 of the Voting Rights Act.[1]

When considering the numerous difficulties encountered by voters attempting to cast ballots on outdated or dysfunctional machines, many of the laws' key provisions, like measures to computerize voter registration lists to assist in accurate and current recordkeeping, come across as commonsense solutions. However, HAVA, as rarely as it is discussed, contains directions for states about the establishment of voter identification standards. Specifically, HAVA recommends that "states should adopt an expansive non-exclusive list of identification to serve as examples of a valid photo identification . . . the list should include forms of identification likely to be possessed by students, disabled, low-income, and immigrant voters and communities of color."[2] Here, certain first-time voters, like those who registered to vote by mail after January 1, 2003, and/or have not previously voted in a federal election within the state or jurisdiction would be required to produce identification at the polls. This call for the creation of minimum identification requirements and the creation of the term *provisional ballot* (the process where a ballot is accepted "provisionally" until election officials can verify the voter's eligibility to vote in the particular precinct at that election) were some of the laws' most significant additions.

While the voter identification clause of the law would not be enforced until the next midterm election (2004), some states became interested in enacting voter identification provisions of their own. In 2006, resulting from the passage of Ohio House Bill 3, *all* Ohio voters were asked to present some form of identification in order to cast a ballot. Presented with the option to furnish materials ranging from utilities bills to driver's licenses, lawmakers did not pursue the all-inclusive photo identification-only route, yet in 2011, the national sentiment began to shift. Between 2011 and 2013, 14 states passed new voter identification measures; however, the chief justificatory claim over the widespread existence of voter fraud remains highly contestable. While evidence is typically absent from many of these allegations, we noticed one unique pattern: the heavy presence of words like "might," "probably," and "perhaps," all indicating the infectious hypothetical nature of these claims. Of the various types of voter fraud (double voting, dead voting, fraudulent addresses, voting by noncitizens, dogs, vote buying, etc.), we found this illusive language to be particularly relevant when investigating allegations of in-person voter fraud. In their groundbreaking report entitled "The Truth about Voter Fraud," Justin Levitt of the Brenan Center for Justice at New York University Law School chronicled these discursive developments well.

With the aim of retracing such allegations to examine the truth behind the headlines, Levitt documents that in many instances "only a tiny portion of the claimed illegality is substantiated—and most remainder is either nothing more than speculation or has been conclusively debunked."[3] Unfortunately, many of the headlines about voter fraud that continue to captivate a great portion of the U.S. public and Grand Old Party (GOP) lawmakers alike are either exaggerated and/or unsubstantiated. Chief among these exaggerations are claims about double voting, that is, the allegation that a voter has either voted twice in the same state, or in some instances, has voted once in one state and again in another. Here is what Levitt and the Brenan Center uncovered.

In Missouri in 2000 and 2002, hundreds of voters were alleged to have voted twice, either within the state or once in Kansas and once in Missouri. The same analysis acknowledged that the "computer files contain many errors that show people voting who did not actually vote." Of 18 Kansas City cases that reporters followed up, 13 were affirmatively shown to result from clerical errors. We are aware of public sources substantiating only four cases (amounting to six votes within the state), yielding an overall documented fraud rate of 0.0003%.

In New Hampshire in 2004, citizens were alleged to have voted twice. In fact, on further investigation, many of the voters who were allegedly listed multiple times on the rolls actually represented different with identical names; others were listed with multiple registrations, but voted only once. We are not aware of any public materials substantiating the claims of double voting.

In New Jersey in 2004, 4,397 voters were alleged to have voted twice within the state, and 6,572 voters were alleged to have voted once in New Jersey and once elsewhere. Many of these alleged double votes were actually flawed matches of names and/or birthdates on voter rolls. Only eight cases were actually documented through signatures on poll books; at least five signatures appear to match. Even if all eight proved to reveal fraud, however, that would amount to an overall double voting rate of 0.0002%.

In New York in 2002 and 2004, between 400 and 1,000 voters were alleged to have voted once in New York and once in Florida. These allegations were also prompted by a flawed attempt to match names and birthdates. We are aware of public sources substantiating only two cases, yielding an overall documented fraud rate of 0.000009%.

In Wisconsin in 2004, dozens of voters were alleged to have voted twice. After further investigations, the vast majority were affirmatively cleared, with some attributed to clerical errors and confusion by flawed attempts to match names and birthdates. There were 14 alleged reports of voters casting ballots both absentee and in person; at least 12 were caught, and the absentee ballot was not counted. There were no substantiated reports of any intentional double voting of which we are aware.[4]

As the investigations continue to reveal, there exists a tremendous gap between fact and fiction. For example, out of the 197 million votes cast for federal candidates between 2002 and 2005, "only 40 voters were indicted for voter fraud, according to a Department of Justice study outlined during a 2006 Congressional hearing. Only 26 of those cases, or about 0.00000013 percent of the votes cast, resulted in convictions or guilty pleas."[5] Unfortunately, for voter ID detractors, these facts are not penetrating headline news.

Instead, what continues to fester includes accusations ranging from deceased individuals as well as noncitizens casting ballots, as suggested by headlines like "Dead Man Voting"[6] and "Among Voters in New Jersey, G.O.P. Sees Dead People."[7] What escaped headlines like these is that yes, the voters had passed, but *after* casting their ballots. One of the earliest examples and investigations brings us back to 1995, where said allegations came under investigation in Maryland. As the study conducted by the Brennan Center recounts, "an exhaustive investigation revealed that of 89 alleged deceased voters, none were actually dead at the time the ballot was cast. The federal agent in charge of the investigation said that the nearest they came was when they found one person who had voted then died a week after the election."[8] Nonetheless, this argument has been revived and investigations have been conducted; however, such alleged activity continues to suffer from insufficient evidence.

This 1995 example only marked the beginning of a long legacy of allegations that continues to consume much attention today. In 2000, nearly 5,500 ballots in Georgia were allegedly cast by deceased voters.[9] Spanning from 1980 to 2000, these allegations were supported by the claim that state voter rolls did not match death lists; however, this headline too was unsupported by any in-depth analysis. As the story developed, a follow-up report was conducted, and the outcome bespoke the allegations within the headlines. Of the nearly 5,550 alleged fraudulent ballots cast, only one instance was substantiated, which was later found to be an error. Here, Alan J. Mandel was confused with Alan J. Mandell.[10] No other evidence of fraudulent votes was alleged following the results of this report. New York, in both 2002 and 2004, had its own allegations of deceased voters casting ballots, much in the same manner as our previous example where a match of voter rolls did not sync with the states death lists. Upon further review, clerical errors were uncovered, but no fraud.[11] As New Jersey announced the same allegations in 2004 regarding 4,755 deceased voters, no public documents substantiated any cases of fraud, whereas no reports were released stating that any of the allegedly deceased voters cast ballots in 2005.[12] And in 2005, 132 votes were alleged to have been cast by deceased voters in Michigan. Under the same premise of mismatched voter rolls and death lists, "a follow-up investigation by the Secretary of State revealed that these alleged dead voters were actually absentee ballots mailed to voters who died before Election Day; 97 of these ballots were never voted, and 27 were voted before the voter passed away. Even if the remaining eight cases all revealed substantiated fraud, that would amount to a rate of at most 0.0027%."[13] While much of the evidence continues to reveal that widespread in-person voter fraud, especially regarding deceased voters, bears no fruit, this has not thwarted the infectious nature of these allegations.

Against the grander backdrop of shifting racial demographics and overall calls for immigration reform, allegations over noncitizen voting has gained a lot of ground, but like our previous examples, this claim too is wholly without merit. Of the allegations and investigations that have transpired over the course of nearly 20 years, the results continue to place a tremendous burden of proof upon those who believe such fraud is widespread. Beginning in 1996, for example, officials in California alleged that 924 noncitizens voted in Orange and Los Angeles counties, including 624 allegedly ineligible voters identified by the Task Force of the House of Representatives investigating the Dornan/Sanchez election. Here, these allegations were supported by unsuccessful attempts at matching immigration lists to voter rolls, whereas in doing so, officials noted that only 71 voters matched name, date of birth, and signature. Upon further review, at least 372 of the voters were officially sworn in before Election Day.[14] To date, there have been no reports of which we are aware that any noncitizen registered or voted. For the sake of argument, however, if all 552 remaining individuals were in fact noncitizens when they cast their ballots, this brings the overall noncitizen voting rate to 0.017 percent. Investigating a similar situation that occurred in 2000, Hawaii officials reported that 553 noncitizens were alleged to have registered to vote. Later, an investigation revealed that 144 people documented that they had become citizens, where at least 61 individuals asked to cancel their registration, while the remaining were stopped at the polls and specifically asked about their citizenship before voting.[15] At the end, officials attributed the registrations to mistake rather than fraud.

In Milwaukee, journalists spent 2001 analyzing 370,000 voting records ranging from 1992 to 2002. While they uncovered four instances in which voter names matched a list of naturalized city residents but appeared to have voted before their naturalization dates, there was no indication of which we are aware that any of these four knowingly voted illegally.[16] Again, for the sake of argument, even if all four matched records of noncitizen votes, this would equate to a noncitizen voting rate of 0.001 percent. In Washington state, documentation from 2004 illustrates that two votes were cast by noncitizens. While there is no record of these individuals knowingly voting illegally, with one individual asking to rescind his vote shortly following the election, the rate of documented noncitizens voting was 0.0002 percent.[17] And finally, we stay in Washington State, as our next example truly underscores the very definition of nativism. In 2005, an unspecified individual asked county offices to investigate the citizenship status of 1,668 registered voters predicated upon their "foreign-sounding names." Despite such ill-mannered intent, there are no reports of which we are aware that any individual on the submitted list was actually a noncitizen.[18]

This revisiting of past reports pertaining to voter fraud is extremely important if one is to have a better understanding of both content and context on multiple levels. Whether it is the claim that the deceased and noncitizens are voting, or that properly registered voters are casting multiple ballots, the evidence simply did not support these early allegations. Since then, especially between 2011 and 2013, some may rightfully ask, "but what about nowadays, what does the data say about recent disputes over the existence of voter fraud?" As calls for voting reform continue to gain momentum, the contentious claim that voter fraud is widespread, like our previous data revealed, is without merit.

Lawmakers in states like Colorado, Florida, Arizona, among others, who claim that voter fraud is alive and well have gone to great mediated lengths to saturate their supporters with this dubious message. Despite press conferences, campaign speeches, press releases, and other venues where lawmakers have turned to reach their audience, their arguments are simply not supported by reality. In his 2013 report about voter fraud in the November 2012 election, Colorado Republican secretary of state Scott Gessler was poised to present findings that revealed 155 possible cases of voter fraud. Like all of the previous examples illustrated, there was more to the story than what initially met the eye. For example, when Gessler presented Boulder County district attorney Stan Garnett a list of 17 names of suspected illegal voters, Garnett's office found that all 17 people were not only citizens, but they were able to easily verify their status to Garnett's office, making Boulder County fraud free. Likening this to a "wild goose chase," Garnett remarked, "local governments and county clerks do a really good job regulating the integrity of elections, and I'll stand by that record any day of the week. We don't need state officials sending us on wild goose chases for political reasons."[19] In Arapahoe County, the state's third most populous county, District Attorney George Brauchler, upon investigating 41 noncitizens for voter fraud, charged four people with misdemeanors, upon investigating election records dating back to 2008.[20] With meager findings, at best, Colorado Democrats have not minced words about voter identification laws and Scott Gessler: "I think he has worked with the Republican Party and secretaries in other states to come up with these schemes to do everything they can to shave off a half-point or 1 percent of the Democratic vote," said Colorado Democratic Party chairman Rick Palacio.[21] Overall, assuming all charges are just, out of more than 3.5 million votes cast during the 2012 election, the fraud findings equates to far less than 0.001 percent of Colorado voters.

As the saga continues, so does the hunt for voter fraud across the country. In Florida, the accusations of voter fraud set the stage for alterations to the law in areas like early voting and voter identification requirements. Creating the voter fraud myth, state GOP lawmakers were determined to find something, even when nothing existed. For example, MTV's Rock the Vote campaign was accused by the state Division of Elections of engaging in criminal activity, specifically regarding 20 registration cases the state flagged as suspicious. Again, as the story holds, the Florida Department of Law Enforcement (FDLE) announced in 2013 that it found no evidence of criminal activity, therefore ending their investigation.[22] The irony in Florida however, is not that voter fraud does not exist, but instead, *who* is committing the fraud. Believe it or not, investigations in the Sunshine state have not found the "usual suspects" (Democrats, communities of color, immigrants, etc.) guilty of fraud, yet Republican organizations have come under significant scrutiny instead. As reported by George Bennett of the *Palm Beach Post*, "the Republican Party of Florida is dumping a firm it paid more than $1.3 million to register new voters, after Palm Beach County Elections Supervisor Susan Bucher flagged 106 'questionable' registration applications turned in by the contractor this month. Bucher asked the state attorney's office to review the applications 'in an abundance of caution' because she said her staff had questions about similar-looking signatures, missing information and wrong addresses on the forms."[23]

Unfortunately, this was not the only reported case involving voter fraud involving the state Republican Party. As reported in March 2013 by the 10-time Pulitzer Prize–winning newspaper, the *Tampa Bay Times*:

> Florida has found that employees of a company once aligned with the Republican Party of Florida engaged in voter registration fraud. The Florida Department of Law Enforcement said Tuesday that two former employees of Strategic Allied Consulting turned in 27 fake voter registration forms. The employees who worked in northeast Florida have been placed on probation since they had no criminal history. The company was hired by Republicans to do voter registration drives in Florida and other states. But last fall the state party fired the company and filed an election fraud complaint against the company with state officials.[24]

In Florida, the irony that began to reveal itself, at least to some, called into question the running theme that Democrats and their allies were responsible for such fraud, as the confirmed cases of fraud pertained to GOP-related groups. Following the 2012 presidential election, the FDLE released the results of their voter fraud investigation to little suspense. Approximately nine months after the ballots were tabulated; the FDLE has little to offer in defense of voter identification proponents, as their results continue to confirm the observation that voter fraud is both rare and more commonly involves clerical error rather than criminal intent. Again, as reported by the *Tampa Bay Times,* "in an inquiry into the Florida New Majority Education Fund, which aims to increase voter registration among underrepresented groups, the FDLE concluded it could make no arrests. In another inquiry, involving Strategic Allied Consulting, a vendor for the Republican Party of Florida, an arrest was made of a man who stole the identity of a former girlfriend's ex-husband. He admitted to fraudulently filling out two voter registration forms. And that was it."[25]

At the end of the day, the truth about voter fraud, at least by the rhetorical standards set forth by supporters, is not important. In Arizona, a state that is no stranger to controversial laws, state Republican lawmakers have pushed for voter identification laws for years, claiming that such a measure would combat fraud by noncitizen voters. While a 2014 federal appeals court ruled that both Arizona and Kansas can continue to vote using a federal form without having to prove citizenship, this ruling only amplified the claims that voter fraud is real and new laws must be enacted. Republican state attorney general Tom Horne, a defender of voter identification laws, argued that "it's important because voter fraud is a significant problem in Arizona," he told the *Arizona Republic,* adding that he believes there "has been what I consider to be a media cover-up of the extent to which voter fraud is a problem in Arizona."[26] Upon an investigation by the *Arizona Republic* newspaper, they revealed 34 court cases, since 2005, in Maricopa County, and even then, there is more than what meets the eye. As the data uncovered, 2 cases involved undocumented immigrants, 12 involved legal residents, 18 involved felons, ironically though none was convicted. A few cases were dismissed; the other suspects pleaded guilty to misdemeanors and served a few months of probation.[27] Horne when confronted with these numbers argued that they prove nothing whatsoever. Instead, he argued that "a lot of them don't get prosecuted" because the county attorneys "have scarce resources and bigger fish to fry"; however, according to the Maricopa County Attorney's Office, over the past nine years there were four cases of voter fraud that the office decided not to prosecute.[28]

Most recently, the headlines surrounding voter identification and in-person voter fraud has taken a peculiar twist. In October 2014, James O'Keefe, the "conservative provocateur" who is best known for his undercover video work against the group ACORN, has surfaced in closely contested Senate races in Colorado, Arkansas, and Kentucky, targeting the staffers and campaigns of Democrats Mark Udall, Mark Pryor, and Alison Lungergan Grimes. Posing as a University of Colorado-Boulder student and LGBT activist, O'Keefe visited the Udall campaign asking if he could volunteer by means of filling out mail in ballots for other college students who had since moved but still received mail on campus. Knowing this was election fraud, campaign staffers declined his request.[29] Later that week at an event for Mark Udall, who was joined by Massachusetts Democratic senator Elizabeth Warren, a woman calling herself "Bonnie" approached another Udall staffer, asking if she could submit blank ballots found in a garbage can, again, the response was "no." The same day, someone identifying themselves as "Nick Davis," accompanied by a "friend" wearing heavy makeup and a mustache, was introduced as a "civics professor" who came to the Boulder office to obtain canvassing information. As suspicions began to run high, photos of O'Keefe, in costume, surfaced on Twitter, only confirming O'Keefe's less-than-sincere tactics.[30]

Upon gaining control of the state capital, Republican lawmakers in Nevada are already poised to enact a voter identification law, despite the absence of actual fraud. Being the first time since 1929 that the state GOP has taken control of both chambers, passage of this proposed bill ought not to face much challenge. When asked if she could point to example of voter fraud in the state that such a law would prevent, Republican secretary of state Barbara Cegavske remarked in a November 2014 interview with MSNBC, "I think the biggest concern that most people have is the absentee ballots," Cegavske said. "I've had people that have reported that they've had family members that are deceased that they found out had voted."[31] Again, citing the aforementioned and thus far unsubstantiated theme of deceased voters casting ballots, along with her overall failure to provide any data or prosecuted cases, much skepticism continues to brew in Nevada. Just days following this breaking story, another development out of Louisiana topped it all. In the only state in the United States that, at the writing of this book, is still waiting to elect its senator (due to a runoff election), state GOP leaders have just launched a group charged with combatting the self-admittedly nonexistent epidemic of voter fraud. Dubbed, the Voter Integrity Program, many dissenters are asking the same questions as those in Nevada, whether or not evidence exists of voter fraud within the state. Steve Hartmann, a spokesperson for the Louisiana Attorney General's Office, when asked about the existence of voter fraud, responded that there have been no "recent complaints" or "instances of this in recent years," yet insists that such a group is needed.[32]

As the investigative reports continue to culminate and the evidence pertaining to voter fraud continues to illustrate that such fraud remains miniscule, only a few arguments have remained accurate over time. Chief among these claims is the belief that voter identification laws, whether acknowledged or not, exist to diminish voter participation among groups who typically sway Democratic. These groups, whether they be African American, Latino, the elderly, those on the lower end of the socioeconomic ladder, or those who are mobility impaired, as the chapters before us will soon illustrate, are all retrogressively impacted by these laws. If the data supported the claims made by GOP lawmakers who are calling for voter identification laws, then this book would approach the topic differently. As it is however, these supporters have failed to "show their work"; they have failed to satisfy any rhetorical burden of proof to prove to dissenters that these efforts are not politically motivated. At no point throughout the lifespan of this book did we uncover *any* evidence by any political group or lawmaker that states (1) voter fraud is a widespread problem downplayed by the media; (2) these reform efforts are actually for the better and not for the worst; and (3) race plays no part in the deliberation of these proposed and enacted laws.

Our Arguments

As of this book's writing, a total of 34 states have passed laws requiring voters to show some form of identification at the polls. As of September 2014, thirty-one of these laws are being enforced, while two have been struck down, and one will not go into effect until 2016. Of the remaining 19 states, they use other methods of voter verification, like checking a voter's signature against information on file. As bills pertaining to the creation of voter identification laws continue to surface across the country, this legislative and legal struggle is far from over. We remain further convinced that not only does race matter in these debates, but this relationship between race and voting rights is as timely and timeless as the struggle over citizenship and the recognition of personhood. Chief among our goals in this book is to highlight not only the past and present underpinning racial dimensions involved throughout the political legacy of voting rights, but more importantly, to illustrate how such past actions continue to guide current controversies pertaining to African American and Latino voting rights. Nowadays, while much of the political rhetoric surrounding changes to voter identification laws employ arguments in defense of so-called voter fraud as their justification, there are considerable reasons to believe that race exists as a significant, albeit downplayed, placeholder within this debate. For instance, since Latinos overtook African Americans in 2004 to become the nation's largest and fastest growing "minority" group and have already displaced whites as the majority in various parts of the county, it would be shortsighted of us not to consider this variable. Our focus, therefore, is the centrality of race as a factor in the political behavior and rhetoric associated with the ongoing debate over voting rights in the United States.

At the core of this book is legislative and judicial analysis, as many of the campaign speeches, press releases, and television appearances made by voter identification proponents are bereft of substantive contributions toward the understanding of this controversy. Therefore, it is the aim of each chapter to fill these voids by means of analyzing various domains housed under the grander umbrella of voting rights/voter identification debates. To this extent, Chapter 1 provides an overview of the political history and development of voting rights in the United States, from past to present. The chapter proceeds by briefly reviewing the development of the right to vote and the acquisition of the right to vote, including an overview of the Voting Rights Act of 1965. Considerable attention will be given to the constitutional safeguards against racial disenfranchisement provided under the act, especially Section 5, and the recently overturned constitutional guidance it provided to freeze election practices or procedures in certain states until they have been subjected to federal review. Next, this chapter briefly turns its attention to discursive formations of voter suppression in regulations and procedures around the country and how these changes affect individuals' right to vote. Here, attention is given to the intersection of race and voting rights and the significant historical and rhetorical contributions made by the Voting Rights Act of 1965. Chapter 2 investigates the laws that currently exist at the state level throughout the United States that restrict the voting rights of convicted felons and assesses the impact on individuals' right to exercise enfranchisement. The following questions are central to the analyses and discussion presented: (1) Who are the convicted felons and to what extent does race and ethnicity emerge as a factor in the designation of persons as such? (2) What impact has criminal incarceration and being branded a felon had on equality of access to the ballot and political justice?

In the chapters that follow, our attention turns toward both past and present landmark cases surrounding voter identification laws. Chapter 3 acknowledges that missing from much cotemporary conversation and political analysis is the landmark 2005 Indiana voter identification law and the fallout it produced—the 2008 Supreme Court case, *Crawford v. Marion County Election Board*. In this case, the nation witnessed two key political/legal developments: (1) the articulation from dissenters that voter identification laws are nothing more than a thinly veiled attempt to disenfranchise low-income Democratic voters; and (2) arguments from supporters who defended the merit of the law as legal assurance against voter fraud. This chapter analyzes the legal and rhetorical nuances involved in this debate, as the *Crawford* decision provided much of the legal arguments used today in defense of voter identification laws. Next, in Chapter 4, Pennsylvania lawmakers too insisted upon the passage of voter identification policy falling in line with the arguments praised by proponents in *Crawford v. Marion County Election Board*. However, this law was made most controversial when Republican state representative Mike Turzai noted that this law would "allow Governor Romney to win the state of Pennsylvania." At that moment, interest began to develop not only in reference to this Pennsylvania law, but possible ulterior motives behind these laws. This chapter dives further into these questions and other allegations by means of *Applewhite v. the Commonwealth of Pennsylvania*. Chapter 5 continues our judicial case studies by means of analyzing two of the most recent and controversial court cases, *Texas v. Holder* and *Shelby v. Holder*. Recent developments in Texas and Alabama continue to link past attempts at voter disenfranchisement with current actions. As the Latino population continues to increase in both states, and in some parts of the Texas outpacing the birthrate of whites, much concern exists over the political longevity of the Republican Party. Because Latinos and other people of color overwhelmingly support the Democratic Party platform, these two attempts at voter identification laws drew both interest and objection. While proponents argued that requiring certain, though not all forms of photo identification will preserve the "integrity" of voting, especially against so-called voter fraud, this chapter argues otherwise. Here, we maintain the argument that shifting racial demographics and political power balances matter, and not necessarily "voter fraud." Chapter 6 provides an update to current trends to the latest developments in voter identification laws. Specifically, our attention will be upon the states that have enacted voter identification legislation following the landmark *Shelby v. Holder* decision along with updates pertaining to felon disenfranchisement. Finally, we offer a brief epilogue on the growth of majority–minority areas throughout the United States.

Notes

1. Pub. Law 107–252 § 301; 42 U.S.C. § 15481.
2. Ibid.
3. Justin Bingham, "The Truth about Voter Fraud," Brennan Center for Justice, November 2007, http://www.brennancenter.org/publication/truth-about-voter-fraud (accessed August 23, 2014).
4. Ibid.
5. Amy Bingham, "Voter Fraud: Non-Existent Problem or Election-Threatening Epidemic?" http://abcnews.go.com/Politics/OTUS/voter-fraud-real-rare/story?id=17213376 (accessed August 23, 2014).
6. Bruce Rushton, "Dead Man Voting," *Riverfront Times* (April 24, 2002), http://www.riverfronttimes.com/2002-04-24/news/dead-man-voting/ (accessed June 14, 2014).
7. David W. Chen, "Among Voters in New Jersey, G.O.P. Sees Dead People," *New York Times,* September 16, 2005, p. B5.

8. Justin Levitt, "The Truth about Voter Fraud," Brennan Center for Justice, November 2007, http://www.brennancenter.org/publication/truth-about-voter-fraud (accessed August 23, 2014).

9. Jingle Davis, "State Plans to Update Voter Lists," *Atlanta J.-Const.,* Feb. 10, 2001, p. 4H.

10. Cox, "The 2000 Election."

11. John Ferro, "Deceased Residents on Statewide Voter List," *Poughkeepsie Journal,* October 29, 2006, http://www.poughkeepsiejournal.com/apps/pbcs.dll/article?AID=2006610290381&template=printart.

12. Cynthia Burton, "No Beyond-the-Grave Balloting Cited," *Philadelphia Inquirer,* November 9, 2005, http://articles.philly.com/2005-11-09/news/254303 38_1_ballots-polling-place-democrats-election-day.

13. Levitt, "The Truth about Voter Fraud," November 2007.

14. Nancy Cleeland, "Hermandad Blames INS For Confusing Illegal Voters," *Los Angeles Times,* January 3, 1997, p. B1; Peter M. Warren, "Jones: 5,087 Registrants Potential Noncitizens," *Los Angeles Times,* October 14, 1997, p. B1; Michael Wagner and Nancy Cleeland, "D.A. Drops Voter Probe After Indictments Rejected," *Los Angeles Times,* December 20, 1997, p. A1.

15. Ishikawa Scott, "Isle Officials Seek Ways to Prevent Illegal Voting," *Honolulu Advertiser,* September 7, 2000, p. A1; Dayton Kevin, "City Steps Up Search for Illegal Voters," *Honolulu Advertiser,* September 8, 2000, p. A1; Ishikawa Scott, "Illegal Voters," *Honolulu Advertiser,* September 9, 2000, p. A1; No Author, "Clerk's Office Allows 153 Naturalized Citizens to Vote in Primary," *AP State & Local Wire, Honolulu,* September 27, 2000.

16. Jessica McBride and Dave Umhoefer, "12 Votes Attributed to Dead People," *Milwaukee Journal Sentinel,* January 22, 2001, p. 2A.

17. Kenneth P. Vogel, "King to Challenge 110 More Votes," *News Tribune,* April 29, 2005 at B2; Brad Shannon, "Rossi's Case Enters Key Phase," *Olympian,* May 1, 2005, p. 1C.

18. Levitt, "The Truth about Voter Fraud," November 2007.

19. Erica Meltzer, "Boulder County DA Stan Garnett Clears All 17 Suspected Illegal Voters," *Daily Camera,* August 14, 2013.

20. Lynn Bartels, "Voter Probe Snares Four," *Denver Post,* November 23, 2013, p. 3A.

21. Robert Barnes, "Colorado May Have Most Closely Watched Election Official," *Washington Post,* September 21, 2012, p. A05.

22. No Author, "No Fraud in Rock the Vote," *Tampa Bay Times,* January 11, 2013, p. 6B.

23. George Bennett, "County Raises Red Flags on 106 Questionable Voter Applications," *Palm Beach Post,* September 26, 2012, p. 1A.

24. No Author, "State Uncovers Voter Registration Fraud," *Tampa Bay Times,* March 6, 2013, p. 8B.

25. Michael Van Sickler, "Two Voter Fraud Cases Close with Meager Findings," *Tampa Bay Times,* September 4, 2013, http://www.tampabay.com/news/politics/stateroundup/two-voter-fraud-cases-close-with-meager-findings/2139886.

26. Mary Jo Pitzl and Yvone Wingett Sanchez, "Federal Judge: Ariz., Kansas Can Require Voters Prove Citizenship," *The Republic,* March 24, 2014, http://www.azcentral.com/story/news/politics/2014/03/19/arizona-kansas-win-voter-citizenship-suit/6613279/.

27. Alia Beard Rau, "Illegal Immigrant Vote-Fraud Cases Rare in Arizona," *The Republic,* November 18, 2013, http://www.azcentral.com/news/politics/articles/20131105arizona-immigrant-vote-fraud-rare.html.

28. Ibid.

29. Valerie Richardson, "Undercover Video Shows Progressives Condoning Voter Fraud in Colorado," *Washington Times,* October 22, 2014, http://www.washingtontimes.com/news/2014/oct/22/undercover-video-progressives-voter-fraud-colorado/.

30. Jon Murray, "Video Activist James O'Keefe Targets Colorado's New Mail Voting Law," *Denver Post,* October 22, 2014, http://blogs.denverpost.com/thespot/2014/10/22/video-activist-james-okeefe-targets-colorados-mail-voting/114385/#more-114385.

31. Zachary Roth, "After Takeover, Nevada GOPers Ready Voter ID," *MSNBC,* November 12, 2014, http://www.msnbc.com/msnbc/after-takeover-nevada-gopers-ready-voter-id.

32. No Author, "Ask the Advocate: Is voter fraud really a problem in Louisiana?" *The Advocate,* November 20, 2014, http://theadvocate.com/news/10719441-123/ask-the-advocate-is.

Chapter 1

Formulating Democracy: Development and Evolution of Voting Rights in America

The year 2015 will mark the 50th anniversary of the Voting Rights Act of 1965. Were it not for the recent developments that undermine the intent and spirit of the legislation, this would be a time of celebration rather than one of dire caution. Voting rights have continually been expanded in the United States since the 1960s, standing as a staunch reflection of the evolving nature and character of American democracy. The expansion of voting rights demonstrates the painfully incremental nature of societal change, as well as the strength that is indicative of the malleability of the system and its capacity to absorb the country's growing multiculturalism and diversity. President Lyndon B. Johnson, a social visionary in his own right, came to understand the fundamental importance of the right to vote for individual dignity, and the dignity of the nation. In his now famous "We Shall Overcome Speech," delivered March 15, 1965, following the violence levied on those planning to march from Selma to Montgomery, he astutely asserted that the framers of the Constitution knew that: "The most basic right of all was the right to choose your own leaders. The history of this country, in large measure, is the history of the expansion of that right to all of our people."[1] President Johnson's understanding and that of the nation thus was becoming increasingly consistent with the foremost goal of the Civil Rights Movement, which was to secure African American[2] political rights, and in particular, their right to cast the ballot freely with the chance of electing the candidate of choice.

Politics in the United States have been and continue to be cyclical in nature. This reality has some unfortunate implications for the consistency of democratic practice. One such implication has to do with the question of inclusion, namely, who will be permitted to participate in the electoral process, when, and with what effect. The country is perpetually engaged in a transitioning democracy, which has long been overwhelmingly controlled by a dominant white majority. Based on white supremacist notions, the entrenched, institutionalized behavior of the dominant group that has long been exercised and accepted will likely be difficult to reverse. However, the demographic changes and electoral shifts currently besetting the United States suggest that it is critical to give serious consideration to understanding these and related issues and to formulating a methodology that not only substantiates but also advances the process of a democracy of inclusion and participation.

In the midst of the nation's rapid population diversification, citizens' belief in the myth of a post-racial American politics and society is pervasive. For many, the election of President Barack Obama has meant that the problem of race (which in reality has much to do with the allocation of social wealth and ultimately power) is a problem of the past. However, there is much empirical evidence demonstrating to the contrary that the measurable gaps in the quality of life experienced by whites and African Americans prevail. On a variety of key measures, in comparison to their white counterparts, in the 21st century, people of color, particularly African Americans, exhibit persistent relative deprivation. Racial and ethnic disparities are present on a wide range of social and economic factors including employment status, educational attainment, income, infant mortality, home ownership, and incarceration, to name a few.[3]

This chapter provides an overview of the political history, development, and evolution of voting rights in the United States. Contemporary developments and practices impacting voting rights need to be examined and understood within the broader historical context of the struggle for social inclusion led by African Americans and the subsequent struggles of other groups, including women and Hispanics seeking assurance of the right to vote. Their initiative reflects the systematic engagement of the country's racist and discriminatory practices with the aim of broadening democratic inclusion and consequently participation in the formation of public policy. Understanding the history and development of voting rights helps clarify the problems, issues, and benefits of current developments, leading ultimately to discovering appropriate policy solutions. We proceed by reviewing the historical development of the right to vote, including the acquisition of the franchise by African Americans and other groups. Focusing on the 1964 Civil Rights Act and the Voting Rights Act of 1965 and its subsequent amendments, our analysis deals with how voting practices in the United States have evolved, been applied, and deteriorated over time. In addition to legislative actions, we consider U.S. Supreme Court rulings and their effects on voting and democracy in the United States. The chapter concludes with a discussion of post-racialism and President Obama's rise to power and an examination of the factors that have prompted largely political conservatives to develop, promote, and endorse measures that have a chilling effect on individuals' right to exercise the franchise.

The political environment within which African Americans, people of color in general, and women have operated has varied throughout history. However, for the most part, those outside of the majority, particularly African Americans, were excluded from participation in the electoral process. Hanes Walton Jr. and Robert Smith have pointed out that:

> For much of their history in the United States, African Americans have been excluded from the normal routine processes of political participation such as lobbying, voting, elections, and political parties. Indeed, in the Republic's more than 200-year history, African Americans have been included as nearly full participants for less than 50 years—the 10-year Reconstruction period from 1867 to 1877 plus the years since the adoption of the Voting Rights Act in 1965.[4]

Thus, to unravel and order the relevant issues, we employ a qualitative historical approach that allows for the partitioning of the political development process in the United States into five major historical periods, thus facilitating comparison between and among each period. These historical periods include Enslavement, Reconstruction, Jim Crow, Civil Rights, and Post–Civil Rights. The nation's transition from the era of Reconstruction to Jim Crow and later from Civil Rights to Post–Civil Rights is instructive given that the former transitional period was successful in virtually eliminating African American political participation, and in the current era of Post–Civil Rights, we unfortunately see such efforts vigorously underway.

Some interesting parallels can be drawn between the Jim Crow era and the contemporary Post–Civil Rights period. Perhaps the most striking similarity is that in each of these eras, broad-based, counter-democratic programs were launched seeking a reversal of the progress made in extending the franchise to those who had been excluded. In recounting what he refers to as "[the] triumph of racism" in the years following Reconstruction, Donald G. Neiman observed:

> During the late 1870s and 1880s southern blacks had refused to accept the Democratic counterrevolution, using political and legal means to defend

their rights. Yet while they had won occasional victories, their positions generally had deteriorated. Beginning in the late 1880s and stretching into the first two decades of the twentieth century, southern Democrats launched a ferocious new offensive that reduced blacks to second-class citizenship.[5]

Thus, during the post-Reconstruction era, white conservatives felt tremendously under siege due to the challenge to white political dominance demonstrated in the aftermath of the Civil War. In response to the challenge, conservatives carried out a "counterrevolution" to restore the political status quo. The conservative reaction involved the use of a variety of measures designed to eradicate the black vote, including poll taxes, literacy tests, the Grandfather clause, and outright fear and terror. The Ku Klux Klan (KKK) notoriously employed terrorism as a means of persuading blacks that it was not in their best interest to vote, as well as convincing liberal whites that it would be contrary to their interests to support black suffrage. While the KKK was initiated in1865 on a relatively small scale in Pulaski, Tennessee, by 1867, the organization operated on an interstate basis as a "highly organized movement."[6] Similarly, in the Post–Civil Rights era, a confluence of tactics designed to stifle the political participation of blacks, Hispanics, and more generally the poor was applied. However, the racial attacks of today generally are better concealed, in some instances due to the nature of institutionalized, systemic approaches. Indeed, American society as a whole and whites as a group generally are less accepting of blatant racial practices. Nonetheless, the improved racial attitudes among Americans have made it easier to sell the notion that voting regulations and enfranchisement policies are race neutral, implying that the effect is the same regardless of race. New barriers abound and some are being developed to effect the retrenchment of individuals' right to vote. Although the impact of certain groups is minimized in the political process, in the end, the whole of society and American democracy are negatively affected. Before broaching the myriad of contemporary problems related to voting and democracy, we first turn our attention to the development and evolution of the right to vote.

Development and Evolution of Voting Rights

The precious right to vote in the United States has deep roots in the nation's historical conception of democracy—a conception fueled largely by the desire of various groups of "newcomers" to be recognized as citizens with a stake in the country's well-being. Those who belong to groups that represent a numerical minority have a deep longing to elect political representation of their own choosing, in defiance of what might otherwise be the "tyranny of the majority." Such aspirations provided much needed momentum to launch and sustain a social change process in the United States that culminated with the Civil Rights Movement. In connection with previous efforts, the movement was dedicated to gaining access to the ballot for African Americans, and more generally the elimination of unequal, second-class citizenship, which was experienced by the group especially in the southern region of the United States from about 1877 to 1964. The development of voting rights has been a protracted process. As such, an historical approach is necessitated for acquiring insight into the current Post–Civil Rights era during which voting rights again appear to wane. In the sections below, we briefly focus on the development of voting rights in the eras of Enslavement, Reconstruction, Jim Crow, Civil Rights, and Post–Civil Rights.

Enslavement

People of African descent are erroneously understood as having been enslaved from the moment they set foot on the shores of America. This widespread misconception is far from the reality of early social practice. Africans, like many poor Europeans, first arrived in America as indentured servants. As such, freedom was a commodity that could be exchanged, earned, used as payment for the acquisition of passage to the New World, or to pay a penalty to society for offenses committed against it.[7] Depending upon locale, along with the acquisition of freedom, there was a chance that suffrage rights would be granted. Social class for some time was most operative in the American political arena, but eventually race became the dominant social construction guiding society's general operation.

The struggle to secure voting rights for all Americans was set into motion with the initiation of the African American struggle to *acquire and use* the franchise as human beings interested in directing their own lives and destiny. From the moment of their enslavement in America, they were possessed by the desire to stand on equal ground in the political process to represent themselves alongside of whites and to have their policy preferences articulated, legislated, and codified. However, the dye cast of this early era called for granting suffrage almost exclusively to white males. Women, Indians, and the majority of blacks were considered unqualified to participate in the electoral process.[8] Also, the uniquely brutal nature of American slavery necessitated complete humiliation and dehumanization, and disenfranchisement served an essential purpose in accomplishing this.

Table 1.1 shows the black population by free-slave status for the period from 1790 to 1860. Data from the U.S. Bureau of Census for the period reveals that in 1790, nationally there were about 60,000 (8%) free blacks among a total black population of 757,000.

By 1860, three years prior to President Lincoln's Emancipation Proclamation, the total number of blacks had grown to almost four and a half million with free blacks totaling 488,000 or 11 percent of the total. At the time, more than half (33,000) of the total free black population resided in the South. In 1790, the bulk of the black population was concentrated in the southern region (690,000), and by 1860, the total number of blacks in the South had grown to more than 4 million including 285,000 free blacks.

TABLE 1.1   Black Population by Free-Slave Status, 1790–1860 (In Thousands)

Area and Year	Total Blacks Number	Free Blacks Number	%	Enslaved Blacks Number	%
United States					
1790	757	60	8	698	92
1800	1,002	108	11	894	89
1810	1,378	186	14	1,191	86
1820	1,772	234	13	1,538	87
1830	2,329	320	14	2,009	86
1840	2,874	386	13	2,487	87
1850	3,639	434	12	3,204	88
1860	4,442	488	11	3,954	89
South					
1790	690	33	5	658	95
1810	1,268	108	8	1,161	92
1830	2,162	182	8	1,980	92
1850	3,352	236	7	3,117	93
1860	4,097	258	6	3,839	94

Source: *The Social and Economic Status of the Black Population in the United States: An Historical View, 1790–1978*. Current Population Reports, Special Studies, Series P-23, No. 80. U.S. Department of Commerce, Bureau of the Census, Second Printing, January 1980, p. 11.

Note: The standard census definition of regions is used. In that definition, the South includes the states of the former Confederacy as well as Delaware, District of Columbia, Kentucky, Maryland, Oklahoma, and West Virginia.

For almost 80 years, from 1787, the year of the Constitutional Convention, to the end of the Civil War in 1865, a total of six (6) states allowed free black people to vote. However, black people could not vote in any state if they were enslaved. In 1776, white men who owned property were granted suffrage, and free black men voted in the states of New Jersey, Pennsylvania, and Maryland. Between 1783 and 1810, only those freed prior to 1783 were allowed the franchise, and after 1810 no black men could vote.[9] Walton and Smith further point out that "between the Revolutionary and Civil Wars, Tennessee in 1834, North Carolina in 1835, and Pennsylvania in 1838, all withdrew the right to vote from 'Free Negroes,'" thus leaving the nonvoting status of blacks in place.[10]

At the beginning of the 19th century, white workers acquired the right to vote as property requirements were eliminated. It was at this time that the right to vote that had been previously extended to blacks was retracted. For example, in New Jersey, Maryland, and Connecticut, laws were passed in 1820 limiting the franchise to white males. Also, in the 1830s, North Carolina and Pennsylvania added the descriptive "white" to the voting qualifications set forth in their state constitutions. This change helped ensure an exclusively white male electorate. After 1819, all states joining the union denied the franchise to African Americans, and by 1855 only Massachusetts, Rhode Island, Vermont, New Hampshire, and Maine, which combined had only 4 percent of the free black population, allowed the group access to the ballot. In contrast to Southern states, New York imposed a minimum property ownership requirement of $200, rather than simply retracting blacks' right to vote. Nonetheless, the voting participation of the state's qualified free black population was effectively reduced. In a manner that served to concretize conditions, New York's white voters, in three statewide suffrage referenda held in 1846, 1860, and 1869, declined to support universal voting rights for "Free Negroes."[11]

As a consequence of their enslavement, persons of African descent were in the unenviable position of having to free themselves from bondage before there could ever be consideration of using the franchise as a group to bring about favorable social and political change. Making matters worse, the Supreme Court's infamous 1857 Dred Scott decision further institutionalized black disenfranchisement and rendered freedom even more distant for African descendants. Chief Justice Taney's declaration made it clear that those who had been sold as slaves were not citizens and that therefore they could not lay claim to any rights and privileges, except those given to them by whites. Ironically, Taney's opinion was a tacit admission that some black people had in fact lived their lives essentially unfettered as American citizens.[12]

Freedmen and abolitionists were eventually able to effectuate and sustain a movement, which in the aftermath of the Civil War in 1865 ushered in the Thirteenth Amendment. This watershed amendment abolished and prohibited slavery and additionally secured a minimal degree of citizenship for former slaves.[13] In 1868, citizenship was clarified along with the explicit legislative hallmarks of "equal protection" and "due process." The Fourteenth Amendment granted citizenship to all people "born or naturalized in the United States," and it extended the protections of due process and equal protection to individual citizens. However, a significant shortcoming of the amendment was that it did not explicitly prohibit vote discrimination on racial grounds.[14] This necessitated and eventually led to passage of the Fifteenth Amendment, which directly addressed the fundamental democratic issue of voting. Ratified in February 1870, the Fifteenth Amendment, which gave suffrage rights to black men, provided that, "[t]he right of U.S. citizens to vote shall not be denied or abridged by the United States or by any State on account of race, color, or previous condition of servitude." Additionally the amendment gave Congress the authority to enforce those rights and regulate the voting process. Since ratification of the amendment, exercise of the franchise has been a fundamental aspect of citizenship rights.[15] Although the Fifteenth Amendment was enacted following a rather difficult ratification process, there was widespread belief that it would be a catalyst for unifying the country behind the rights of freed slaves and their involvement in the political process. However, in later years, the U.S. Supreme Court interpreted the amendment very narrowly, and thus, in earnest, initiated the disenfranchisement of black voters. The Court's narrow interpretation encouraged policies such as poll taxes and literacy tests, which were implemented throughout the South, and by the early 1900s, black Americans were facing a struggle for the right to vote.[16]

Thus, the early history of voting rights expansion in the United States is mixed in terms of its trajectory. Consequentially, the expansion of voting rights to African Americans was reliant on the use of the social movement as a crucial mechanism for gaining access. The informal participation exerted by African Americans and their white coalition partners in the early phase of voting development, for the most part, was their only option for bringing about constitutional democratic change. In the 20th and 21st centuries, social movements continued to be a necessary strategy for gaining and guaranteeing the right to vote of African Americans, Latinos, and other groups. The ebb and flow of American democracy and the incremental nature of the system have dictated the utility of the social movement, which in the 21st century is enhanced by the power of computers, digital communications, satellite technologies, and notably, social media. In the absence of the capacity for formal political participation, the aggrieved will develop and apply alternative processes and means to gain access to the ballot box.

Reconstruction

The struggle for the franchise persisted for decades beyond the end of the Civil War. Even after the war was over, the Southern states refused to recognize the rights of freedmen. Rather, the South as a region wanted to continue to direct its destiny within the context of historical social relations, with no intention whatsoever of allowing freed slaves to participate in the political process. The resistance to passage of the Fifteenth Amendment, and therefore black voting, is illustrated by the fact that the state of Tennessee was the only Southern state to initially adopt and ratify the Fifteenth Amendment. For the remaining Southern states, voting rights was addressed through the Military Reconstruction Act of 1867. This legislation was one of three Reconstruction acts passed at the end of the Civil War as the United States sought to rebuild the union. It was enacted despite a veto by President Johnson. The major goals of the act included rebuilding the governments of the Southern states and ensuring the civil rights of free blacks in state-level politics and political processes. The act further decreed that Southern states were to be divided into five regional military districts and placed under the control of the U.S. military. Military commanders placed in charge of these districts were given significant power. Also of note is that along with ensuring basic freedoms for black Americans, the law was used as a means to punish Southern states. The Republican-controlled Congress wanted assurances that the former Confederate states were fully aware of the new order, and that from this point forward, things would be different. Freed slaves, for example, were now to become a part of society, able to exercise their rights as citizens to be involved in the political processes along with all other Americans.[17]

While there was strong emphasis on gaining access to public accommodations, the earliest of the civil rights bills passed by Congress, the Civil Rights Act of 1875, illustrates that extending the franchise to those excluded from public accommodations access was an important objective.[18] However, this legislation fizzled as Reconstruction declined, in part due to the removal of federal troops placed in the South for the protection of the rights of black citizens. After only eight years, the act was struck down by the Supreme Court's ruling in the Civil Rights Cases of 1883, which explicitly declared that while the Fourteenth Amendment prohibited discrimination by the states, it did not cover discrimination by individuals and private businesses (Walton and Smith, 2012, 36).[19]

Jim Crow

Despite the passage of the Fifteenth Amendment, black voting rights suppression persisted. The passage of the Compromise of 1877 ushered in the decline of Reconstruction, which collapsed under the pressure of the development and institutionalization of wide-ranging measures to restrain the free exercise (registration and voting) of the black franchise. In attempting to restore white supremacy in line with the desire of Southerners to maintain political power, a wide range of schemes and mechanisms were employed including the "Grandfather Clause, white primaries, preprimaries, poll taxes, reading and interpretation tests, multiple ballot boxes, single-month registration periods, party instead of state administered primaries, single-state party systems, evasion, economic reprisals, terror, fraud, corruption, violence, mayhem, and murder."[20]

State-level attempts to permanently institutionalize not only race-based segregation but also the disenfranchisement of virtually everyone except white males point to one of the most critical developments of the era. Between 1890 and 1908, ten (10) Southern states wrote new constitutions with provisions that enshrined literacy tests, poll taxes, and grandfather clauses. The model approach was that developed by the state of Mississippi; it called explicitly for blacks to be penalized as a racial group.[21] Walton and Smith refer to the period from 1890 to 1901 as the "era of disenfranchisement" during which "the states of the Old Confederacy adopted new state constitutions that prevented, prohibited, or manipulated African Americans out of their voting rights."[22]

Later on, some Southern states used the white primary to minimize or eliminate the threat of black voting. The rise of the white primary as an electoral device signified a unique period of exclusion, originating in 1923 when the Texas legislature passed a statute preventing blacks from voting in the Democratic Party primaries. As an electoral device, the white primary was employed in one-party states where the primary nominee was certain to prevail in the general election; it effectively denied the right to vote to African Americans. Following a series of cases challenging the white primary, the U.S. Supreme Court, in *Smith v. Allwright*, 321 U.S. 649 (1944) held that since the state of Texas regulated primaries, the practice of barring black voters from voting in the primaries must be considered as state action and as such was unconstitutional. This translated to the Democratic Party no longer being able to operate as if it were a "private" club or organization.[23] The upshot of the ruling was its facilitation of the transfer of African American's political allegiance from the Republican Party to the Democratic Party. Stephen F. Lawson has explained:

> Since the white primary had erected a solid fortress keeping blacks out of the polling booths, its demolition opened the ironclad doors to the most important election in southern politics. The decision arrived at a time when the majority of blacks had recently abandoned their historic attachment to the GOP for the party of Franklin Roosevelt. For Negro Republicans in the South, the one-party system was a mighty cross to bear in addition to the poll tax and literacy tests. The opening of the Democratic primary coming as most blacks were joining the New Deal coalition presented opportunities for participation in politics missing since the 1890s.[24]

However, while the Supreme Court's decision in *Smith v. Allwright* (1944) signified a substantive shift in the direction of securing black voting rights, it did not portend the end of the structural impediments that were in place to prevent voter access and exercise of the franchise. For the remainder of the 20th century, and consistent with the past, African Americans advocated for their voting rights as a crucial aspect of citizenship. During this period, the major recurring voting rights impediments included malapportionment, annexation, consolidation, run-off elections, and at-large or multimember election systems. This new phase of vote suppression, however, unhinged some important changes in the legal environment in the form of a series of new and increasingly strong national laws eventually enacted explicitly to address racial discrimination in the political process.[25]

Thus, progressive changes in the political environment, particularly the fall of the Democratic primary, helped to alter perceptions of the electoral power of African American voters. As a device to shrink the exercise of the vote among blacks, the white primary, which had been an indispensable tool for the maintenance of white supremacy and Dixiecratic power, withered away between 1944 and 1952 after considerable resistance, lending indispensable momentum to the rise of the Civil Rights era.[26]

Civil Rights Era

The Civil Rights era was one of tremendous hope and promise. After World War II ended, many black soldiers returned home from their stations overseas, only to discover that despite their service to the country, they would still be treated as second-class citizens. With the zeal to challenge and transform society, many began to sense that the time was right to participate in the political arena not only through informal mechanisms but by casting the ballot wherever possible. As a group, African Americans began to realize that if they could cast their votes as a bloc, there might well be opportunities to essentially direct electoral outcomes. President Franklin D. Roosevelt's New Deal initiative was welcomed by blacks as it created essential social programs and employment opportunities in aftermath of the Great Depression, which had decimated Americans generally, with even heavier consequences for African Americans and the poor. Perhaps unknowingly, Roosevelt lent credence to African Americans' belief that they could change electoral outcomes by voting as a bloc. However, while he recognized that he needed the support of black voters, Roosevelt also realized that race had to be minimized (he even refused to support anti-lynching legislation) in order to hold the New Deal coalition together.[27] Despite his downplaying of racial issues, Roosevelt managed to engender the optimism and support needed to encourage African Americans to commit to the Democratic Party for more than 70 years—and they did so, despite the party's role in hastening the decline of the first Reconstruction.

Among the major accomplishments of the Civil Rights era is the passage of the 1964 Civil Rights Act; however, to view this legislation discretely would suggest that such historical developments are noncumulative. Nor should this legislation be assumed unrelated to the development of voting rights. While the Civil Rights Acts have largely been seen in terms of their contribution to the development of access to public accommodations, they have also played a pivotal part in securing the right to vote. Almost 80 years following the enactment of the 1875 Civil Rights Act, which was overturned by the 1883 Civil Rights Cases, the Civil Rights Act of 1957 was passed. Significantly, this legislation gave the federal government the authority to obtain an injunction against any threatened or actual interference with voting rights. The 1957 act stipulated further that U.S. district courts exercise jurisdiction over such suits and that the customary requirement that plaintiffs first exhaust available state and judicial remedies would no longer apply.[28]

Three years later, the Civil Rights Act of 1960 was passed. The content of the bill explicitly suggested that the problem of protecting the voting rights of people of African descent had not been resolved by the passage of previous legislation, including the 1875 and 1957 legislative actions. The Civil Rights Act of 1960 addressed this persistent problem by providing for the appointment of federal "voting referees" in order to safeguard blacks' right to vote without discrimination. The 1960 act further authorized federal district courts to enlist qualified voters for all state and federal elections in locales where systematic disenfranchisement had occurred. Giving more teeth to the legislation was the provision that the U.S. Department of Justice could challenge those cases in which individuals had been denied their voting rights.[29]

The 1964 Civil Rights Act provided for even greater comprehensive federal oversight of voting than had been demonstrated by prior legislation. This act required voting registrars to apply consistent standards for applicants regardless of race mandated that literacy tests be in writing and defined a sixth-grade education as a refutable presumption of literacy. The 1964 act also permitted the U.S. attorney general to sue upon written complaint by aggrieved individuals.[30]

J. Morgan Kousser (2000, 33–40) points out that there are a number of similarities between the 1964 Civil Rights Act and the 1875 Civil Rights Act, which was swept away with the decline of Reconstruction. Remarkably similar to the 1964 legislation, the 1875 act stipulated in part:

> That all persons within the jurisdiction of the United States shall be entitled to the full and equal enjoyment of the accommodations, advantages, facilities, and privileges of inns, public conveyances on land or water, theaters, and other places of public amusement; subject only to the conditions and limitations established by law, and applicable alike to citizens of every race and color, regardless of any previous condition of servitude.[31]

In contrast, the 1964 Civil Rights Act reads as follows:

> All persons shall be entitled to the full and equal enjoyment of the goods, services, facilities, privileges, advantages, and accommodations of any place of public accommodation, as defined in this section without discrimination or segregation on the ground of race, color, religion, or national origin.[32]

The differences in the language of the two bills lie in the specificity of the 1964 act, particularly the reference to segregation, which is not mentioned in the 1875 legislation. Also notably, unlike its 20th-century descendent, the 1875 Civil Rights Act did not include any provisions regarding voting and enfranchisement. Interestingly, the 1875 act was passed almost strictly along partisan lines and was rather weak legislation, although there was negotiated support from a few Democrats, who in turn were able to force the removal of language in the bill that integrated churches and schools. Moreover, the act was passed in the lame duck session of Congress following the Republicans' loss of 47 percent of its seats in the House of Representatives.[33] Ironically, these developments marked the end of the "First Reconstruction," which depending upon the Southern state, lasted up to a decade.

While it is clear that the modern Civil Rights Acts helped enable the inclusive, guaranteed exercise of the franchise, it was the Voting Rights Act (VRA) of 1965 that reaped the boldest legislative achievements in the struggle for black enfranchisement. One indication of the strength of this legislation in contrast to the 1964 Civil Rights Act was Title I's declaration that it was unlawful to attempt to deny the right to vote, which had been granted to all people by the Fifteenth and Nineteenth Amendments. In effect, the Civil Rights Act held that any voter qualifications must be equally applied to all persons. For example, if literacy tests were going to be used to establish voter qualifications, they would have to be administered to everyone in order to comply with the law.[34]

A major distinction therefore between the Civil Rights Act and the Voting Rights Act is that the latter rendered illegal the determination of voting qualifications on the basis of race or color. In contrast, the Civil Rights Act essentially held that any qualifications must be applied in a color-blind manner. Critically important in the Voting Rights Act is a feature giving the federal government discretionary authority to act on behalf of the aggrieved. In instances in which local registrars refused to comply with the guarantees of the Fifteenth Amendment, the federal government was empowered to take the action necessary to ensure compliance.[35]

However, there are some other differences between the Civil Rights and Voting Rights Acts. Several of the provisions of the latter legislation are temporary, requiring periodic reauthorization. Section 2 of the act prohibits any "voting qualification or prerequisite to voting, or standard, practice or procedure" employed by any state or political subdivision "to deny or abridge the right of any citizen of the United States to vote on account of race or color." Of the temporary provisions of the law, two have been controversial. Overturned by the U.S. Supreme Court during spring, 2014 by virtue of the invalidation of Section 4, Section 5 has been highly controversial. Referred to as the preclearance provision, it obliged the majority of the Southern states, as well as other jurisdictions, to receive advance approval of changes to election procedures by the Department of Justice or the U.S. District Court for the District of Columbia. Under the statute, federal approval required proof that the proposed change would not have an intentional impact with respect to abridgement or denial of the right to vote due to race or membership in a language minority group.[36] Along with Section 5, Section 203 of the Voting Rights Act, which was added in 1975 when the law was renewed, requires jurisdictions to provide multilingual ballots where there are large populations of non-English-speaking persons.[37] The implications of this development are discussed in more detail below.

The immediate impact of the 1965 Voting Rights Act on access to the political process was enormous. Table 1.2 illustrates the impact. The table shows that the rate of African American voter registration in the former Confederate states increased substantially for the period from 1947 to 1966. While the effects of the legislation were strong in terms of impact on black voter registration throughout the former Confederate states, Georgia exhibited the lowest percentage change for the period (28.8%), and Alabama the highest (50%). Although the effects of the act were felt across the country, the impact of the legislation was most clear in the registration and voting patterns of African Americans in the southern region of the United States. Illustrating this point is U.S. Bureau of Census data, which reveals that in the 1964 presidential election, 72 percent of African Americans in the regions of the Northeast, Midwest, and West voted. In contrast, however, only 44 percent of African Americans in the South cast ballots. By 2008, black turnout in the South reached 66 percent, exceeding that for all other racial groups in the region.[38]

As an intervention strategy against white domination, the passage of the Voting Rights Act dramatically altered the political landscape, especially that in the South. Ironically, the success of this legislation helped to hasten the onset of the Post–Civil Rights era. While it was clear that the legislation was having a positive effect, there were many blacks and whites who considered the battle for equality to be over. This was evinced by the strong surge in black voter registration and participation, and later, the growth in the number of black elected officials contributed to fueling these perceptions. The illusion of success engendered by the passage of the act prompted

TABLE 1.2   Percentage of Voting Age African Americans Registered to
Vote in Southern States, 1947–66

State	1947 (%)	1952 (%)	1956 (%)	1966 (%)	Overall % Increase
Alabama	1.2	5	11	51.2	50
Arkansas	17.3	27	36	59.7	42.5
Florida	15.4	33	32	60.9	45.5
Georgia	18.8	23	27	47.2	28.4
Louisiana	2.6	25	31	47.1	44.5
Mississippi	0.9	4	5	32.9	32
North Carolina	15.2	18	24	51.0	45.8
South Carolina	13.0	20	27	51.4	48.4
Tennessee	25.8	25	27	71.7	46.9
Texas	18.5	31	37	61.6	43.1
Virginia	13.2	16	19	46.9	33.7

Source: Adapted from Hanes Walton Jr., *Black Politics: A Theoretical and Structural Analysis*
(New York: J.B. Lippincott Company, 1972), p. 4.

political complacency on the part of those who had helped bring about the
change, leading to an opportunity for the opposition to regroup and mobilize to counter the historic expansion of the right to vote. Not only did black
voting participation substantially increase, but notable was also the steady
increase in the number of black elected officials throughout the country
and especially in the South. Both of these trends were clearly associated
with the Voting Rights Act of 1965 and subsequent amendments in 1970,
1975, and 1982. These legal developments combined with the trend of diversity in the United States have fashioned an era of post-racialism in which
racial equality is presumed, and charges of racism and racial discrimination
are interpreted to be a presentation of victimization to gain the sympathy
of the public. It was inevitable in such a climate that the significance of race
would continue to diminish in the public discourse and ultimately be re-
flected in the implementation of so-called race-neutral policies.

Post–Civil Rights Era

In many respects, the 21st century is but an echo of the past. Among the
social and political developments in the Post–Civil Rights period is the
so-called era of post-racialism. Similar to Reconstruction, the Post–Civil

Rights era is one of the most productive periods of political empowerment for African Americans in terms of voting, office seeking, and winning political office. The period began simultaneously with the decline of protest politics and the rise of formal black electoral participation, which had been operationalized through the Civil Rights Movement. However, in a manner similar to that of Reconstruction, the Post–Civil Rights era thus far has exhibited a political and social volatility with grave implications for democratic practice in the United States.

The era of Post–Civil Rights is marked by several features, including the continued expansion of the electorate, as well as the continued growth of black office-holding in the United States, and especially in the South. Perhaps the apparent momentum of black political participation has led to a third prominent characteristic of the Post–Civil Rights era: the minimization of race as a factor in American society. What this meant, of course, is that race and racial differences would no longer provide a basis for challenging discrimination and social inequalities. The growing emphasis on so-called "race-neutral" policies helped to further obscure and obfuscate recognition of legitimate cases of racial discrimination and inequality. Although the courts generally remained supportive of African American voting rights in the early decades of the Post–Civil Rights era, the nation's growing diversity (especially electoral) provided an opportunity to essentially set aside black issues, thus making it clear that as a numerical minority, African Americans would no longer be a dominant consideration.

In 1970, five years following the passage of the Voting Rights Act, amendments were made extending the right to vote to 18-year-old citizens, and prohibiting the use of literacy as a condition to voter registration. Five years later, in 1975, an amendment was passed which permanently prohibited literacy tests. This amendment also renewed the act for an additional seven years. These key modifications to the 1965 legislation widened further the reaches of American democracy, facilitating exercise of the franchise by not only African Americans, but also other groups including Hispanics, Filipinos, Chinese, and Japanese.[39] Abigail Thernstrom has suggested, however, that in 1975, Congress departed radically from the statute's original aim of black enfranchisement by conceding the argument of the Mexican-American Legal Defense and Education Fund (MALDEF) that Hispanics should be afforded the same "extraordinary" protection that African Americans had been given. Specifically, MALDEF questioned whether there was any real difference between, for example, Alabama and Texas if both were engaged in changing voting rules that would yield discriminatory results. It was pointed out that while Alabama must seek federal approval to draw new district maps, relocate polling places, and annex areas outside of municipal limits, Texas, without federal restraint, could freely adopt at-large voting, redraw city council districts, or make any other changes to the electoral system that it deemed was fitting. Thus, while broadening the racial group coverage of the Voting Rights Act, the 1975 reauthorization and amendment process not only changed the trigger for coverage but also redefined "literacy test" to include English-only ballots in Texas, Arizona, and Alaska, along with designated counties in California, Florida, and South Dakota.[40]

In 1982, Congress extended the Voting Rights Act by 25 years, a decision heavily motivated by the consensus that Sections 2 and 5 of the act should be renewed. The 1982 extension strengthened the climate for the 1990 round of redistricting, which in turn, enhanced black electoral fortunes in the House of Representatives, which grew from 15 to 27 nationally and from 4 to 14 in the South. It was the vigorous enforcement of Section 5 that buttressed the electoral capacity for growth in black office-holding during the period, much of which can be attributed to the change from single-member districts, reapportionment, and court challenges to actions believed to violate the Voting Rights Act.[41]

The climate for black political fortunes was challenged, however, with the Supreme Court's ruling in *Mobile v. Bolden,* 446 U.S. 55 (1980), which required plaintiffs to prove "discriminatory intent" on the part of state and local governments in implementing or modifying electoral districts. About six years later, the Court in *Thornburg v. Gingles,* 478 U.S. 30 (1986) determined that dilution of the black vote in North Carolina was unconstitutional based on multimember district schemes that resulted in inequality in the opportunities at the disposal of black and white voters to elect their preferred representatives. The case challenged a North Carolina redistricting plan, which in the eyes of voting rights advocates ignored the opportunity to establish a majority–minority district. While redistricting had proven effective as a means for achieving population equalization among districts, the Gingles challenge revealed that it could be used by state legislatures to undermine the Voting Rights Act. Following the Gingles ruling, in excess of 90 percent of legal challenges to municipal at-large elections were victorious.[42] Specifically, Gingles stipulated that in order to prevail, plaintiffs must demonstrate the following: (1) lingering effects of past discrimination, (2) the extent of racially polarized voting in the electoral jurisdiction, (3) racial bias in election campaigns, and (4) patterns of racial bloc voting over extended periods of time. Gingles resulted in the Supreme Court upholding the 1982 amendments to the Voting Rights Act, thus "validat[ing] the fundamental democratic principles of participation, representational choice, and equal access to the electoral arena" (Hill and Reddix-Smalls, 2002, 14–15).[43] Both the *Mobile v. Bolden* and *Thornburg v. Gingles* decisions paved the way for a number of important legal challenges dealing with reapportioned districts at the local, state, and congressional levels.

Following the Gingles ruling, the justice's potential to vacillate or be ambivalent became apparent. Practically speaking, the decision seemed to signal that the Supreme Court would no longer be the principal institutional shield of African Americans against relentless forces bent on undermining the political gains of the Civil Rights Movement. This tendency was revealed when another turning point was unveiled with the decision in *Shaw v. Reno,* 509 U.S. 630 (1993). This important case took aim at shaping how the Court would view the basis for enfranchisement. However, a split ruling, with Justice Sandra Day O'Connor serving as the swing vote, in the end, was of no comfort to liberals and progressives, many of whom were taken aback by the narrow 5–4 ruling. O'Connor's pivot to support the conservative wing of the Court rested in large part on the argument that the district in question had been drawn in an irregular shape. In her written opinion, O'Connor rejected the assumption that because people happened to be of the same race that they necessarily "think alike, share the same political interests and will prefer the same candidate." She further asserted that the district that was drawn was "so bizarre on its face that it is unexplainable on grounds other than race," thus suggesting that the same scrutiny applied to other state laws also be applied to redistricting (*Shaw v. Reno,* 509 U.S. 630, 1993).[44]

In his dissent of the Court's majority opinion, Justice Stevens framed the ruling as a decision that would undermine the equal protection clause of the Fourteenth Amendment. The ruling forced the states that had drawn such districts to demonstrate adherence to the Court's "strict scrutiny" of such districts. Thus, with the Shaw decision, the stage was set for a number of cases that would challenge the establishment of minority–majority districts in the states of Florida, Georgia, Louisiana, and Texas. It was decided that there should be a full trial to consider a challenge that was being made contesting two North Carolina majority–minority districts. Focusing on the irregular shapes of these districts, the Court determined that one of the North Carolina districts was inexplicable on grounds other than race, and as such, was evidence of "racial gerrymandering" and "political apartheid" in violation of the Equal Protection Clause of the Fourteenth Amendment.[45]

The Shaw ruling laid the groundwork for a series of cases that would come before the Court to contest majority–minority congressional districts in Florida, Georgia, Louisiana, and Texas. In 1995, the Supreme Court in *Miller v. Johnson,* 515 U.S. 900 used the reasoning in Shaw to show that race was the principle factor in drawing Georgia's Eleventh District. Thus, the Court determined that the drawing of the Eleventh District was "narrowly tailored," in violation of "strict scrutiny" that the Court had imposed.[46] *Bush v. Vera,* 517 U.S. 952 came before the Supreme Court one year later. In this case, it was found that three majority–minority congressional districts—two African American and one Latino—had employed race as the main factor in drawing district boundaries. Consequently, it was determined that the districts did not pass the strict scrutiny test of the Court due to Texas' failure to specifically focus on remedying "identified discrimination" founded on a "strong basis in evidence."[47]

Shaw v. Hunt, 517 U.S. 899 (1996), known also as *Shaw II,* ruled invalid North Carolina's redistricting plan because the message had been conveyed by the government that political identity could be based primarily on race. In the end, the Court's finding in *Shaw II* combined with the rulings from *Shaw I, Miller, and Bush* to prevent the continued ascendancy of African Americans to elected office. These cases have proven instrumental in redefining the role of the Court and their use of the Constitution to guarantee state processes for legislative representation, and ultimately they have helped stifle the growth in black office-holding that was initiated with the enactment of the Voting Rights Act.[48]

The next opportunity for action on the Voting Rights Act was in 2007, the year during which the Section 5 preclearance provision was set to expire. Sections 6 through 9 included the observer provisions, which authorized the federal government to send federal election examiners and observers to certain jurisdictions covered by Section 5, where there was evidence of voter intimidation. While Sections 6 through 9 were permanent, their utilization was primarily through the Section 5 preclearance provision. Anxious to avoid a partisan confrontation, the Republican-controlled Congress again renewed Section 5 for another 25 years, setting it in place through the year 2032. One year before it expired in July 2006, George W. Bush signed the Voting Rights Act extension, which had passed with a strong bipartisan vote of 98–0 in the Senate and in the House 390–33. Some Southern lawmakers, as to be expected, were opposed; they argued that race relations in their states had changed considerably since the 1965 act. The Bush administration's renewal of the legislation left the following states under federal oversight: Alabama, Alaska, Arizona, Georgia, Louisiana, Mississippi, South Carolina, Texas, and Virginia. This remained the situation until the passage of the U.S. Supreme Court's 2014 ruling striking down key provisions of the Voting Rights Act that had been instrumental in securing and protecting the voting rights of African Americans and other minorities.[49]

Democratic Practice and Diversity in the Era of Post-Racialism

The contraction of democratic practice that is occurring simultaneously with the nation's growing diversity is increasingly entangled with the immigration issue, in part due to the growing political empowerment of Hispanics, Asians, and other nonwhite numerical minorities in the electoral arena. In fact, immigration has emerged as a partisan issue with tremendous import for conservatives who seem preoccupied with the notion that diversity may be a threat to their capacity to acquire and maintain political power. Even while declarations of the view that America has entered a post-racial era abound, the Post–Civil Rights period features attempts by diversity opponents to minimize or eliminate voter participation, especially among African Americans and people of color, but in actuality, anyone who opposes the conservative agenda. Inevitably, the reality of the racial dimensions of this power struggle easily renders the argument of a post-racial America null and void.

Interestingly, while the contention of a post-racial United States is strong among the populous, the contraction of democracy in the Post–Civil Rights period features race as a declining consideration in politics and policy-making. The changed context of race and the attendant decline of racial politics enabled forces opposed to inclusion to develop, refine, and impose new obstacles, which in some ways are a throwback to the barriers erected to prevent exercise of the franchise imposed in the Jim Crow period. Indeed, Jim Crow and the modern era are strikingly similar with respect to the hijacking of public policy to achieve the political objectives of social forces aiming to acquire and/or maintain their power base. To the detriment of the nation, such tactics facilitate democratic erosion and the lack of inclusiveness of political participation. The major recurring voting rights impediments in place in the era of Post–Civil Rights include malapportionment, annexation, consolidation, run-off elections, and at-large or multimember election systems. More than a decade ago, political science professor Dianne

Pinderhughes warned of the decline of the public sector nationally, and the impact of markets on democracy. She lamented:

> as long as African-Americans were excluded entirely from Citizenship, or were legally segregated within the polity, public sector power, authority and values remained relatively stable. Having admitted African-Americans fully (at least in theory) to the public sector, we watched whites exit geographic and political spaces African-Americans had recently entered. At the same time, we watched the reconstruction of political values about the meaning of that public space; in fact one could assert that people have behaved *as if* government and the public sphere had become polluted by African-Americans' presence.[50]

Thus, ironically one of the consequences of black empowerment is the commandeering of the public sector for use on behalf of a largely segregated private sector, or at least one that in the 21st century, will largely continue to be off limits to African Americans. The danger lies in the fact that the Civil Rights Movement not only enhanced the citizenship and political voice of African Americans, it did so too for Asians and other non-Europeans and expanded it for indigenous populations. The question is whether all groups regardless of skin color will have access to the levers of government and policy-making to influence outcomes in regard to economic issues.[51]

The election of President Barack H. Obama, the first African American to occupy the American presidency, is an impressive milestone achievement, not only nationally but also internationally since he arguably holds the most powerful political office in the world. Obama's election helped to promote the idea within and without that race is no longer significant and that race neutrality has been achieved in the United States. Despite the optimism engendered by his rise to power, the 2008 election outcome was a catalyst for the American political right to challenge the inclusive public policies that have opened up the electoral arena to African Americans, Hispanics, Asians, other immigrant groups, and the poor. In light of the trend of diversity, the concern among Republican operatives may be manifested in the belief that their power will likely be diminished as the voting electorate becomes increasingly nonwhite. Rather than opt to make changes to their policy positions that would attract nonwhite voters, the current power base of conservatives, the Republican Party, has remained stalwart in its posture, thus reinforcing the need to minimize nonwhite interests and consequently devalue their voting participation. This has occurred primarily through the erection of barriers to voting rights and by the apparent decision not to commit time or resources to gain more supporters from among the traditionally oppositional and relative newcomers to electoral participation.

As a defining feature of the Post–Civil Rights era, Barack Obama's election signified the optimism of U.S. citizens about the full extension of democratic practice and the elimination of racial obstacles not only in politics but also in the society at large. A multitude of analysts and pundits stressed that if elected, President Obama would advance the United States to an era of post-racialism. At least popularly, the term "post-racial era" is largely defined as a period when race or skin color no longer serves as an essential basis for the distribution of the wealth, power, and social resources. More broadly, however, the term implies the persistence of an institutionalized racial differentiation of wealth, power, and resources. In the Post–Civil Rights era, racial differences persist on such basic quality of life measures as income, rates of infant mortality, home ownership, high school and college graduation, etc. As a group, African Americans lag behind whites and others, and race is still a major feature of the sociopolitical landscape. Given that similar patterns are present in government, a "post-racial" president is mandated to eradicate institutional racism in government by taking positions and making decisions to bring about racial parity. Ironically, to take such action requires the acknowledgment of race and/or the conspicuous absence of diversity, since it comprises the empirical basis upon which institutional change can be reasonably advanced and assessed.

President Obama's rise to power occurred in the midst of the nation's devaluation of government and the public sector. The racial dynamics associated with the decline of the public sector and government has added a layer of complexity to understanding the problems and successes of the Obama presidency. As a result of overt and institutionalized racism, he has faced tremendous resistance from opponents committed to the charge of containing the growth and influence of the federal government. Pinderhughes points out that public sector decline has had several consequences. First, due to budget reductions over the years the public sector has grown smaller. Second, increased legitimacy accorded the private sector has lent itself to the suggestion that the federal government is incapable of serving the public efficiently and effectively. Third, the social emphasis has shifted from engendering collective values to emphasizing more strongly the ideals of individualism, choice, and competition. A fourth critical outcome of the public sector's decline is that the "definition of the national polity was reframed so as to make public space considerably less useful and hospitable to groups not already economically entitled."[52] The latter effect is especially troubling given the suggestion that African Americans could well likely find themselves on the economic periphery.

Catalysts for New Voting Restrictions

In the 21st century, an evolutionary shift in population and consequently electoral participation began in the United States. Demographers have projected that emerging patterns of nonwhite subgroups and their growing registration and voting patterns will likely be sustained well into the future. Such developments have clear implications for political party positioning in the electoral arena to attract the support of new entrants to the process of democratic participation. However, when a well-situated vocal minority is operating within a mainstream political party, it can potentially wreak havoc thus minimizing the chances of striking a balanced position for the sake of the party. The climate of intense partisanship in Washington, D.C., prompts questions regarding the political motivations of conservatives, primarily Republicans, who seek to change public policy on the erroneous basis that race is no longer a factor in the United States. If given free reign, the effort will continue to effectively undercut American democracy by limiting and constricting citizen access to exercise of the franchise. One can easily surmise that the Republican Party may have calculated that its policy positions are misaligned with the needs and issues of the nation's rapidly growing and emerging nonwhite voting groups.

Research has established that young African Americans are the most politically engaged of any other racial or ethnic group. They are considered the most likely to get out and vote, as well as to actively participate in politics and the political process. Indeed, all ethnic groups show a trend suggesting that the more highly educated are the most likely to vote and participate in the political process. Hence, one motivation for the current disenfranchisement initiatives is likely the existing and potential voting strength of African Americans and nonwhites. Table 1.3 shows the composition of the voting population and eligible electorate by race and Hispanic origin for the period from 1996 to 2012. The data shown for the period reveal steady growth among nonwhites in terms of their representation as a percentage of eligible voters and those who actually vote. On the other hand, for the specified period, as a percentage of the eligible electorate and as a percentage of the voting population, the proportion of whites respectively declined between 1996 and 2012 from 79.2 to 71.1 percent and from 82.5 to 73.6 percent in these categories. These trends sound an alarm to those interested in maintaining the status quo and governance standards that neglect inclusiveness. These patterns indeed may signify the decline of existing regimes of white domination, in both political and economic terms, and thereby indicate to conservatives the need for strong action in regard to reshaping electoral standards, but not necessarily its policy positions, which are the true motivation for an individuals' support in a democratic republic.

TABLE 1.3 Composition of the Voting Population and Eligible Electorate by Race and Hispanic Origin: 1996–2012

Year/Race and Hispanic Origin	% Eligible Electorate	% Voting Population
2012		
White, non-Hispanics	71.1	73.7
Blacks	12.5	13.4
Hispanics	10.8	8.4
Asians	3.8	2.9
2008		
White, non-Hispanics	73.4	76.3
Blacks	12.1	12.3
Hispanics	9.5	7.4
Asians	3.4	2.6
2004		
White, non-Hispanics	75.2	79.2
Blacks	11.9	11.1
Hispanics	8.2	6.0
Asians	3.2	2.2

(*Continued*)

TABLE 1.3   (Continued)

Year/Race and Hispanic Origin	% Eligible Electorate	% Voting Population
2000		
White, non-Hispanics	77.7	80.7
Blacks	12.2	11.7
Hispanics	7.1	5.4
Asians	2.5	1.8
1996		
White, non-Hispanics	79.2	82.5
Blacks	11.9	10.8
Hispanics	6.1	4.7
Asians	2.1	1.7

Notes: Federal surveys now give respondents the option of reporting more than one race. Therefore, two basic ways of defining a race group are possible. A group such as Asian may be defined as those who reported Asian and no other race (the race-alone or single-race concept) or as those who reported Asian regardless of whether they also reported another race (the race-alone-or-in-combination concept). Eligible electorate refers specifically to citizens 18 years of age and older, or the citizen voting-age population. Voting population refers to the number of voting-age citizens who actually reported casting ballots.

Source: U.S. Census Bureau, Current Population Survey, November Select Years.

Since the 2000 presidential election, the country has undergone significant growth in its nonwhite population, most notably revealed in the electoral participation that has tended to outpace that of whites. Changes in the composition of the voting population shows that nonwhites have grown significantly in their representation among the nation's eligible voters and as a proportion of those who actually vote. Table 1.4 shows changes in voter turnout by race and Hispanic origin for the period from 1996 through 2012. In comparison to white voters, overall the figures reveal strong increases in nonwhite voting for each of the presidential elections held since 1996. In the United States in 2010, non-Hispanic whites voted at a higher rate (49%) than blacks (43%). In 2004, non-Hispanic whites voted at a higher rate (67%) than blacks (62%). Over four voting cycles, the difference remained more or less constant between black and white voting percentages. Although these numbers show a steady state in the demographics of the voting base, the African American community has achieved at least two significant milestones in recent history, which will be discussed later.

Long-term trends suggest a steady pattern, with no dramatic increase or decrease in the voting behavior of African Americans. Traditionally, however, voter turnout increases when there is a presidential election. In 2008, African American youth voted for candidate Barack Obama at a significantly increased rate. Since then, however, there has been a steady decline in voter turnout in general. This declining trend corresponds with the steady decline of voter confidence and trust in America's political leadership.

TABLE 1.4   Voter Turnout by Race and Hispanic Origin: 1996–2012 (In thousands)

Year/Race and Hispanic Origin	Total Votes Cast	Net Change from Previous Presidential Election
2012	**Number**	**% Change**
Total	132,948	1,804
White, non-Hispanics	98,041	−2,001
Blacks	17,813	1,680
Asians	3,904	547
Hispanics	11,188	1,443
2008		
Total	131,144	5,408
White, non-Hispanics	100,042	475
Blacks	16,133	2,117
Asians	3,357	589
Hispanics	9,745	2,158
2004		
Total	125,736	14,910
White, non-Hispanics	99,567	10,098

(Continued)

TABLE 1.4   (Continued)

Year/Race and Hispanic Origin	Total Votes Cast	Net Change from Previous Presidential Election
Blacks	14,016	1,099
Asians	2,768	723
Hispanics	7,587	1,653
2000		
Total	110,826	5,809
White, non-Hispanics	89,469	2,865
Blacks	12,917	1,531
Asians	2,045	304
Hispanics	5,934	1,006

Notes: Federal surveys now give respondents the option of reporting more than one race. Therefore, two basic ways of defining a race group are possible. A group such as Asian may be defined as those who reported Asian and no other race (the race-alone or single-race concept) or as those who reported Asian regardless of whether they also reported another race (the race-alone-or-in-combination concept).

Source: Adapted from U.S. Census Bureau, Current Population Survey, November Select Years.

Figure 1.1 illustrates the changing makeup of the electorate in the United States for the period 1996 through 2012. Specifically, it illustrates voting rates in presidential contests by race and Hispanic origin from 1996 through 2012. The bottom graph shows differences between the shares of the voting population and eligible electorate by race and Hispanic origin for the same period. As the line graph shows, in 2012, a historical milestone was achieved for the first time in presidential election history when African American voter turnout exceeded that of any other group. The voting rates for the period 1996 to 2012 for Hispanics and Asians have steadily increased respectively from 45 to 48 percent and from 44 to 47 percent. Noteworthy is the almost two-percentage point decline in voting for Hispanics between 2008 and 2012. This can be explained by the heightened anti-immigration rhetoric and increased deportation activity, which created a climate of intimidation threatening even to legitimate voters.

African American voting long lagged behind that of other racial and ethnic groups. The difference reached a high point in 1972 when it measured 10.9 percent. Since that time, however, the difference has fallen dramatically, and in 2000, the difference was only 1.2 percent. For the first time in 2008, the trend was reversed, and black citizens voted at a 2.6 percent greater rate than all other citizens. The trend culminated in 2012 when African American voter turnout exceeded that of white Americans. Although African American voters comprised only 11 percent of the electorate, they

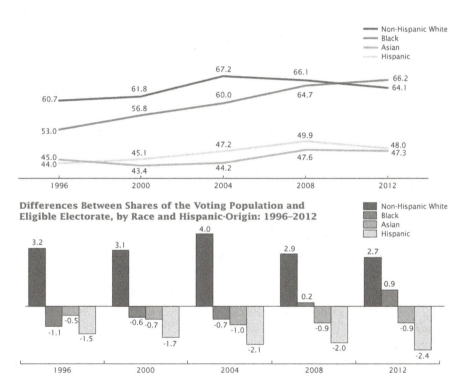

FIGURE 1.1.   Voting Rates in Presidential Elections, by Race and Hispanic Origin: 1996–2012

Note: The top portion of this graphic shows voting rates over time by race groups and Hispanics. The bottom portion shows these subpopulation's shares of the eligible electorate compared to their shares of the actual voting population. For example, in 2012 the non-Hispanic white share of the voting populations was 2.7 percentage points higher than the non-Hispanic white share of the eligible electorate.

Source: U.S. Census Bureau, Current Population Survey, November Select Years.

accounted for 13 percent of 129 million ballots cast in 2012, roughly the same as in 2008 according to exit polls. Moreover, consistent with historical patterns, about 93 percent of African American voters cast their ballots for Barack Obama, the Democratic candidate (U.S. Census, 2013). As illustrated in Figure 1.1, there may be sound reasoning for the conservative wing of the nation to be concerned with the loss of political power. In 2012, black voters cast ballots at a rate higher (66.2) than whites (64.1), leaving a residual race gap of 2.1 percent.

Right Wing Reaction

As has already been demonstrated, suppression of the right to vote is not new to American politics. In fact, one might even argue that vote suppression is intrinsic to the culture of American politics, which by its very nature is a tug of war between democratic and anti-democratic forces seeking to win political power by virtually any means. Since the timing with which the imposition of new voting restrictions were intensified (following the 2008 presidential election) appears to coincide with the opportunity to reelect the nation's first African American president, one cannot escape the notion that race and diversity may have been principal motivating factors for the imposition of a new wave of restrictive voting measures.

During 2011, new laws were enacted in states around the nation to restrict the right to vote. The Brennan Center for Justice at New York University School of Law estimated that more than 5 million Americans could be affected by the new rules—a number larger than the margin of victory in two of the last three presidential elections. New photo ID laws, proof of citizenship laws, laws making it harder to register to vote, for example, ending Election Day voter registration, reducing early and absentee days, and making it more difficult for the voting rights of felons to be restored were among the kinds of changes made prior to the 2012 election. The Brennan Center for Justice based its projection of more than 5 million voters on six key projections outlined below:

1. New photo ID laws for voting would be in effect for the 2012 election in five states including Kansas, South Carolina, Tennessee, Texas, Wisconsin, and that 3.2 million voters would be affected.
2. New proof of citizenship laws would be in effect in Alabama, Kansas, and Tennessee (two of which will also have new photo ID laws), and that 240,000 additional citizens and potential voters will be affected by new proof of citizenship laws.

3. Laws passed by two states, Florida and Texas, would restrict voter registration drives, causing all or most of those drives to stop. Based on 2008 voter registration drives, it was estimated that 202,000 voters would be affected as a result of voter registration drives being made extremely difficult or impossible under new laws.

4. In Maine, 60,000 voters would be affected in jurisdictions where Election Day voter registration was repealed because Maine abolished Election Day registration. (Based on 2008 Election Day voter registration.)

5. The early voting period would be cut by half or more in three states (Florida, Georgia and Ohio). Based on this activity in 2008, The Brennan Center projected that one to two million voters would be eliminated under new laws limiting or eliminating early voting.

6. Finally, it was projected that at least 100,000 disenfranchised citizens who might have regained voting rights by 2016 would likely remain disenfranchised because of efforts taken to make it more difficult to restore the right to vote to convicted felons. For example, Florida and Iowa made it substantially more difficult or impossible for people with felony convictions to get their voting rights restored. The Sentencing Project, a Washington, D.C., voter restoration advocacy group, found that in Virginia one in five (20%) African Americans had lost the right to vote because of a felony. At the time, the rate in Virginia was one of the highest in the country, only trailing Florida (23%) and Kentucky (22%). It is important to note that in Virginia, even the completion of sentence and being off parole does not automatically result in restoration of voting rights; voting rights can only be restored by the governor.

Initiatives to restrict the right to vote led to a number of important legal challenges made by citizens and community groups. We discuss the status of these challenges in the final chapter of this book. These challenges and their attendant outcomes suggest that the country has entered a period of voting decline, more broadly, democratic contraction that is consistent with historical patterns. Our consideration of the development of voting rights in the United States necessarily takes into account strongly the cyclical and repetitive reinforcing patterns of enfranchisement, disfranchisement, and enfranchisement that prominently characterize the historical nature of voting. Voting, however, must not be viewed strictly from a quantitative perspective as impediments to voting can come in many forms. As demonstrated in the recent North Carolina legislation on voting registration, there are many means and causes behind the disenfranchisement of the voting public. Clearly, the North Carolina law is an attempt to erode the voter base of the Democratic Party. We examine in some detail this and other cases around the country demonstrative of the erosion of voting rights and democracy in the next chapters of this book.

Notes

1. Lyndon B. Johnson, "We Shall Overcome" speech delivered before a Joint Session of Congress, March 15, 1965. Also see Sean Connolly, *The Right to Vote* (North Mankato, MN: Smart Apple Media, 2006).

2. Throughout this book, the terms African American, black, and people of African descent are used interchangeably.

3. See Brad Plumer, "The ten charts show the black-white economic gap hasn't budged in 50 years, *Washington Post,* August 28, 2013, http://www.washingtonpost .com/blogs/wonkblog/wp/2013/08/28/these-seven-charts-show-the-black-white-economic-gap-hasnt-budged-in-50-years/

4. Hanes Walton Jr. and Robert C. Smith, *Black Politics: A Theoretical and Structural Analysis* (New York: J.P. Lippincott Company, 1972), 96.

5. Donald G. Neiman, "Equality Deferred, 1870–1900," in *The Civil Rights Movement,* ed. Jeffrey O.G. Ogbar (Boston: Houghton Mifflin Company, 2003), 31–32.

6. Benjamin Quarles, *The Negro in the Making of America* (New York: Macmillan, 1969), 139–40.

7. See Wolfe, B., & McCartney, M. Indentured Servants in Colonial Virginia. (2012, December 6). In *Encyclopedia Virginia.* Retrieved from http://www .EncyclopediaVirginia.org/Indentured_Servants_in_Colonial_Virginia (accessed March 23, 2014). Also see Billings, Warren M. *The Old Dominion in the Seventeenth Century: A Documentary History of Virginia, 1606–1700.* Revised Edition. Chapel Hill: University of North Carolina Press, 2007.

8. Steven F. Lawson, *Black Ballots: Voting Rights in the South, 1944–1969* (New York: Columbia University Press, 1976), 1.

9. Center for Voting and Democracy, 2009, http://archive.fairvote.org/ righttovote/timeline.htm (accessed October 30, 2014).

10. Hanes Walton Jr. and Robert C. Smith, *American Politics and the African American Quest for Universal Freedom,* 6th ed. (New York: Longman, 2012), 177.

11. Ibid.

12. Ibid. See also Manning Marable and Leith Mullings (eds.), "No Rights That a White Man Is Bound to Respect: The Dred Scott Case and Its Aftermath," in *Let Nobody Turn US Around,* 2nd ed. (New York: Rowman & Littlefield, 2009).

13. The House Joint Resolution proposing the 13th amendment to the Constitution, January 31, 1865; Enrolled Acts and Resolutions of Congress, 1789–1999; General Records of the United States Government; Record Group 11; National Archives.

14. The House Joint Resolution proposing the 14th amendment to the Constitution, June 16, 1866; Enrolled Acts and Resolutions of Congress, 1789–1999; General Records of the United States Government; Record Group 11; National Archives.

15. The House Joint Resolution proposing the 15th amendment to the Constitution, December 7, 1868; Enrolled Acts and Resolutions of Congress, 1789–1999;

General Records of the United States Government; Record Group 11; National Archives.

16. Neiman, "Equality Deferred, 1870–1900."

17. See Benjamin Quarles, *The Negro in the Making of America,* 11th Printing (New York: Collier Books, 1976), 133.

18. Neiman, "Equality Deferred, 1870–1900."

19. Walton and Smith, 2012, 178; also see Walton, 1992, 33–54.

20. Walton and Smith, 2012, 178.

21. Lawson, 1976, 11.

22. Walton and Smith, 2012, 178.

23. See Lucius J. Barker, Mack H. Jones, and Katherine Tate, *African Americans and the American Political System,* 4th ed. (Upper Saddle, NJ: Prentice Hall, 1999), 124–25; also see Richard M. Valelly, *The Two Reconstructions: The Struggle for Black Enfranchisement* (Chicago: University of Chicago Press, 2004), 150.

24. Lawson, 1976, 53.

25. Hill and Reddix-Smalls, 2002, 15.

26. Valelly, 2004, 150.

27. Lawson, 1976, 53.

28. Hill and Reddix-Smalls, 2002, 15.

29. Valelly, 2004, 150.

30. Hill and Reddix-Smalls, 2002, 15.

31. *U.S. Statutes at Large,* vol. 18, 335, cited in J. Morgan Kousser, "What Light Does the Civil Rights Act of 1875 Shed on the Civil Rights Act of 1964?" in *Legacies of the 1964 Civil Rights Act,* ed. Bernard Grofman (Charlottesville, VA: University of Virginia, 2000), 33.

32. Civil Rights Act of 1964, Title II, Section 201[a], Public Law 88–35, July 2, 1964.

33. Kousser, 2000, 36.

34. Civil Rights Act of 1964, Title I.

35. Ibid.

36. See Abigail Thernstrom, "Redistricting, Race, and the Voting Rights Act," *National Affairs,* 1–8, August 20, 2014, http://www.nationalaffairs.com/publications/detail/print/redistricting-race-and-the-voting-rights-act (accessed August 20, 2014); see Hill and Reddix-Smalls, 2002.

37. Walton and Smith, 2012, 216.

38. Thom File and Sarah Crissey, Voting and Registration in the Election of November 2008, *Current Population Reports,* July 10, 2012, http://www.census.gov/prod/2010pubs/p20-562.pdf (accessed November 9, 2014).

39. Rickey Hill, "The Voting Rights Act of 1965: Consequences and Challenges after 30 Years," in *American National and State Government: An African American View of the Return of Redemptionist Politics,* 2nd ed. ed. Claude W. Barnes, Samuel A. Moseley, and James D. Steele (Dubuque, IA: Kendall/Hunt Publishing Company, 2007). Also see Hill and Reddix-Small, 2002.

40. Thernstrom, August 20, 2014.

41. Hill and Reddix-Smalls, 2002, 15.

42. Richard H. Pildes, "The Politics of Race, review of Quiet Revolution in the South," *Harvard Law Review* 108 (April 1995): 1364, 1373.

43. Hill, 2007. Also see Barnes, Moseley, and Steele, eds., 2007. Also see Hill and Reddix-Small, 2002, 14–15.

44. Hill and Reddix-Smalls, 2002, 15.

45. Ibid.

46. Ibid., 16.

47. Ibid.

48. Ibid.

49. Thernstrom, 2014, 5. Also see Chris Danielson, *The Color of Politics: Racism in the American Political Arena Today* (Santa Barbara, CA: Praeger, 2013).

50. Dianne Pinderhughes, "Past Patterns and Lessons Learned: Continuing Efforts at Participation in Empowerment Policy," in *Beyond the Color Line: Race, Representation, and Community in the New Century,* ed. Alex Willingham (New York: Brennan Center for Justice at New York University Law School, 2002), 82.

51. Ibid.

52. Ibid., 81–82.

Chapter 2

Felon Disenfranchisement and Voting Rights

Since the turn of the century, felony disfranchisement has been used increasingly in combination with changes in voting regulations, which generally tend to make it more difficult to vote for many African Americans, Hispanics, and other nonwhites including immigrants, the homeless, and poor people. The disenfranchisement of currently and formerly incarcerated citizens is but one form of voting discrimination, and it is the primary focus of this chapter. Other prevalent contemporary forms of voting discrimination include the use of at-large elections to dilute the vote of minority groups, voter intimidation and deception, language barriers, disability barriers, and voter purges that require duly qualified citizens to reregister to vote.[1] Use of these tactics dynamics invariably lead to reasoning that given the pattern of racial voting in the United States since the 1930s, the current motivations and pattern of vote suppression are also likely to be race based. Thus, it is imperative to examine the diverse and evolving laws that exist at the state level throughout the United States restricting the voting rights of convicted felons.

In this chapter, we assess the impact of the designation "convicted felon" on individuals' right to exercise the franchise and examine current developments projected to impact positively or negatively the chances that citizens convicted of crimes will be stripped of the right to vote. Following a brief examination of felony disenfranchisement, we address the following broad questions, which serve to guide our analysis and discussion: (1) Who are the convicted felons, and to what extent and how does race and ethnicity factor in the designation of persons as such? and (2) What impact has criminal incarceration, and being branded a felon, had on equality of access to the ballot and political justice?

The history of voting inclusion in the United States demonstrates that there long has been a variety of motivations and approaches pursued to undercut the constitutional principle of one person, one vote. As our approach, analysis, and discussion of felony disfranchisement develops, it is important to keep in mind that temporally, the Post–Civil Rights era coincides with several related policy developments and societal trends. Foremost among these was an enhanced focus on law and order, which was a fundamental theme dominating national politics in the 1980s. The theme of law and order continued into the 1990s, and remains a strong current among office-seekers and politicians generally who seek to project themselves as "tough on crime."

Understanding Felony Disenfranchisement

What is felony disenfranchisement? The answer to the question is vital for the development of programs and strategies to rectify a problem that subverts the practice of democracy. It is appropriate to begin by clarifying the meaning of "disenfranchisement." Disenfranchisement is the result of actions and/or policies that prevent those who are eligible to vote from being able to vote. When persons who are eligible to vote *are legally barred* based on public policy from casting their rightful ballot, the situation is known as *de jure* disenfranchisement. In contrast, *de facto* disenfranchisement is evident when individuals otherwise eligible to vote opt not to do so due to longstanding community practices that serve to discourage not only voting, but also voter registration. For example, institutionalized local practices involving misinformation, confusion, deception, and lack of voter registration and voter access may be routine developments, which due to their long-term persistence have gone largely unchallenged in the political arena. In effect, citizens are denied the right to vote under these conditions. Felony disenfranchisement is therefore a form of *de jure* disenfranchisement since it involves the application of laws that prevent individuals from voting due to a conviction for the commission of a felony.[2]

Moreover, disenfranchisement is viewed as a "collateral consequence" imposed for the commission of a crime that reaches the level of felony, as defined by state law. As a "collateral consequence," disenfranchisement can be either temporary or permanent, depending upon the jurisdiction. Cherie Dawson-Edwards notes that, "Due to their original intent, collateral consequences, such as felon voting restrictions, are still held to be civil in nature, but increasing evidence shows that over time their results have become punitive."[3] In either case, felon disenfranchisement policies can have a significant effect on the outcome of political contests.[4] Depending upon the state, such policies may well be intimidating, thus affecting citizens' motivation to register to vote, vote, or pursue elected office.

Policy makers who endorse the use of felon disenfranchisement laws are quick to point out that such laws are "race neutral." Race-neutral laws, by definition, apply to all citizens in the same manner rather than to any specific racial group.[5] David Wilson, Michael Owens, and Darren Davis point out that, "States commonly adopt and enforce criminal justice policies, such as capital punishment, mandatory minimum sentences, 'Three Strikes' laws, and social welfare policies like bans on cash and food assistance for poor families that primarily affect individual felons."[6]

While the connection between race and criminal prosecution in the United States is evident, the compounding issue is that the incarceration of African Americans has been vastly disproportionate to their representation in the population and consistently greater than the rate of incarceration for whites. These circumstances have prevailed at least since the era of the Civil War.[7] Over the course of approximately the past four decades, the criminal justice system in the United States has experienced tremendous systematic expansion disproportionately at the expense of black males, but broadly penetrating to society at-large. Laws permanently banning voting by ex-felons represent the most obstructive, if not most insidious, form of felon disenfranchisement. For example, more than a third of the states had laws disenfranchising ex-felons in 1850, and by 1920, three-fourths of the states banned voting by ex-felons. It was not until the decades of the 1960s and 1970s that states began to take action to relax the application of felon disenfranchisement provisions.[8] The current policy environment, however, is particularly repressive for African Americans. According to the Sentencing Project, self-described as working for "a fair and effective U.S. criminal justice system," "[f]elony disenfranchisement is an obstacle to participation in democratic life which is exacerbated by racial disparities in the criminal justice system, resulting in 1 of every 13 African Americans unable to vote" (2012).[9]

Criminal (In)Justice and Voting: A Historical Overview

There is a lengthy world history illustrating the use of the criminal justice system to revoke individuals' political rights. The practice extends back to English, European, Greek, and Roman law. It was based on the belief that the penalty of disenfranchisement was appropriate retribution for the commission of crime against society and that such a penalty would motivate individuals to abide by the law.[10] The idea behind the loss of these rights was that disfranchisement would be a condition brought on by the crime committed, and thus, that there was a debt that had to be paid to society. Europeans brought with them to the New World the practice of "civil death," which was instituted in instances where criminal offenses were committed. Civil death entailed the loss of personal property, the loss of the right to testify in court, loss of standing to engage in contractual relations, as well as the loss of the right to the franchise. Over time, civil death as a practice declined; however, felon disenfranchisement remained in place in a number of locales.[11]

The franchise in the United States prior to the Civil War was generally limited to white males, although there was a minute subgroup of blacks that could meet existing property requirements where they existed. One researcher points out that, "The United States Constitution of 1787 neither granted nor denied anyone the right to vote. Over time, states granted suffrage to certain groups and erected barriers to prevent other groups from voting."[12] Thus, it was not until the passage of the Fourteenth Amendment in 1868 that African Americans were legally designated citizens, and the right to vote was extended only to black men two years later in 1870 with the passage of the Fifteenth Amendment. The rise of Reconstruction intensified the pressure to maintain state power and white domination. States and municipalities that had enacted Black Codes (which essentially recast Slave Codes of the previous period) later enlisted Jim Crow laws to stifle black political enfranchisement.[13]

While the struggle for access to the ballot is largely a story of the progression of U.S. society, paralleling this legacy is the evolution of a criminal justice system that is used to limit the exercise of the franchise, especially among subgroups that have been deemed a threat to the dominant group. Social scientists have demonstrated that race is critical in bringing about the adoption and promotion of policies that prevent felon voting.[14] It is fascinating that the general conditions present in the contemporary period parallel those of the Reconstruction era during which both the Fourteenth and Fifteenth Amendments were enacted. The apparent government support for black enfranchisement during Reconstruction signaled to whites that the first major post-slavery challenge to their political dominance was underway. Consequently, white backlash within and external to formal political structures emerged with a vengeance in the form of local resistance to the amendments, the rise of the Ku Klux Klan, and the use of terror, lynching, and racial violence to preclude any possible shift toward black governmental influence and power. Alongside use of the aforementioned extra-systemic measures was the expansion of *de jure* limits on the voting rights of criminal offenders, a form of institutional resistance during Reconstruction to the possible shift in the racial balance of power.[15] During this period, one of most effective and widely applied methods of containing black voting was criminal disenfranchisement, which according to the Sentencing Project, continues to be the primary factor in explaining the disproportionate disenfranchisement of African American adults.[16]

Indeed, there is mounting evidence that *de jure* limits on felon voting today likely have a deleterious effect on election outcomes and that they undermine democratic practices. Specifically, the charge is that the system of justice is systematically and institutionally stacked against people of color, particularly African Americans and Latinos, who represent in the minds of many, perhaps the most pressing and salient threat to the status quo of U.S. politics. This perception, prevalent among Americans generally and whites in particular, is based primarily on the combined presence of the two groups, and in the case of Latinos, their growing numbers in the population. However, the problem and effects of the incarceration of members of these two groups is a significant societal issue with broad implications for winning and losing elections. Unfortunately, such measures appear to be a manifestation of the nation's resistance to diversity and inclusion, which is seen by many as a threat to the "American way of life." In attempting to understand the nature and practice of prison incarceration, we must consider both the extent and pattern of application to discern how they occur and who is affected. The broad social and political contexts within which felon disenfranchisement policies are operationalized may also shed light on their application and persistence. Below, we briefly focus on the 2008 and 2012 election and reelection, respectively of Barack Obama, to better understand the context and motivations for felon disenfranchisement.

The election of Barack H. Obama in 2008 to the U.S. presidency is perhaps the most potent symbol of African American political power to evolve since the onset of the Civil Rights Movement, which culminated in the enactment of the 1964 Civil Rights Act and the Voting Rights Act of 1965. While he was endorsed by the majority of voters, more than 95 percent of black voters supported his candidacy, which was the highest proportion among any of the racial groups. Similar to the era of Reconstruction, a strong negative reaction in the form of white backlash ensued from the corridors of white political power as a response to Obama's overwhelming success. Despite his successful candidacy, once in power, and especially following the defeat of the Democratic Congress in the 2010 midterm elections, Obama encountered tremendous institutional resistance. Nevertheless, following the 2008 election, there was much discussion among social scientists, policy makers, pundits, and laypersons regarding whether his victory meant that the United States had entered a new post-racial era. The declaration that the United States was embarking upon an era of post-racialism diverted attention from Obama's race and racial issues. In effect, post-racialism diminishes the reality that Obama was the first person of African descent to capture the position of "leader of the Western world." It also minimized the implications of his achievement for the political power of African Americans as a group.

Even though race was not directly an issue in either the 2008 or 2012 presidential campaigns, the strength of the minority–majority coalitions assembled by the Obama campaigns were likely quite disconcerting for the Republican Party. The coalitions that solidified his victories in 2008 and 2012 were similar, and they were consistent with Democratic presidential coalitions that materialized since the 1960s. Walton and Smith report that:

> There were majorities among minorities, including 95 and 93 percent of blacks; 66 and 71 percent of Latinos; and 66 and 73 percent of Asian Americans in 2008 and 2012 respectively. Obama also won a majority of the Jewish vote, although it was down from 86 percent in 2008 to 78 percent in 2012. coalition consisted of 80% non-whites and 39% of the white majority. Nevertheless, Jews were the only discrete white demographic group won by Obama in 2012. In 2008, he also won the white youth vote (18–29), but in 2012 he lost it by a margin of 44–51. . . . Overall, Obama's minority-majority coalition was constituted by 80 percent nonwhite minorities and 39 percent of the white majority, with minorities constituting 26 percent of the electorate in 2012, up from 25 percent in 2008. Obama's percent of the white majority was the lowest since Walter Mondale's 35 percent in 1984 and his percent of the minority vote was the highest since Jimmy Carter's 82 percent in 1976.[17]

Moreover, Walton and Smith point out that:

> Obama's "rainbow" coalition was enhanced by the size and support of the Latino and Asian American electorates. The Latino share of the electorate increased from 9 to 10 percent between 2008 and 2012 (the exit polls actually show a decline in Obama's black support from 95 to 93 percent).[18]

Hence, the implications of the Obama victory are clear. Walton and Smith contend further:

> The expansion of support for Obama among Latinos and Asian Americans is significant for the future prospects of a progressive rainbow coalition in the United States since these groups are the fastest growing segments of the electorate while the white majority steadily declines . . . If the 2012 Obama vote is an indicator, this part of the rainbow is not only growing but perhaps trending in a left-liberal Democratic direction.[19]

Thus, it is plausible that it was the nature and depth of Obama's minority–majority coalition that prompted political opponents to take action. However, the initiation of Obama's second term was associated with a decline in the frequency and vehemence with which interested publics would assert that the United States had transitioned to a more progressive and more inclusive era of post-racialism. This may be due to the calculated and successful attempts by conservative politicians and their mass media counterparts to attack and ridicule President Obama in a manner unprecedented in the experience of United States' presidents. The objective of such ridicule was not simply to undermine the Obama coalition, but also to diminish President Obama himself by framing him as one of the "other," thus distinguishing him from dominant political elites. The attacks on Obama ranged from allegations that he is not a U.S. citizen and that he is a member of the Muslim religion, to the overt unprecedented disrespect levied by Senator Joe Wilson in the midst of his speech on health care. About 40 minutes into the president's speech, which was delivered on September 2, 2009, before a joint session of Congress, Senator Joe Wilson pointed at the president and angrily shouted, "You lie!"[20] Wilson's intrusion was the first time a U.S. president had been interrupted out of order and procedure to be called a liar by a member of Congress. Wilson's behavior along with the allegation that the president had lied about health care helped frame Obama in a manner that would justify in the minds of those so inclined the disrespect and maltreatment dealt by the political opposition.

President Obama's election as the first black president and the revivification of voter-suppression efforts did not occur by happenstance. Nineteen states implemented new voting restrictions between 2011 and 2012, and since 2013, nine states under the Republican Party's control have adopted policies that make voting more difficult. Following the Supreme Court's June 2013 ruling that diluted the Voting Rights Act, 8 of 16 of the states previously covered by Section 5 had passed or implemented new voting restrictions by late spring of 2014.[21] The juxtaposition of attacks on the president with the protracted expansion of felon disenfranchisement demonstrate a multipronged approach to diminish African American political power and influence at its height in the Post–Civil Rights era. The attacks were intended also to contain the vote of Latinos, who have been growing as a proportion of the voting electorate.

As a political tactic, the reversion to felon disenfranchisement began about four decades ago, not long following the passage of the Voting Rights Act. While states over the past decade generally had taken steps to reduce the harshness of felon disenfranchisement laws, the appearance of Barack Obama on the national political scene, in some quarters, rather than generate anticipation and excitement, instead caused dire consternation. Nonetheless, the hype of U.S. post-racialism and colorblindness was facilitated by the Obama presidency, which helped create the context to substantiate the myth of colorblindness that has been used to help justify felon disenfranchisement. Michelle Alexander explains how this works:

> In the era of colorblindness, it is no longer socially permissible to use race, explicitly, as a justification for discrimination, exclusion, and social contempt. So we don't. Rather than rely on race, we use our criminal justice system to label people of color "criminals" and then engage in all the practices we supposedly left behind. Today it is perfectly legal to discriminate against criminals in nearly all the ways that it was once legal to discriminate against African Americans. Once you are labeled a felon, the old forms of discrimination—employment discrimination, housing discrimination, denial of the right to vote, denial of educational opportunity, denial of food stamps and other public benefits, and exclusion from jury service—are suddenly legal. As a criminal, you have scarcely more rights, and arguably less respect, than a black man living in Alabama at the height of Jim Crow. We have not ended racial caste in America; we have merely redesigned it.[22]

Thus, *de jure* disenfranchisement in the form of felon disenfranchisement is highly injurious to the practice of democracy. Given the impact of felon disenfranchisement on the right to vote and the likely associated consequences of future loss of employment, loss of income, educational opportunity, and public benefits to which citizens are generally entitled, practically speaking, "Civil Death" is the result temporarily, if not permanently. Moreover, the erroneous promotion of felon disenfranchisement as colorblind or race neutral runs contrary to diversity efforts seeking to bind the society because the results of such policies lay bare the unequal treatment and racial disparities that exist with respect to the loss of voting rights. The situation is clearly reminiscent of institutional circumstances extending back to the days of Jim Crow when the law of the land dictated second-class citizenship for persons of African descent. Ironically, however second-class status was frequently also imposed on poor whites and other nonblacks, although the system instilled within many whites the belief in their own superiority over black people regardless of their economic circumstance. In the sections below, we turn our attention to the state's role in felon disenfranchisement and the process of African American criminalization. The present composition of convicted felons is also discussed, along with the impact of *de jure* disenfranchisement on voting and elections.

States and Felon Disenfranchisement

In the United States, a "state's rights" orientation governs decisions regarding conditions for the return of the rights of an individual due to current or previous felony convictions. Each state has its own view about to whom voting rights should be restored and when, thus engendering a complex maze of laws and practices that operate in a manner contrary to the federal guarantees of the Constitution and other legislative and court actions. Since each of the 50 states can make their own laws regarding whether and how individuals branded felons will participate in the political process through voting, an unevenness, consequently unfairness, exists nationally with regard to the conditions of voting, and the right to do so.[23] While standing on the sidelines the federal government has in effect colluded with the states in re-institutionalizing a system that virtually guarantees that the voter rolls will be diminished. Without federal collusion, it is unlikely that felon disenfranchisement among African American and Latinos could have flourished. Indeed, federal involvement in the criminal justice realm over the past almost half a century has been vital to the development of state-level criminal justice policies and practices that prevent voting by not only those serving sentences, but also those who have fulfilled their debt to society.

The Criminalization of African Americans

While the association of African Americans with crime has long been a tactic employed to negatively frame select individuals and the group as antisocial, the Civil Rights Movement, and later the Black Power Movement provided the necessary stimuli for the re-intensification of black criminalization. The 1965 Watts' riots marked the re-intensification of the criminalization of African Americans and black men particularly, which had been underway for some time nationally with tremendous vigor and

effectiveness. The situation in Watts, which emerged in part because of negative relations between the black community and the Los Angeles Police
Department (LAPD), stemmed from perceptions that the police harassed
and repressed local citizens without due cause. Supported by the proliferation of civil riots and urban rebellions in the late 1960s and early 1970s,
local police departments became increasingly militarized. During this period, Special Weapons and Tactics (SWAT) commands with the capacity to
inflict overwhelming force were established.

The interest and emphasis of the federal government in social control
was demonstrated by the passage of two important bills by Congress. First,
antiriot provisions were included as part of the 1968 Civil Rights Act. These
provisions called for severe penalties for those convicted of crossing state
lines or using interstate communications facilities to incite riots. The second key piece of legislation passed was the Omnibus Crime Act of 1968,
which had been framed as part of the nation's response to the urban unrest
of the 1960s. The bill established a national training center to instruct local
law enforcement in riot-control techniques, as well as provided funding
to improve local riot-control initiatives.[24] Thus, the federal government's
antiriot efforts targeted toward the major urban centers, many of which
had been virtually abandoned by whites for the suburbs, were effectively
aimed at communities that were predominantly black. The process of black
criminalization persisted for the duration of the presidential terms of both
Richard Nixon and later Ronald Reagan, who promoted strong programs
of "law and order" to counter growing crime, much of which was tied to the
drug trade in major U.S. cities. However, Danielson points out that,

> white politicians exploited the specter of black criminality to frighten white
> constituents. In Boston, for example these fears played into white opposi-
> tion to court-ordered busing. And just as the split between blacks and or-
> ganized labor and blacks and Jews over affirmative action played into the
> hands of conservatives and weakened liberalism, so too did liberals' attempts
> to rationalize crime and lawlessness with poverty and other sociological
> explanations.[25]

The association of African Americans with heinous criminal activity received prominent national attention during the 1988 presidential campaign
featuring George H.W. Bush and Michael Dukakis. According to Barker,
Jones, and Tate, "[George Bush's] 1988 campaign against Democratic nominee Michael Dukakis bore a close resemblance to Nixon's law and order

campaign in 1968, which some thought was a coded message that capitalized on whites' racial prejudices against blacks."[26] To help cement his victory for the Republicans, the specter of Willie Horton Jr. was deployed as a tactic to instill fear among whites and activate them in the presidential election on behalf of the Republican Party. Horton was a black man from Massachusetts who served 10 years for first-degree murder. While on furlough in April 1987 he escaped to Maryland and entered the home of Clifford Barnes and Angela Miller, a white couple engaged to be married. Horton brutally raped Miller and terrorized Barnes, who managed to escape and call police.[27] The Horton case stands as a prominent example of how race is conflated by politicians, office seekers, and mass media, respectively, seeking to maintain political power, acquire political power, or attract viewers. In each instance, the repeated association of black people with criminal activity leaves an impression that plays over and over in the minds of some whites, eventually extending into the political arena.

During the 1980s, African Americans and Latinos were arrested and incarcerated at extraordinarily high levels, based primarily on policies promulgated during the administrations of presidents Ronald Reagan (1980–1988) and George H.W. Bush (1988–1992). According to the American Civil Liberties Union (ACLU), by 1990 the population of inmates in the United States stood at 1,139,803 or 455 per 100,000 persons—a rate significantly higher than that for South Africa, which at the time was second only to the United States in imprisoning its own citizens.[28] The growth in the black prison population was buoyed by strong public support for activist courts that would be firm in dealing with the commission of crime. Studies revealed that between 1969 and 1974, Americans' belief that the courts were too lax in administering "justice" increased, respectively, from 75 to 82 percent.[29]

The increased attention to enforcement and incarceration was propelled by the declaration of a "War on Drugs," which was centered primarily in the major urban areas of the United States. It has been pointed out that:

> While this phenomenon [the war on drugs] is best remembered for its association with crack cocaine in the 1980s, it actually began with New York and the Rockefeller Drug Laws of 1973. Governor Nelson Rockefeller, a moderate Republican, embraced a tough-on-crime approach to appease party conservatives. While he demonstrated this most vividly in his violent crushing of the Attica prison rebellion in 1971, he also signed into law legislation enacting lengthy prison terms for selling narcotics.[30]

With the onset of the crack epidemic in the 1980s, the devastating effects of the War on Drugs on African American life hinged on the racial disparity in the usage of crack cocaine versus cocaine in powder form. Studies have shown, for example, that African Americans have received substantially longer sentences for possession of crack cocaine compared to the sentences meted out for their white counterparts who use cocaine in powder form. Michelle Alexander points out that although the launch of President Ronald Reagan's War on Drugs had little to do with the emergence of crack cocaine, the rapid proliferation of the drug in Los Angeles and cities nationwide created a ripe atmosphere for the promotion of the War on Drugs. The media campaign launched by the Reagan administration was quite impactful as part of the strategy to garner the support of the public and members of Congress. Indeed, the drug war was initiated in 1982, and the crack cocaine epidemic followed in1985, enabling substantial increases in funding for the initiative and simultaneously fueling racial disparities in drug convictions and sentences resulting in felony records.[31] Moreover, the budget climate emphasizing austerity with regards to social programs, particularly education, complemented the War on Drugs.

With the future for federal support of education beginning to dim, the push for federal reform of welfare policies was initiated in the 1990s. On the watch of President Bill Clinton, the explosion of black incarceration coincided with these reforms, leaving many former beneficiaries and their families without the necessary social safety net essential for successful transition from welfare or unemployment to work. Overall, the cumulative misery of many African Americans did nothing to offset the potential to become entangled with crack cocaine. If anything, the increasingly dire economic conditions that were being faced in many communities caused many more individuals to turn to the use of crack cocaine and other illegal drugs. The resultant criminalization of African Americans generally and black males particularly invigorated and sustained the War on Drugs by providing a constant flow of persons branded with the label "felon," thus the opportunity to impose penalties that would strip one of their voting rights. More importantly however, it provided the opportunity to suppress voting by a segment of the population typically believed to be in opposition to Republicans who recently have been the major proponents of felon disenfranchisement.

Variability and Impact of State Policies

During 2011, the United States incarcerated 716 people per 100,000 population—the most extensive system and practice of imprisonment in the world. Over the past 40 years, expansion of the population of prisoners resulted in the denial of voting rights to an estimated 5.85 million Americans due to policies that prevent voting by those who have committed felonies.[32] As of 2012, there were almost 1.5 million people in state and federal institutions and an additional 744,500 people in local jails, for an overall prisoner total of 2.2 million.[33] The effects of incarceration surfaced in the 2008 presidential election undercutting the constitutional principle of one person, one vote, and possibly influencing the outcome in very close races. An estimated 5.3 million Americans (representing about 1 in 40 adults) were unable to vote in the 2008 election because they had been convicted of a felony. Of this number, more than 676,000 were women, and 2.1 million were persons who had already satisfied the term of their sentence. Among those excluded from voting were 1.4 million African American men.[34] In 2014, 7.7 percent of African American adults, or 1 out of 13, had their right to vote revoked—a rate that is four times the 1.8 percent rate of non–African Americans. The racial disparity is amplified in the states of Florida (23%), Kentucky (22%), and Virginia (20%), where at least one in five African American adults are unable to vote due to the commission of a felony.[35] Nationally, an estimated 2.2 million African Americans are deprived of the right to vote due to their involvement with the criminal justice system, and of these, more than 40 percent have satisfied their sentences. These dismal statistics bear out the fact that the laws imposing felony disenfranchisement tend to have a disproportionate effect on African Americans.[36]

Hispanics are also incarcerated at rates disproportionate to their representation in the nation's population and at rates that substantially exceed those of whites; however, Hispanic incarceration rates are markedly lower than those for African Americans. In 2012, the Bureau of Justice Statistics reported alarmingly differential rates of incarceration for African American men (more than six times greater than for whites) and Hispanic men (almost two and a half times greater than whites). Males between the ages of 30 and 34 years comprised the majority of the prison population in 2011. Within this age range, 1,115 white men were incarcerated per 100,000 men in the population. Among African American and Hispanic men the rates were astoundingly higher at 7,517 and 2,762, respectively, per 100,000. Delving deeper into the demographics of the incarcerated it is evident too that the racial disparities are highest among more youthful black men of ages 18 and 19, who are more than nine times more likely than white men of the same age to be incarcerated. In contrast, Hispanic men of ages 18 and 19 are 3.5 times more likely than white men of the same age to be imprisoned.[37]

Among the regions of the country, the South has the largest concentration of persons disenfranchised due to conviction for the commission of a felony. Table 2.1 shows the top 10 states as of 2010 that had the highest incidence of disenfranchised voters. Also, Southern states comprise 7 of the top 10 states with the highest disenfranchisement levels. Three western states (Wyoming, Nevada, and Arizona) comprise the bottom four states, along with Georgia, with the lowest rate of disenfranchisement among the top 10.

Table 2.2 presents felony disenfranchisement laws by state and for the District of Columbia. The table is organized based on the following arrangements that serve generally to guide decisions regarding the restoration of voting rights to one who has been convicted of a felony: (1) no restriction; (2) prison; (3) prison and parole; (4) prison, parole, and probation; and (5) prison, parole, probation, and post-sentence. The data relative to state-level policies reveal that there are only two states, Maine and Vermont, that do not impose any restrictions whatsoever on the right to vote, including those presently incarcerated and those required to meet the conditions of parole, probation, or special post-sentence conditions. The remaining states and the District of Columbia do impose restrictions on the voting rights of incarcerated persons or those formerly convicted of a felony; however, the severity of restriction varies from state to state. Thirteen states impose the most severe voting rights restrictions.

TABLE 2.1 Disenfranchisement by Top 10 States

Rank	State	Number of Voters Disenfranchised (#)	Percentage of Voters Disenfranchised (%)
1	Florida	1,541,602	10.42
2	Mississippi	182,814	8.27
3	Kentucky	243,842	7.35
4	Virginia	451,471	7.34
5	Alabama	262,354	7.19
6	Tennessee	341,815	7.05
7	Wyoming	25,657	5.99
8	Nevada	86,321	4.24
9	Arizona	199,734	4.19
10	Georgia	275,866	3.83

Source: Christopher Uggen, Sarah Shannon, and Jeff Manza, "State—Level Estimates of Felon Disenfranchisement in the United States, 2012." The Sentencing Project, Washington, D.C.

TABLE 2.2   United States' Felony Disenfranchisement Laws by State and District of Columbia

State	No Restriction	Prison	Prison/ Parole	Prison/ Parole/ Probation	Prison/ Parole/ Probation/ Post-Sentence
Maine	X				
Vermont	X				
Dist. of Columbia		X			
Hawaii		X			
Illinois		X			
Indiana		X			
Michigan		X			
Montana		X			
North Dakota		X			
Ohio		X			
Oregon		X			
Massachusetts		X			
New Hampshire		X			
Pennsylvania		X			
Utah		X			
California			X		
Colorado			X		
New York			X		
Connecticut			X		
Alabama				X	
Alaska				X	
Arkansas				X	
Georgia				X	
Idaho				X	
Kansas				X	
Louisiana				X	
Maryland				X	
Minnesota				X	
Missouri				X	
New Jersey				X	
New Mexico				X	

(Continued)

TABLE 2.2   (Continued)

State	No Restriction	Prison	Prison/ Parole	Prison/ Parole/ Probation	Prison/ Parole/ Probation/ Post-Sentence
North Carolina				X	
South Carolina				X	
Oklahoma				X	
Texas				X	
Washington				X	
West Virginia				X	
Wisconsin				X	
Arizona					X
Delaware					X
Florida					X
Iowa					X
Kentucky					X
Nevada					X
Mississippi					X
Nebraska					X
Rhode Island					X
South Dakota					X
Tennessee					X
Virginia					X
Wyoming					X

Source: Compiled based on information retrieved from the website of The Sentencing Project, Washington, D.C., *U.S. Felony Disenfranchisement Laws by State,* September 12, 2014, www.sentencingproject.org/template/page.cfm?id=13.

In these states, the right to vote is not restored even after completion of the prison sentence and having satisfied any requirement of probation or parole. The Sentencing Project of Washington, D.C., estimates that about 45 percent of the disenfranchised reside in these 13 states. On the other hand while a minority of disenfranchised voters are jailed or imprisoned, 75 percent remain disenfranchised on parole or probation following completion of their sentences.[38] The two most restrictive categories of felon disenfranchisement are dominated by the former confederate states, suggesting an association between the restrictiveness of felon disenfranchisement policies and geographic region. This is important to note because the long legacy of black social and political repression that operated openly in the southern region of the United States based on the assertion of states' rights, until passage of the Civil Rights Act and the Voting Rights Act in 1964 and 1965, respectively.

The second most restrictive category, comprising the states of Arkansas, Georgia, Louisiana, North Carolina, South Carolina, and Texas, represent almost one-third of those requiring the disenfranchisement of persons currently incarcerated, or on parole or probation. Also included in this category are the peripheral South states of Maryland and West Virginia. The most restrictive category includes the former confederate states of Alabama, Florida, Mississippi, Tennessee, and Virginia, which represent 5 of the 12 states that revoke the right to vote from individuals who are in jail or prison, on parole or probation, or have completed their sentences. Delaware and Kentucky are included also among the states with the harshest felon disenfranchisement policies, regardless of the completion of prison time, parole, or probation.[39]

Examples of inconsistencies in state felon disenfranchisement policies are numerous. However, it is worthwhile also to note that in some states, persons convicted even of misdemeanors are subject to various penalties. Specifically, anyone convicted of a misdemeanor in Idaho, Illinois, Indiana, Kentucky, Michigan, Missouri, South Carolina, and South Dakota may not vote while incarcerated. Moreover, Kentucky and Missouri require an executive pardon before persons convicted of certain misdemeanors (referred to in Kentucky as "high misdemeanors" and in Missouri as "elections-related misdemeanors") can ever vote again. In Iowa, persons convicted of "aggravated" misdemeanor cannot vote while incarcerated. In contrast to Missouri, which requires an executive pardon for the restoration of the right to vote in cases of elections-related misdemeanors, in West Virginia, those who are convicted of certain elections-related misdemeanors cannot vote while incarcerated; however, all others are permitted to vote by absentee ballot. Also, in Washington, D.C., certain election, lobbying, and campaign finance-related crimes (which may be misdemeanors) are defined as felonies for the purpose of disenfranchisement; others with misdemeanor convictions may vote by absentee ballot while incarcerated. In the remaining 40 states, individuals are permitted to vote by absentee ballot while incarcerated for any misdemeanor.[40]

While state disenfranchisement penalties for conviction of a misdemeanor can yield disenfranchisement in some states, state disenfranchisement laws for the conviction of a felony are more poignant; the differences are quite significant. A case in point is Alabama, a state in which violent offenses such as murder, rape incest, and sexual crimes against children are firmly dealt with in the criminal justice system. Thus, a felon's right to vote in these instances may not be restored. Alternatively, the state of Arizona restores the rights of felons immediately after fulfillment of the penalty for the first offense. However, second-time offenders must apply to regain their rights after reintegration. Similar to Alabama, the state of Delaware views the commission of crimes of violence such as murder, manslaughter, and felony sex abuse as a basis to permanently disqualify someone from voting. In addition to crimes of violence, people convicted of bribery in public administration and improper influence or abuse of public office are also ineligible to have their right to vote restored.[41] In April 2013, Delaware repealed a voter disenfranchisement provision eliminating the five-year waiting period and allowing automatic restoration of voting rights after completion of full sentence, including probation and parole.[42]

While it is evident that the states have been looking at their policies with an eye toward reform, not all of them are necessarily interested in relaxing penalties that have revoked the right to vote. For example, individuals are permanently disenfranchised in Florida unless they are given discretionary executive clemency. Although Florida underwent developments under Governor Charlie Crist resulting in the liberalization of felon disenfranchisement, recently a tougher stance has been taken by instituting a five-year waiting period. Upon taking office in 2011, Crist's successor Rick Scott amended the Clemency Board rules to limit sharply voting rights restoration. The changes instituted by Governor Scott had a devastating effect on the restoration of voting rights. During Crist's term, from 2007 to 2011, 155,312 people had their right to vote restored. However, under Scott's leadership, in 2011, the state's Board of Executive Clemency only returned the right to vote to 78 people, and in 2012, the number of people who had the right to vote reinstituted totaled 342.[43]

The state of Iowa is another case in which felon disenfranchisement was relaxed, only to be later reasserted. In 2005, Iowa governor Tom Vilsack signed an executive order modifying the state's felony disenfranchisement policy from a lifetime penalty with the possibility of gubernatorial pardon to a policy allowing automatic restoration of voting rights upon completion of sentence. Vilsack's policy reduced the number of disenfranchised in Iowa by 81 percent or about 100,000 people. However, with the election of Terry Branstad to the office of governor in 2011, the policy was reverted to the process of executive review on a case-by-case basis. By 2013, 8,000 individuals had satisfied the terms of their convictions; however, less than a dozen of these individuals had their voting rights restored since Governor Branstad's election to office.[44]

The state of Kentucky also has a strict restoration policy. Its policy directs that the right to vote can be returned only when the governor confers an executive pardon following the completion of sentence. On the other hand, Mississippi is even stricter. It does not permit restoration of rights if any of the following crimes were committed: murder, rape, bribery, theft, arson, obtaining money or goods under false pretense, perjury, forgery, embezzlement, bigamy, armed robbery, extortion, felony bad check, felony shoplifting, larceny, receiving stolen property, robbery, timber larceny, unlawful taking of a motor vehicle, statutory rape, carjacking, or larceny under lease or rental agreement. It is quite curious, however, that drug-related offenses are omitted from the foregoing list. In order to have the right to vote restored following the completion of sentence, one must personally persuade their representative to sponsor legislation on their behalf to restore their right to vote, and both legislative chambers must then pass the bill. They do, however retain the right to vote for president.[45]

Felons in Nebraska are returned the right to vote automatically two years following the completion of prison sentence and all probation and parole requirements. Those convicted of the crime of treason are ineligible to have the right to vote. In Nevada on the other hand, the right to vote is restored automatically if one was not a violent offender or a second time (violent or nonviolent) offender. The right to vote belonging to these offenders can only be restored by returning to the court in which they were convicted.[46]

In March 2012, South Dakota enacted legislation revoking the right to vote from convicted felons serving terms of probation only allowing those who have served all of their parole along with their sentence to vote. Prior to this change, only those on parole or incarcerated were ineligible to vote. In contrast, however, felon disenfranchisement policy in the state of Tennessee has been consistent since 1981. The law allows individuals who have not been convicted of a serious felony (e.g., murder, rape, treason, and voter fraud) to seek reinstatement of voting rights by applying to the state Board of Probation and Parole.[47]

The situation in Virginia also illustrates the volatility of felon disenfranchisement policy as a consequence of gubernatorial change, particularly in instances where control shifts from one political party to another. The Commonwealth of Virginia has long been among those states with the harshest felon disenfranchisement laws, barring those with felony records from voting for life. As is the case in Iowa, in Virginia, those convicted of a felony are not permitted to vote for the duration of their lives. In a demonstration of unusual Republican leniency, Governor Bob McDonnell, in July 2013, modified state policy such that voting rights would be automatically restored on an individual basis for those convicted of nonviolent felonies, no longer under the state's supervision, without pending felony charges, and without any financial obligations that have been imposed by the court. It was projected that the change could restore the right to vote to as many as 100,000 people.[48] Governor McDonnell's Democratic successor, Terry McAuliffe, publicly announced on April 18, 2014, that additional changes would be made to Virginia's disenfranchisement policies. Specifically, the change stipulated that those convicted of nonviolent felonies (including drug crimes) would have their right to vote automatically restored under the following circumstances: term of incarceration and all probation or parole have been satisfied; a zero balance for any court costs, fines, or restitution imposed by the court; and no pending felony charges. Those convicted of violent felonies, crimes against children, and election law offenses are required to wait three years before they can apply to the governor for the restoration of their voting rights.[49]

In the state of Washington, the voting rights of convicted felons can be restored by reregistering to vote following the completion of sentence and any parole or probation obligations. However, individuals who have "willfully failed to make three payments in a 12 month period" on any fine required by the court may be subject to having their right to vote revoked. On the other hand, Wyoming requires those convicted of a first-time nonviolent felony to petition the Board of Parole in order to have their right to vote reinstated following a five-year period after completion of sentence; all others must apply directly to the governor following completion of sentence to have their voting rights restored.[50]

Thus, felony disenfranchisement laws in the United States constitute a maze of regulations governing the right to vote. As indicated in the foregoing discussion, while the right to vote can be restored in many states following revocation, the process varies considerably from state to state. This problem may be compounded by the fact that many of the individuals who have been convicted of a felony lack knowledge and/or are unaware that their right to vote may be restored. Moreover, election officials are often confused about state law perhaps contributing to the preliminary conclusion that in those states that continue to disenfranchise only 1 percent or less to 16 percent have the right to vote returned.[51] In the section that follows, we consider the role that a state's political culture plays in the persistence and severity of felon disenfranchisement policies.

The Role of Political Culture

Given that the United States operates based on a federal system of government, an important question is, why do states differ so widely in the requirements, persistence, and severity of felon disenfranchisement laws? In that vein, it is fair also to ask whether the federal government ought to play a stronger role in ensuring the right to vote in elections at all levels of government, as well as bringing about consistency in the reinstatement of the right to vote in instances in which it has been revoked. In 1966, Daniel Elazar advanced the notion that in the United States political subcultures were regionally distributed. He points out that east to west migratory patterns moving across the North American continent enabled the development of political culture. According to Elazar, the migration of people across the country tended to follow "lines of least resistance which generally led them due west from the immediately previous area of settlement."[52] Consequently, the people who migrated as a group were likely to remain together as a "community." These communities formed a unified political ideology and a political culture that was based on historical experience, societal values, and lifestyle.[53] While Elazar's theory has been controversial over the years among social scientists, it nonetheless sheds light on the behavior of states in regards to felon disenfranchisement.

Elazar points out that political culture influences "the particular pattern of orientation to political action in which each political system is embedded." Accordingly, his theory posits that political culture in the United States comprises three major subcultures, which he applies to various regions of the country. These include the individualistic, moralistic, and traditionalistic subcultures. The traits associated with each subculture are distinctive; however, geographically, given migratory patterns, political cultures may overlap. For moralists, the role of government is to provide for the public good and to be concerned for the public welfare. In other words, the idea of moralists is that the public good will be served by the positive developments brought about by officials upon which moral obligations have been placed. Thus, moralistic cultures tend to support a high degree of government intervention politically, economically, and socially.[54]

On the other hand, individualists tend to focus on private concerns and work to limit community involvement in politics. Under the individualist culture, politicians seek to control government through the use of a "spoils system," and in the process, they endeavor to enhance their own social, economic, and political status. In contrast to the moralistic culture, there is less concern for the public good. In this case, democracy functions as a marketplace where politicians rely on public demand and follow strict utilitarianism. Limiting community activity and encouraging individual initiative create a marketplace where private enterprise eclipses the public good.[55]

The traditionalistic political culture is an elitist construct, which gears the society toward the objective of maintaining the status quo. Traditionalism promotes the notion of established hierarchy in which those at the top control the reins of governmental power. Because of their desire to maintain the status quo, there is little initiative on the part of traditionalists to be inclusive. Thus, participation is limited and governmental change is discouraged. Individualists are similar to moralists in that they recognize government as a positive force in society but one limited to an elite few.[56]

The fact that the 11 traditionalistic states of the former confederacy fall in the bottom tiers of voting restrictions for felony conviction reflect that the sociopolitical residue of Jim Crow continues to reside on the national landscape. A recent study investigating the effects of political culture on felon disenfranchisement policies found that "even slight changes in a state's political culture have a substantial impact on their probability of adopting more or less restrictive felon disenfranchisement policies." More specifically it was found that "as the political culture of a state moves away from moralistic views and towards more traditionalistic views the probability of the state adopting more restrictive felony disenfranchisement policies increase."[57]

Jim Crow segregation, a pervasive Southern policy that was traditionalistic in orientation, extended roughly from the turn of the century until the mid-1960s. There is at least one important parallel that can be drawn between modern disenfranchisement practices and the Jim Crow system: the goal to control some subpopulation of individuals deemed problematic to society's dominant group. In the case of Jim Crow, the goal was control of the black population. Control was exerted primarily in two ways, which had personal costs associated with them, to hinder black political organization. The first entailed an encompassing system of debt bondage. Second, physical violence and force were openly employed to ensure compliance to the exploitative economic relationship that existed between black farmers and white creditors.[58] In contrast, felon disenfranchisement is used as a mechanism to influence levels of nonwhite electoral political participation, particularly registration and voting. Depending upon how political party interests can benefit, the felon disenfranchisement "pressure valve" is either loosened or tightened such that the outcomes of close elections may be tilted in one partisan direction or another. It may be that "control" is still important among the states of the former confederacy, as suggested by the fact that the voting restrictions meted out by these states for felonious offenses are generally much harsher than those in other regions of the country (see Table 2.1). It has been pointed out that, "Historically, felon disfranchisement has built on the laws of the Jim Crow era; black men at the turn of the century would be disqualified from voting if they were convicted of crimes, often petty or property-related crimes rather than violent ones."[59]

In 1890, the state of Mississippi ratified a new constitution and which became the model for disenfranchisement. The Mississippi Constitution of 1890 stipulated that,

> Every inhabitant of this state, except idiots and insane persons, who is a citizen of the United States of America, eighteen (18) years old and upward, who has been a resident of this state for one (1) year, and for one (1) year in the county in which he offers to vote, and for six (6) months in the election precinct or in the incorporated city or town in which he offers to vote, and who is duly registered as provided in this article, and who has never been convicted of murder, rape, bribery, theft, arson, obtaining money or goods under false pretense, perjury, forgery, embezzlement or bigamy, is declared to be a qualified elector, except that he shall be qualified to vote for President and Vice President of the United States if he meets the requirements established by Congress therefore and is otherwise a qualified elector.[60]

Thus in the aftermath of Reconstruction, the Mississippi Constitution emerged as a vital tool in helping to return the control of state politics to whites. Specifically, this was accomplished in part by the stipulation that black men would lose the right to vote if they were convicted of bigamy, arson, petty theft, and fraud.[61] There are indications that the problem of control is manifested in the present. For example, black felons, particularly those in Southern locales, may be reluctant or hesitant to register to vote, due to "their fear of local authorities. This situation is reminiscent of the fear black men and women in the South had of trying to vote in the 1950s and 1960s."[62] Below Next, we go beyond the consideration of political culture to explore and discuss the role and dynamics of partisanship and race in the formation and persistence of state felon disenfranchisement.

Factors Influencing Felon Disenfranchisement

Felon disenfranchisement laws are formulated within the context of a state's political culture. Consequently, political culture, as noted above, can affect the harshness of penalties imposed by such laws. The historical relations among the races are exacerbated by the problem of political culture, which has facilitated the modern disenfranchisement of blacks, Latinos, and others who traditionally have been subjected to vote suppression. Political partisanship is important also in decisions that states make about the enfranchisement of felons. However, in the same manner as race, partisanship may be used tactically in reference to felon disenfranchisement, which can affect winning and losing elections. Moreover, the racial motivations have been revealed attitudinally, and these in turn have been shown to influence politics, policy formation, and resistance to policy reform. Specifically of note are "racial resentment" and "racial threat," both of which researchers have shown play an important role in shaping the opinions of citizens about felon voting rights. The concept of racial resentment takes into account that racism has largely evolved from overt to covert. As a concept, "racial resentment captures Whites' disdain for Blacks' seemingly illegitimate demands on society and the opportunities offered by public and private institutions to those who are undeserving."[63]

When individuals have free access to register to vote, along with the capacity to cast the ballot as they see fit with reasonable assurance it will be counted, the direction and momentum of history may be subject to change. However, race and partisanship appear increasingly important to maintaining disenfranchisement policies in general, especially when a country is undergoing diversification in a manner reshaping the dominant group into the new minority.

Political Partisanship

On April 11, 2014, in a speech before Reverend Al Sharpton's National Action Network, President Barack Obama finally raised the specter of partisanship and the role it is playing in the political arena. In this speech he stated that "The right to vote is threatened today in a way that it has not been since the Voting Rights Act became law nearly five decades ago. Across the country, Republicans have led efforts to pass laws making it harder, not easier, for people to vote."[64] The President's speech emphasized that Democratic leaders had embraced the cause of voting rights. Obama's attorney general Eric Holder has been instrumental in bringing the issue of felon disenfranchisement and voting rights to the forefront. The Department of Justice has been unusually active in dealing with the issue in general and in 2013 filed lawsuits opposing new voting restrictions in Texas and North Carolina.[65] There have been a number of studies that examine the conditions incentivizing political parties to seek electoral changes. For example, a 1991 study by Baschart and Comer concluded that when there is unified control by a political party over the redistricting process, the results of redistricting will tend to favor that political party.[66] During 2005, an important study by Antoine Yoshinaka and Christian R. Grose examining the change or repeal of felon disenfranchisement policies between 1960 and 1999 was published. Positing that one political party likely will gain electorally from felon disenfranchisement while the other loses, the study found that in "states where the government was under unified control of the Democratic Party were more likely to repeal disenfranchisement provisions pertaining to the voting rights of felons and ex-felons." The authors point out further that, "these results suggest that suffrage laws were made more inclusive when (1) the Democrats were in power at the state level; and (2) their hold on power was relatively weak. These findings suggest that parties change elections laws if the potential political costs of doing so are outweighed by perceived benefits."[67] Thus, it is likely that political parties become involved in the process of changing voting rights and election laws when they believe they can benefit from the change. This perspective is prudent given the reality that democracy (of which the right to vote is inherently part) should be, if it is not, an issue of nonpartisan dimensions. In the end, the objective of the political party in an electoral contest is to win elections, and both the Democrats and Republicans reasonably desire to do so.

Racial Resentment

As a "race-neutral" policy, felon disenfranchisement operates in a society that is undergoing a transition from blatant racism to a form of racism that operates with principally based covert mechanisms. Regardless of the overt or covert nature of racist expression, such behavior is nonetheless indicative of the disdain that one might have for minority group members. Even though structural and economic changes that have occurred roughly since the second half of the 20th century have contributed to reduced overt racism and racial practices, "current 'race neutral' language and policies remain socially and culturally embedded in the discriminatory actions of the past."[68]

The concepts "racial resentment" and "racial threat" are employed by social scientists to understand the dynamics of contemporary racism. Racial resentment is defined by David Wilson and Darren Davis as the "animosity" or "irritation" that whites may feel toward blacks who they believe are gaining an unfair and undeserved opportunity at their expense. Similarly, Kinder and Sanders have defined racial resentment as the belief that "Blacks do not try hard enough to overcome difficulties they face and they take what they have not earned."[69]

David Wilson and his colleagues, in an important nationally representative study, contend that race-neutral policies in the criminal justice realm, such as felon disenfranchisement, are intertwined with perceptions about African Americans. Their research examined the contention that "attitudes toward policies restoring the political rights of felons are expected to be similar to attitudes toward other race-neutral criminal justice issues, and more generally, to those of race-conscious policies."[70] Wilson and his colleagues maintain that the association between crime and race is governed by the racial stereotypes that whites hold about blacks. Accordingly, "Despite being race neutral, criminal justice statutes, unintentionally or not, become a code for communicating racial information without appearing overtly racist."[71] Specifically of interest to the study was how racial resentment "affects attitudes about the extent to which society should restore political rights to felons." The researchers also examine the interaction of political ideology with racial attitudes and investigate how such interaction can "bias collateral consequences for felons in the mind of the body politic."[72]

Several important findings emerged from this study. First, it found that racial resentment was the main factor influencing attitudes regarding the reinstatement of political rights for felons. Findings revealed that with an increase in the levels of racial resentment, individuals are less likely to endorse action by Congress to restore felons' political rights. It was also found that despite the level of racial resentment, conservatives are more likely than liberals to be against reinstating the political rights of felons. A third key finding from the study revealed that contrary to their expectations, while liberals with low racial resentment are more supportive than their conservative counterparts, "as feelings of racial resentment increase among liberals, their attitudes toward restoring rights to felons begin to mirror those of conservatives, especially conservatives with high racial resentment."[73]

Unfortunately, these findings do not portend well for the eradication of felon disenfranchisement policies as they are due to the "race-crime-ideology convergence." This phenomenon occurs when crime and criminal behavior become intertwined with stereotypes about African Americans and the views of liberals and conservatives achieve a point of intersection, especially in instances of high racial resentment.[74] In the end, it appears that despite claims made about race-neutral felon disenfranchisement policies and collateral consequences, such "policies producing the consequences and race become essentially non-separable in the minds of non-African Americans, who tend to conflate criminality with Blacks."[75] Hence, felon disenfranchisement will likely continue for the foreseeable future with varying degrees of collateral consequences imposed and the tacit approval of an ambivalent public.

Racial Threat

The paranoia of Southern whites in dealing with those formerly enslaved inspired V. O. Key's black-belt hypothesis which can be used to shed additional light on our understanding of the contemporary sociopolitical setting in which the states appear to operate in a manner to "control" and "keep in their place" in the electoral arena, burgeoning African American and Latino subpopulations. The contemporary racial threat thesis is a variation of the black-belt hypothesis, which references the problem of the "southern black belts" in the Jim Crow era as being one of how to ensure the dominance of the white minority over the black majority. In 1949, Key wrote, "It is the whites of the black belts who have the deepest and most immediate concern about the maintenance of white supremacy. Those whites who live in counties with 40, 50, 60, and even 80 per cent Negro share a common attitude toward the Negro."[76]

The contemporary racial dynamics that are related to the exercise of the franchise bear a striking resemblance to the post-Reconstruction era states, especially those of the South, which sought to eradicate the influence of African Americans in local, state, and national politics. Following the Civil War, states and local jurisdictions, in their zeal in some cases to recapture political power, imposed sweeping Black Codes followed by the institution of a range of Jim Crow laws intended to stifle black political and social participation and the acquisition and maintenance of power. The rise of the Ku Klux Klan signified that whites were willing to employ extra-systemic measures to maintain white supremacy and specifically dominate the black population.

"Racial threat" is a concept employed by social scientists, particularly political scientists and sociologists, to understand the role of racial dynamics in the formation of policy-making processes.[77] It involves the specialized utilization of group threat theories, which posit that in circumstances in which subordinate groups obtain power at the cost of a dominant group, the subordinate group will be perceived as a threat by the dominant group.[78] Racism and racial threats can evolve with social change, for example, economic growth. Such social changes, however, may have only a temporary or intermittent effect. For example, despite the enactment of milestone civil rights and voting rights legislation in the mid-1960s, research has shown that slavery and Jim Crow continue to exert a residual influence on the development of current "race-neutral" policies, notwithstanding society's growing rejection of overt racism.[79]

While the research dealing with the connection between racial threat and felon disenfranchisement practices is very limited, there is an important 2005 study conducted by Angela Behrens, Christopher Uggen, and Jeff Manza, which analyzes the origin and development of state felon disenfranchisement laws. In doing so, they utilize an "event history analysis," which takes into account the racial composition of state prisons and other measures of racial threat. Specifically of interest was "whether, and how, racial threat influences the passage of restrictive state felon disenfranchisement laws."[80] The fundamental conclusion reached by the study is that "the racial composition of state prisons is firmly associated with the adoption of state felon disenfranchisement laws. States with greater nonwhite prison populations have been more likely to ban convicted felons from voting than states with proportionally fewer nonwhites in the criminal justice system."[81] This important finding suggests that there are racial dynamics that play out with respect to the harshness of the felon disenfranchisement policies established by the states. It also reinforces previous theory and research concerning the use and influence of race in a political context whereby policies are declared by the governing entity to be racially neutral.

Roadblocks and Prospects for Reform

Nationally, there has been a growing political consensus supporting the eradication of policies and practices of felony disenfranchisement. However, there are still a number of obstacles that must be overcome if real progress is to be achieved in the relatively near future. The most substantial barriers to bringing about the reform of felony disenfranchisement laws are: (1) the persistence of political partisanship as a factor governing ideas and positions on the issue; (2) the complexity and diversity of felony disenfranchisement laws and the inconsistencies and complexity frequently associated with the reinstatement of an individual's right to vote; (3) inconsistent communication among state agencies; (4) underfunded parole boards (related to the issue of partisanship); and (5) the prevalence of racialized opinions in society, which tend to sustain and encourage bias in politics and systemic and institutionalized discrimination. These barriers combine in a manner that results in the maintenance of the status quo with respect to felony disenfranchisement.

Over the past decade and a half, increasing attention has been given by the states to reforming a system increasingly seen as unfair and destructive to U.S. democracy. The National Conference of State Legislatures (2014) suggests that among its members, significant progress has been accomplished toward the reform of laws dealing with felon voting rights, especially those imposing permanent disenfranchisement and an extraordinary burden to an individual's right to have their vote restored. In its website, the organization points out that, "[b]etween 1996 and 2008, 28 states passed new laws on felon voting rights."[82] The state-level actions taken during this period include: (1) the repeal of lifetime disenfranchisement laws for some ex-offenders by seven states; (2) two states restored the voting rights of probationers; (3) data sharing among agencies was improved in seven states; and (4) the process for regaining voting rights was simplified in twelve states.[83] The range of laws is attributable in part to the diversity of the peoples, culture, and histories of the various states and regions of the country, which to the degree possible have been knitted together by the structural arrangement of federalism. While these developments are generally encouraging, state and local political culture, along with historical context and partisanship, will continue to provide fuel and influence public policy. In the end, further clarification and guidance from the federal level will likely prove essential in bringing about enhanced consistency and fairness with respect to the application of state felon disenfranchisement policies.

Notes

1. Rachel Evans and Joanna E. Cuevas Ingram, *Voting Rights Barriers and Discrimination in Twenty-First Century California: 2000–2013* (San Francisco: Lawyers' Committee for Civil Rights of the San Francisco Bay Area, 2014), 4.

2. Ibid., 8.

3. Cherie Dawson-Edwards, "Enfranchising Convicted Felons: Current Research on Opinions Towards Felon Voting Rights," *Journal of Offender Rehabilitation* 46, no. 3/4 (2008): 15.

4. Angela Behrens, Christopher Uggen, and Jeff Manza, "Ballot Manipulation and the 'Menace of Negro Domination': Racial Threat and Felon Disenfranchisement

in the United States, 1850–2002," *American Journal of Sociology* 109 (2003): 559–660.

5. Lynn Eisenberg, "States as Laboratories for Federal Reform: Case Studies in Felon Disfranchisement Law," *New York University Journal of Legislation & Public Policy* 15, no. 2 (2012): 545–46.

6. David C. Wilson, Michael L. Owens, and Darren W. Davis, "How Racial Attitudes and Ideology Affect Political Rights for Felons," Unpublished paper (2014): 6, http://www.academia.edu/6255670/How_Racial_Attitudes_and_Ideology_Affect_Political_Rights_for_Felons (accessed November 1, 2014).

7. Behrens et al., "Ballot Manipulation and the 'Menace of Negro Domination,'" 560.

8. Ibid., 564.

9. Christopher Uggen, Sarah Shannon, and Jeff Manza, "State-level Estimates of Felon Disfranchisement in the United States (Washington, DC: The Sentencing Project, 2012), 1, http://www.sentencingproject.org/doc/publications/fd_State_Level_Estimates_of_Felon_Disen_2010.pdf (accessed November 3, 2014).

10. Jeff Manza and Christopher Uggen, "Punishment and Democracy: Disenfranchisement of Nonincarcerated Felons in the United States," *Perspectives on Politics* 2, no. 3 (2004): 492.

11. National Conference of State Legislatures, "Felon Voting Rights," 2014, http://www.ncsl.org/research/elections-and-campaigns/felon-voting-rights.aspx#background (accessed October 23, 2014).

12. Behrens et al., "Ballot Manipulation and the 'Menace of Negro Domination,'" 561.

13. C. Vann Woodward, *The Strange Career of Jim Crow*, 3rd ed. (New York: Oxford, 1955, 2001).

14. Behrens et al., "Ballot Manipulation and the 'Menace of Negro Domination,'" 560.

15. Ibid., 560–61.

16. The Sentencing Project, *Felony Disenfranchisement*, 2014, www.sentencingproject.org/template/page/cfm?id=133 (accessed September 3, 2014).

17. Hanes Walton Jr. and Robert C. Smith, *American Politics and the African American Quest for Universal Freedom*, 7th ed. (Boston: Pearson, 2015), 186–87.

18. Ibid., 188.

19. Ibid., 189.

20. Emily Friedman, "Did Joe Wilson's 'You Lie' Outburst Cross the Line on Congressional Courtesy?" ABC News, September 10, 2009, http://abcnews.go.com/Politics/rep-wilsons-liar-shout-violated-congressional-courtesy/story?id=8537370 (accessed September 22, 2014).

21. Ari Berman, "Republicans Used to Support Voting Rights—What Happened?" *The Nation*, April 15, 2014, http://www.thenation.com/blog/179325/democrats-support-voting-rights-republicans-should-too (accessed October 2, 2014).

22. Michelle Alexander, *The New Jim Crow: Mass Incarceration in the Age of Colorblindness* (New York: The New Press, 2010), 2.

23. National Conference of State Legislatures, "Felon Voting Rights," July 15, 2014, http://www.ncsl.org/research/elections-and-campaigns/felon-voting-rights .aspx (accessed September 6, 2014).

24. Doug McAdam, *Political Process and the Development of Black Insurgency, 1930–1970* (Chicago: University of Chicago Press, 1982), 222–23.

25. Chris Danielson, *The Color of Politics: Racism in the American Political Arena Today* (Santa Barbara, CA: Praeger, 2013), 49–50.

26. Lucius J. Barker, Mack H. Jones, and Katherine Tate, *African Americans and the American Political System*, 4th ed. (Upper Saddle, NJ: Prentice Hall, 1999), 220.

27. Danielson, *The Color of Politics,* 54–55.

28. Cited in Jarvis Tyner, "Crime-Causes and Cures," in *Let Nobody Turn Us Around: Voices of Resistance, Reform, and Renewal,* 2nd ed, ed. Manning Marable and Leith Mullings (Lanham, MD: Rowman & Littlefield 2009), 612.

29. Danielson, *The Color of Politics*, 49.

30. Ibid., 144.

31. Alexander, *The New Jim Crow,* 5.

32. Uggen et al., "State-Level Estimates of Felon Disfranchisement in the United States," 2012.

33. The Sentencing Project, *Felony Disenfranchisement.*

34. Ibid.

35. Evans and Ingram, *Voting Rights Barriers,* 2014, 8.

36. Ibid.; Jean Chung, *Felony Disenfranchisement: A Primer* (Washington, DC: The Sentencing Project), http://www.sentencingproject.org/docL/publications/ fd_Felony%20Disenfranchisement%20Primer.pdf 2013 (accessed August 23, 2014).

37. E. Ann Carson and William J. Sabol, "Prisoners in 2011" (December 2012), NCJ 239808, United States Department of Justice, Office of Justice Programs, Bureau of Justice Statistics, Washington, DC, http://www.bjs.gov/content/pub/pdf/ p11.pdf (accessed November 28, 2014).

38. Ibid.

39. Ibid.; Chung, *Felony Disenfranchisement.* Also see Procon.org, "State Felon Voting Laws," updated July 15, 2014, http://felonvoting.procon.org/view.resource .php?resourceID=000286&print=true (accessed August 20, 2014).

40. Ibid.; Chung, *Felony Disenfranchisement.* Also see ProCon.org, "State Felon Voting Laws."

41. Ibid.

42. The Sentencing Project, "Democracy Imprisoned: A Review of the Prevalence and Impact of Felony Disenfranchisement Laws in the United States," September 2013, Washington, DC, 5–6.

43. Ibid., 6.

44. Ibid.

45. Ibid.; Chung *Felony Disenfranchisement*; ProCon.org, "State Felon Voting Laws."

46. Ibid.

47. Ibid.

48. Ibid.; The Sentencing Project, "Democracy Imprisoned," 5.

49. Ibid.; ProCon.org, "State Felon Voting Laws." Also see The Sentencing Project, "Democracy Imprisoned," 5.

50. Ibid.; ProCon.org, "State Felon Voting Laws."

51. The Sentencing Project, "Democracy Imprisoned," 4–5. Berman, "Republicans Used to Support Voting Rights—What Happened?."

52. Daniel J. Elazar, *American Federalism: A View from the States* (New York: Thomas Y. Crowell, 1966), 99.

53. Daniel J. Elazar, *The American Mosaic: The Impact of the States* (New York: Harper and Row, 1994).

54. Daniel J. Elazar, *American Federalism: A View from the States*, 3rd ed. (New York: Harper and Row, 1984), 117–18.

55. Ibid., 115–17.

56. Ibid., 118–19.

57. Daniel S. Murphy, Adam J. Newmark, and Phillip J. Ardoin, "Political and Demographic Explanations of Felon Disenfranchisement Policies in the States," *Justice Policy Journal* 3, no. 1 (2006): 14.

58. McAdam, *Political Process and the Development of Black Insurgency, 1930–1970,* 88.

59. Danielson, *The Color of Politics,* 147.

60. Mississippi Constitution of 1890, Article 12, Section 241.

61. Neil R. McMillen, *Dark Journey: Black Mississippians in the Age of Jim Crow* (Urbana and Chicago: University of Illinois Press, 1989), 47.

62. Danielson, *The Color of Politics,* 147.

63. Berman, "Republicans Used to Support Voting Rights," 1.

64. Ibid. Also see Janell Ross, "Where Voting Rights are Under Attack," August 5, 2013, http://www.theroot.com/articles/politics/2013/08/voting_rights_under_attack_states_move_to_change_laws.html (accessed August 20, 2014).

65. Harry Basehart and John Comer, "Partisan and Incumbent Effects in State Legislative Redistricting," *Legislative Studies Quarterly* 16, no. 1 (1991): 63–79. Also see a study that examines the enactment of restrictive voting laws directed at third parties by the major political parties, by Michael Lewis-Beck and Peverill Squire, "The Politics of Institutional Choice: Presidential Ballot Access for Third Parties in the United States," *British Journal of Political Science* 23, no. 3 (1995): 419–27.

66. Antoine Yoshinaka and Christian R. Grose, "Partisan Politics and Electoral Design: The Enfranchisement of Felons and Ex-Felons in the United States, 1960–1999," *State and Local Government Review* 37 (2005): 49–60.

67. Behrens et al., "Ballot Manipulation and the 'Menace of Negro Domination,'" 568. Also see Tali Mendelberg, *The Race Card: Campaign Strategy, Implicit Messages, and the Norm of Equality* (Princeton, NJ: Princeton University Press, 2001).

68. Wilson et al., "How Racial Attitudes and Ideology Affect Political Rights for Felons."

69. Ibid.; Donald R. Kinder and Lynn Sanders, *Divided by Color* (Chicago: University of Chicago Press, 1996). Also see Donald R. Kinder and David Sears, "Prejudice and Politics: Symbolic Racism Versus Racial Threats to the Good Life," *Journal of Personality and Social Psychology* 40 (March 1981): 414–31.

70. Ibid.; Wilson, Owens, and Davis, 7.

71. Ibid.

72. Ibid., 11.

73. Ibid., 20.

74. Ibid., 20–21.

75. Ibid., 19–20.

76. See V. O. Key, *Southern Politics in State and Nation* (Knoxville, TN: The University of Tennessee Press Knoxville, 1984 (1949)), especially 4–10.

77. Behrens et al., "Ballot Manipulation and the 'Menace of Negro Domination.'"

78. Ibid.

79. Ibid., 568–69. Also see Michael K. Brown, *Race, Money and the American Welfare State* (Ithaca, NY: Cornell University Press, 1999); and Michael Goldfield, *The Color of Politics: Race and the Mainsprings of American Politics* (New York: New Press, 1997).

80. Behrens et al., "Ballot Manipulation and the 'Menace of Negro Domination.'"

81. Ibid.

82. National Conference of State Legislatures, "Felon Voting Rights."

83. Ibid.

Chapter 3

On the Birth of Voter Identification Laws: *Crawford v. Marion County*

Missing from much contemporary conversation and political analysis pertaining to the spread of voter identification laws is an account of the political and legal actions that led to the 2008 Supreme Court case, *Crawford v. Marion County Election Board*. In 2005, Indiana state legislators sought to blaze a new political path by means of defining and articulating the merits of requiring voters to provide government-issued photo identification in order to cast a ballot. Passing on a party line vote of 31–17, with Democrats arguing the side effects of voter intimidation and disenfranchisement of poor and elderly constituents, state senate Republicans clung to the belief that such a legal shift is needed to aid in the prevention of voter fraud.[1] To this extent, as Martin DeAgostino recounts, "Republicans refused to bend on the chief Democratic demand, that the bill recognize alternative forms of ID such as current utility bills, bank statements or pay stubs," leading both supporters and dissenters to agree that "the proposed legislation would be among the most restrictive in the country."[2]

Best known as Public Law (P.L.) 109, the bill's chief architect, state Republican senator Victor Heinold expressed that, "I'm proud that Indiana is leading the way on this," insistent upon the belief that this measure will ensure every eligible voter's voice is heard and counted.[3] When the dust settled, the Indiana General Assembly passed P.L. 109, an Act to amend existing state election law by means of requiring voters to satisfy all of the following:

(1) The document shows the name of the individual to whom the document was issued, and the name conforms to the name in the individual's voter-registration record.

(2) The document shows a photograph of the individual to whom the document was issued.

(3) The document includes an expiration date, and the document:
    (A) is not expired; or
    (B) expired after the date of the most recent general election.
(4) The document was issued by the United States or the state of Indiana.[4]

As seen here, Indiana state legislators introduced measures that took many voters by surprise, as P.L. 109 represented a drastic shift in state election law. On a grander scale, P.L. 109 garnered the attention of many observers. Meanwhile, in 2004, lawmakers in Arizona created the Arizona Taxpayer and Citizen Protection Act, requiring voters to present both photo identification and proof of citizenship. This proposition differed from P.L. 109 in that Arizona voters, not just lawmakers, decided the fate of this proposition. The Act secured 56 percent of the electorate, including 47 percent of self-identified Latino voters, 51 percent of independents, and even 42 percent of Democrats.[5] However, in Indiana under the leadership of then newly elected Republican governor Mitch Daniels, many state residents, along with various civil rights groups, began to question the depth and breadth of P.L. 109. Moreover, these inquires brought into question whether or not a "problem" actually existed that warranted such an expansion of election law, or if this "solution" was addressing a "problem" that only existed in the minds of Republican lawmakers. Upon failure to produce data to support the leading claim that voter fraud was prevalent in Indiana, and thus producing only anecdotal evidence, P.L. 109 caused much controversy.

This line of skepticism toward P.L. 109 also reflects the sentiments surrounding the passage of P.L 105, as well as the subsequent legal challenges. For some, this new measure was no different than the political attempts sought after the Civil War to disenfranchise certain segments of the population, chiefly, those who were more likely to support Democratic candidates. As Chandler Davidson recounts, these "laws were often presented as high-minded attacks on fraud—efforts to 'purify' the electorate that would inconvenience 'vote sellers' or the ignorant and 'shiftless'."[6] Yet, when fast forwarding to our current political climate, Davidson argues that, "unlike today, when proponents of voter identification must strain mightily to find the rarest examples of fraud, particularly in-person voter fraud at the polls," we continue to see great interest and partisan support of these measures.[7] Needless to say, P.L. 105 was met with great concern given the ambiguity surrounding the existence of voter fraud in Indiana. While a 2005 U.S. Senate policy committee report claimed that "voter fraud continues to plague our nation's federal elections, diluting and canceling out the lawful votes of the vast majority of Americans," this so-called problem existed only in the minds of some, causing a disconnect between some lawmakers and those they serve. This interplay between "problem" and "solution" and "fact" and "fiction" continues to challenge the prevalent assumption regarding the rampant nature of voter fraud. With these concerns in mind, along with the allegations of constitutional overstep, especially regarding the First and Fourteenth Amendments, we have the ingredients for a long-enduring legal storm. To begin, we first revisit *Indiana Democratic Party v. Todd Rokita,* followed by its appeal with the United States Courts of Appeal, and finally, its Supreme Court case.

Indiana Democratic Party v. Todd Rokita

With much controversy surrounding the highly partisan passage of P.L. 105, a law that many felt infringed upon the constitutional assurance of equal access to the polls, violated the Equal Protection Clause of the Fourteenth Amendment, and violated the First Amendment, dissenters sought to halt the new law. From the outset, Judge Sarah Barker took a peculiar approach in articulating what she believed to be both the issues and evidence at hand. In her view, the plaintiffs' fight to dismantle Indiana's new measure contained many oversights and generalities, weakening their argument. According to Judge Barker, the "plaintiffs, for example, have not introduced evidence of a single, individual Indiana resident who will be unable to vote as a result of Senate Enrolled Act (SEA) 483 or who will have his or her right to vote unduly burdened by its requirements," later adding, "in so doing, plaintiffs' case is based on the implied assumption that the court should give these constitutional and statutory provisions an expansive review based on little more than their own personal and political preferences."[8] To add clarity to what is otherwise a fairly ambiguous articulation of the plaintiffs' dispute, Judge Barker quickly reviewed the numerous facial challenges. In her opinion,

> Plaintiffs have mounted a facial challenge to the validity of SEA 483, raising a variety of related issues about the voter ID Law, including that is substantially burdens the fundamental right to vote, impermissibly discriminates between and among different classes of voters, disproportionally affects disadvantaged voters, is unconstitutionally vague, imposes a new and material requirement for voting, and was not justified by existing circumstances or evidence.[9]

Defendants, on the other hand, deny the existence of these hurdles, instead arguing SEA 483 is "justified by legitimate legislative concern for in-person voting fraud and a reasonable exercise for the State's constitutional power to regulate the time, place and manner of elections."[10] Given the overarching argument of retrogression by the plaintiffs, followed by the outright denial of discriminatory intent and effect by the defendants, matters were both complicated and controversial. With the politically charged atmosphere and highly mediated attention surrounding the case, Judge Barker knew that many eyes were upon every move of the court, which, in turn, produced a very peculiar summary judgment.

Informed by the belief that hastily and poorly constructed foundational arguments were guiding the chief claims argued by both plaintiffs and defendants, Judge Barker found it necessary to explain, before rendering a decision, how these shortcomings harmed much of the evidence entered into the case. In her words:

> We pause at the outset to remark that our task in ruling on the complicated issues in this case has been impeded, not so much by the expensive scope of the litigation as by the hap-hazard "shot gun" approach utilized by the attorneys in raising these difficult issues and then leaving them unsupported by evidence or controlling legal precedent. The briefing was fraught with inaccurate citations to the record, mischaracterized evidence in the record, and misrepresented holdings in the case law. Particularly troublesome was the fact that two sets of plaintiffs consistently spoke independently of another often raising the same argument but in slightly different fashion and without informing the court whether they were adopting or incorporating the claims of their co-plaintiffs. Plaintiffs also made no apparent effort to match individual plaintiffs to specific claims or arguments. What the court faced, as a result, was the gargantuan task of sorting through the hodge-podge of individual plaintiffs, their claims, and their evidence and then trying to make sense of it all. To require the Court to sort everything out and make sense of it is a dereliction of counsels' responsibilities and an abuse of the court's scarce resources. Nonetheless, we have done the best we can under the circumstances.[11]

Not pleased by the manner and quality of submitted evidence, the court sought to bring clarity to this "deluge of data" by grouping the facts of the case into seven categories. This grouping consisted of: "(I) Indiana election law and procedures, (II) Requirements for obtaining photo identification documents from the BMV, (III) Evidence regarding voter fraud, (IV), Evidence about potential impacts of SEA 483 on Indiana voters, (V) the Defendants, (VI) the Plaintiffs, and (VII) the . . . 'Brace Report'." The first two categories, while strictly factual, provide the perfect springboard into understanding how the court erred in granting the defendants motion for summary judgment.

Indiana election law and procedures are key culprits in this case, as ease and access to the ballot are essentially at the center of this case. The proposed changes to state law would require "citizens voting in-person at precinct polling places on election day, or casting an absentee ballot in person at a county clerk's office prior to election day, to present . . . valid photo identification."[12] More specifically, "Indiana voters are required to produce acceptable photo identification before signing the poll book. SEA 483 applies to voting at both primary and general elections. SEA 483 does not apply, however, to receiving and to casting an absentee ballot sent by the county to the voter through U.S. Mail; or to a voter who votes in person at a precinct polling place that is located at a state licensed care facility where the voter resides."[13] If a voter is unable to produce acceptable photo identification, a member of the precinct election board can "challenge" the voter. If "challenged," the voter must sign an affidavit attesting their identity, whereby allowing the voter to cast a provisional ballot. However, in order for the provisional ballot to be counted, the voter must appear before the circuit court clerk or county election board to prove their identity. If successful, the ballot will be opened, processed, and counted. Otherwise, the only other way provisional ballots can be counted is if: "(1) the person is indigent and is 'unable to obtain proof of identification without payment of fee'; or (2) has a religious objection to being photographed."[14] Oddly enough, two observations arise. First, neither indigency nor religious objection affidavits are available to voters on Election Day; instead, they are only available at election board offices the day following the election. Second, the law is very ambiguous on how it defines who qualifies as "indigent," as this is a key claim levied by the plaintiffs that the proposed changes to existing state election laws disenfranchise those at the bottom rungs of the socioeconomic ladder.

Prior to these proposed changes, a voter seeking to cast a ballot would need only to present themselves to the election clerks, proceed to sign the poll book, where at that point, the voters' signature would be compared to a previously photographed copy, before being allowed to cast a ballot, baring no discrepancies in the signatures. Under the proposed changes in the law, those individuals who do not possess "acceptable" forms of photo identification would then become a part of another grim reality, either the 82 percent of the provisional ballots cast in Marion County in 2004 that were not counted, or the 15 percent of all statewide provisional ballots that were counted.[15] Either way, the desire not to fall into either category presents itself as a pressing case, leading many plaintiffs to argue that this is simply the plight of poor or "underprivileged" voters in Indiana, as they are the demographic who would not be allowed to cast ballots on Election Day.

In order to avoid these complications, defendants maintain that obtaining an "acceptable" form of photo identification, like a state-issued driver's license, is the simple solution. Upon further review of this claim, it is imperative to establish what the required documents are for obtaining photo identification in the state. The Indiana Bureau of Motor Vehicles (BMV) requires all driver's license applicants or nonlicense identification-card applicants present either one primary or one secondary document along with one proof of Indiana residency requirement. Alternatively, applicants can submit two primary documents and one proof of Indiana residency. In accordance with state law, a primary document is used to verify identity, date of birth, and citizenship, which may include a U.S. birth certificate with a stamp or seal, documents showing that the person was born abroad as a U.S. citizen or is a naturalized citizen, a passport, or a U.S. military or merchant marine photo identification. Secondary documents in nature consist of items including, but not limited to: a bank statement, a certified academic transcript, a major credit or bank card (Master Card, VISA, American Express, and Discover only), and U.S. veteran's universal access ID card with a photo. While this list is not exhaustive, its purpose is to better situate both the content and context of Indiana voters. Regarding documents that establish proof of Indiana residency, applicants must present proof of a residential address, excluding post office boxes. Included in this list are items like a change of address confirmation from the U.S. Postal Service, an Indiana property deed or tax assessment, a current bill or benefit statement, along with an Indiana residency affidavit, among other options.

Establishing the governing policies and procedures pertaining to obtaining "acceptable" forms of photo identification places us on firmer ground to understand and assess the numerous moving parts in this case. Pursuant upon the aforementioned details, the BMV provided the court with an assessment of what it articulated to be potential difficulties in obtaining photo identification. Interestingly enough, this represents the initial and one of the steepest points of departure in this case, as the BMV claims that "there are persons who do not currently have a driver's license or identification card . . . however [the BMV] has not been able to determine the appropriate number of Indiana residents of voting age who are without an Indiana driver's license or identification card."[16] Plaintiffs, on the other hand, dismiss the BMV's claim of an inability to determine how many Indiana residents of voting age do not possess acceptable forms of photo identification. For instance, according to court documents, "plaintiffs further note that a survey released on October 28, 2005, by AARP Indiana reports that 3% of Indiana registered voters over the age of 60 do not have a driver's license or identification card."[17] Testimony from the executive director of the Indianapolis Resource Center for Independent Living (IRCIL), for instance, explained to the court that it is very common for persons with disabilities to not possess identification, especially those required under the law in question.[18]

The court's line of questioning pertaining to the possible impact this law could have on Indiana voters is multi-tiered. In addition to providing data sets and expert testimony that affirms the existence of a retrogressive impact on voters, plaintiffs also provided two expert reports. In the first report, authored by Professor Marjorie Hershey of Indiana University, the plaintiffs submitted the potential negative impacts that the implementation of the law would bring. The findings of the report paint a grim portrait of widespread disenfranchisement through the imposition of additional requirements. Through Dr. Hershey's eyes, the implementation of this law would likely "decrease voter turnout, particularly among voters of lower socioeconomic status." He later adds that, "the costs imposed by SEA 483, in terms of time, transportation, fees and obtaining all of the necessary information, threaten to be most difficult for the disabled, homeless, persons with limited income, those without cars, people of color, those who are part of 'language minorities', and the elderly."[19] In addition, plaintiffs cited both formal and informal surveys that support Hershey's findings. At this point, it is very important to note the continuity among findings pertaining to the negative impact this law would have across various demographic groups, as these early findings still remain consistent among plaintiffs over voter identification laws. As mentioned earlier, the court accepted these findings without fault. However, this was not the case for the plaintiff's second and final expert report.

Referred to as the "Brace report," this analysis affirmed many of the denied impacts the new law would place upon potential voters, chiefly that poor, elderly, and people of color would be impacted overwhelmingly. According to the findings of the report,

At least 51,000 registered voters and as many as 141,000 registered voters in Marion County, and up to 989,000 registered voters in the state of Indiana, do not currently possess a BMV-issued driver's license or photo identification. Brace also claims to have determined that registered voters who reside in census block groups with a median household income of less than $15,000 are more than twice as likely not to possess photo identification as are registered voters who reside in census group blocks with a median household income of more than $55,000.[20]

Upon entering this report into evidence, the court made a peculiar assessment, dismissing much of the report's finding. Through the court's eyes, "we have not included the Brace Report in our determinations because we view the analysis and conclusions set out in it as utterly incredible and unreliable," later reminding us of federal rule of evidence 702, adding that admitted evidence must be the product of reliable principles and methods applied to the facts of the case, whereas it was in the court's view that the Brace report drew "obviously inaccurate and illogical conclusions," failing to "qualify the statistical estimates based on socio-economic data." While it would take many pages and a noticeable deviation to discuss and analyze the statistical models called into question within the Brace report, it is important to note the court's quick dismantling of the plaintiffs' arguments and evidence pertaining to voter impact. However, these actions pale in comparison to the court's assessment of the chief claim that produced this law in the first place: so-called voter fraud.

Pursuant upon the belief that voter fraud was an issue, both plaintiffs and defendants submitted arguments that paint contrasting pictures over this contested reality. Through the court's eyes, these arguments unfold like this, "(A) plaintiffs note that there is no evidence of any instance of in-person voter fraud in Indiana; (B) Defendants counter that, even though there is no evidence of voter fraud as such, there is significant inflation in the Indiana voter registration lists; and in any event, based on reports documenting cases of in-person voter from other states, (C) Defendants maintain that voter fraud is or should be a concern in Indiana."[21] Following down this misguided path, defendants:

> Concede that the State of Indiana is not aware of any incidents or persons attempting to vote, or voting, at a place with a fraudulent or otherwise false identification. Plaintiffs further note that no voter in Indiana history has ever been formally charged with any sort of crime related to impersonating someone else for purposes of voting. Plaintiffs further contend that no evidence of in-person voting fraud was presented to the Indiana General Assembly during the legislative process leading up to the enactment of SEA 483.

Plaintiffs do note, however, there is evidence of absentee voter fraud in Indiana and that pervasive fraud regarding absentee balloting led the Indiana Supreme Court to recently vacate the results of the mayoral election in East Chicago.[22]

There are many unsettling admissions by both the court and the defendants that remain peculiar against the grander backdrop of establishing a burden of proof to support the need of a voter identification statute. Obviously, one of the first questions one must grabble with is whether or not the nonexistence of in-person voter fraud elevates the statute in question to the level of immediate statewide implementation. For instance, the court notes that the state of Indiana submitted several polls indicating voter concern about the existence of fraud at the ballot box. The state entered into evidence a 2000 Rasmussen Report's poll that showed that 59 percent of voters believed there was "a lot" or "some" fraud in elections. Moreover, the state cited a similar Gallup Poll that illustrated 67 percent of adults polled had only "some" or "very little" confidence in the way the votes are cast in our country, later concluding that a 2004 Zogby poll found that 10 percent of voters believed their votes were not accurately counted, resulting in the Baker-Carter Commission findings that found the perception of voter fraud "contributes to low confidence in the system."[23]

The evidence submitted on behalf of the state of Indiana, at best, severely lacks merit and relevance. First, while the defendants conceded that they were not aware of any in-person attempts of voter fraud, it was the plaintiffs who noted the existence of voter fraud via absentee balloting. This is a very important point, because as we recall, the proposed changes in state law *do not* apply to receiving and to casting an absentee ballot sent by the county to the voter through U.S. Mail. If cases of voter fraud exist in the form of absentee ballots, why does this law not directly address this exposed vulnerability? It appears rather incongruent to provide a "solution" to the nonexisting problem of in-person voter fraud while disregarding the actual trouble with absentee voter fraud. Next, the notion of voter perception needs to be called into question as to whether or not the polling data entered into evidence even establishes or assists in satisfying any burden of proof, especially given the context of national sentiment in 2000. As we all recall, the fiasco in Florida surrounding the presidential election between George W. Bush and Albert Gore gave way to much voter frustration. More specifically, the time period when the polling data was used must be understood in the context of the national situation surrounding Florida's

2000 election night problems, especially as it pertains to usability and ballot design flaws. Whether we revisit the troubles experienced with the punch card voting machines, which gave way to terms like "hanging," "dimpled," and "pregnant" chads, to the debates over how best to calculate those votes, the year 2000 must be understood within this context. Additionally, when discussing factors like low voter confidence, it is not only inaccurate to attribute that to voter fraud but would also behoove anyone to omit the national sentiment surrounding the 2000 presidential election, especially as it relates to the Florida fiasco.

The state's truncated use of the Baker-Carter Commission's elementary finding that the perception of voter fraud "contributes to low confidence in the system" by no means supports the standing of the defendant's claim. With the understanding that no reported cases of in-person voter fraud exist in Indiana, and without specificity in the report to Indiana, what then are we to make of this "finding?" While it is true, according to court documents, that the state "also produced evidence of published books and media reports discussing allegations and instances of in-person voter fraud in several other states," if none pertain to Indiana, a state with no evidence of such fraud, what standing should we grant to this? If voter fraud represents a growing problem, as supported by tangible evidence and not hunches, then it is a matter worth resolving. However, within the context of Indiana, the defendants appear to be shouting fire when no smoke exists.

In the plaintiffs' final attempt at supporting the claim that Indiana's new voter identification law is not only retrogressive but it also oversteps its constitutional boundaries, the safeguards of the First and Fourteenth Amendments were called into question. Although the court moved quickly to dismiss these claims, with attention to the Equal Protection Clause, the court provided a thorough, albeit severely flawed rationale for their dismissal. Without wasting time, the court opined that the plaintiffs "have failed to demonstrate that strict scrutiny of SEA 483 is warranted, primarily because they have totally failed to adduce evidence establishing that any actual voters will be adversely impacted by 483."[24] Through the court's eyes, strict scrutiny, defined as the legal review process in which a "regulation is necessary to serve a compelling state interest and that is narrowly drawn to achieve that end," is not warranted.[25] While the court dismissed the findings of the Brace report, offering no rejoinder to the summary findings by Professor Hershey and the numerous testimonies, it becomes increasingly difficult to accept the court's position that plaintiffs have "totally failed to adduce evidence establishing that any actual voters will be adversely impacted by 483." The equal protection clause of the Fourteenth Amendment prohibits states from denying any person within its jurisdiction the equal protection of the laws, whereas according to the plaintiff's evidence, all articulate the presence of discrimination in the laws application. Typically, questions or legal challenges pertaining to possible violations of the equal protection clause arise when states or laws in general grant access or rights to one group to engage in an activity while denying other individuals the same access or rights.

With respect to strict scrutiny, the court executed a calculated, but again, flawed maneuver in not fully addressing the matter. As defined previously, the application of strict scrutiny to a proposed or existing law may only be applied "to serve a compelling state interest and that is narrowly drawn to achieve that end," whereas within the context of this case, voter fraud would be the compelling state interest, while photo identification would be the narrowly drawn solution to answer that compelling interest. Because the courts will only strictly scrutinize a law if it has been shown to discriminate, whether along the lines of race, national origin, or, in some situations, non-U.S. citizenship, by denying this expert reports and testimony asserting this reality, the court maneuvered a deeply flawed exit strategy in order to avoid grappling with this reality. The defendant's admission that no in-person voter fraud exists, in turn questions the compelling state interest upholding the relevance of this law, and what is perhaps most surprising is the court's overall denial of retrogressive impact caused by the law.

Not convinced of any forms of retrogression caused by the law, the court sought to make this painfully clear to the plaintiffs. As viewed by the court, "despite apocalyptic assertions of wholesale voter disenfranchisement, plaintiffs have produced not a single piece of evidence of any identifiable registered voter who would be prevented from voting pursuant to SEA 483 because of his or her inability to obtain the necessary photo identification."[26] Furthermore, opined the court, "plaintiffs have failed to produce any evidence of any individual, registered or unregistered, who would have to obtain photo identification in order to vote, let alone anyone who would undergo any appreciable hardship to obtain photo identification in order to be qualified to vote."[27] In the court's final blow before granting defendants' motion for summary judgment, the court delivered its dismissal to plaintiffs' claim that the proposed law amounts to nothing short of a poll tax for certain populations. In their sweeping claim, the court asserted, "we do not view the photo identification requirement of SEA 483 to be a poll tax . . . the

BMV may not impose a fee for the issuance of [an original, renewal, or duplicate] identification card to an individual . . . who . . . does not have a valid Indiana driver's license . . . thus, by statute, any individual who meets the age eligibility requirement to vote can obtain photo identification form the BMV without paying a fee."[28]

In direct response to the associated costs in obtaining the needed primary and secondary documents, transportation logistics, among other variables entered into evidence by plaintiffs, the court was not swayed. The court asserted that the "cost of time and transportation" cannot qualify as a poll tax because "these same 'costs' also result from voter registration and in-person voting requirements . . . plaintiffs provide no principled argument in support of this poll tax theory."[29] Here, we reject the court's claim in all its forms. For example, data would be needed to support the claim that the same logistical 'costs' exist between in-person voting and registering to vote. It is implied, not stated, that there are an equal number of polling places as there are BMV offices, and more importantly, that these offices are open during normal business hours, which is inaccurate. In Albany, Indiana, their BMV facility opens only on Wednesdays and Fridays; in Albion, they open only on Tuesdays and Thursdays; and in places like Alexandria and Anderson, they are open five days a week. If the BMV is central in assisting citizens with compliance of the new law, then every location must hold identical hours to assure that residents, regardless of location, have the same window of opportunity to access these services. Unfortunately, this understanding of equal access did not register in the court's mind, as they granted defendants motion for summary judgment.

Crawford v. Marion County Election Board

This bizarre turn of events sparked a motion for appeal by the plaintiffs. Not pleased by the dismissal of some and admission of other evidence, the appeal was met by the U.S. Court of Appeals, Seventh Circuit in 2006 and was granted judgment in 2007. In what was a fairly brief assessment of the law in question, juxtaposed with the challenges raised by the plaintiffs, the court wasted no time in upholding the lower court's motion for summary judgment on behalf of the defendants. Oddly enough, the court's rationale was quite synchronized with the ruling from the lower court, including a series of very peculiar claims. Writing the court's majority opinion, Judge Richard Posner affirmed various objections raised by the plaintiffs, including an acknowledgment that "the Indiana law will deter some people from voting." Moreover, Judge Posner also affirmed the positive correlation between socioeconomics and voter access to the polls. He writes:

> No doubt most people who don't have photo ID are low on the economic ladder and thus, if they do vote, are more likely to vote for Democratic than Republican candidates. Exit polls in the recent midterm elections show a strong negative correlation between income and voting Democratic, with the percentage voting Democratic rising from 45 percent for voters with an income of at least $200,000 to 67 percent for voters having an income below $15,000. Thus the new law injures the Democratic Party by compelling the party to devote resources to getting to the polls those of its supporters who would otherwise be discouraged by the new law from bothering to vote.[30]

Upon first glance, one would be led to believe that such a strong admission by the court would occupy a heavy presence in how the court weighs the claims of the case; however, this could not be further from the truth. Despite the acknowledgment of the plaintiff's cornerstone claim of widespread disenfranchisement, the court was still not convinced of the new law's severity. On the claim that Indiana's voter identification law would thwart access to the polls, the court responded by opining, "there is not a single plaintiff who intends not to vote because of the new law—that is, who would vote were it not for the law."[31] From the standpoint of the court, the plaintiffs have thus far been unable to identify any specific person who would be deterred from voting, especially given the allowances the law affords to those who are deemed "indigent" have a religious objection to being photographed, or reside in a nursing care facility.

In the court's initial dissent against the plaintiffs' appeal, the rationale becomes more peculiar. Against the grander backdrop of the charges alleged by the plaintiffs, Judge Posner sought to articulate how such allegations of discrimination do not rise to the merit of judicial consideration, let alone, ordering an injunction against the law. On the first charge of obstructing voter access to the polls on account of having to produce photo identification, Judge Posner opined:

> There is not a single plaintiff who intends not to vote because of the new law— that is, who would vote were it not for the law. There are plaintiffs who have photo IDs and so are not affected by the law at all and plaintiffs who have no photo IDs but have not said they would vote if they did and so who also are, as far as we can tell, unaffected by the law. There thus are no plaintiffs whom

the law will deter from voting. No doubt there are at least a few such people in Indiana, but the inability of the sponsors of this litigation to find any
such person to join as a plaintiff suggests that the motivation for the suit is
simply that the law may require the Democratic Party and the other organizational plaintiffs to work harder to get every last one of their supporters to
the polls.[32]

In what reads as a fairly strange reading of the case Judge Posner is not
convinced that those without photo identification would not vote on account of the new law. Here, the shortcomings in reasoning exist on multiple levels. As seen by the court the physical absence of plaintiffs who
possess no photo identification and plan not to vote as a result of the law's
retrogressive impact illustrates that the negative consequences of the law,
as argued by the plaintiffs, are merely a political stunt on behalf of the state's
Democratic caucus. Failure to bring plaintiffs before the court who are directly disenfranchised as a result of the law existed as reason enough for
the court to believe, "there thus are no plaintiffs whom the law will deter
from voting." With judicial precedence established in Supreme Court cases
like *Burdick v. Taskushi,* the court found that "election laws will invariably
impose some burden upon individual voters. . . . to subject every voting
regulation to strict scrutiny and to require that the regulation be narrowly
tailored to advance a compelling state interest, as petitioner suggests, would
tie the hands of States seeking to assure that elections are operated equi-
tably and efficiently."[33] However, with no evidence that Indiana elections
were plagued by systemic failures, chiefly, in-person voter fraud, the burden
of proof to even establish that a compelling state interest exists remains
shrouded in controversy.

As noted by the court in its initial deliberation in *Indiana Democratic
Party v. Todd Rokita,* state supporters of the new law, despite failing to present evidence of a compelling state interest, received the benefit of much
doubt. In objecting to the plaintiffs' association between the state's voter
identification law and a poll tax, Judge Posner offered the argument that:

> The Indiana law is not like a poll tax, where on one side is the right to vote
> and on the other side the state's interest in defraying the cost of elections or
> in limiting the franchise to people who really care about voting or in exclud-
> ing poor people or in discouraging people who are black. The purpose of the
> Indiana law is to reduce voting fraud, and voting fraud impairs the right of
> legitimate voters to vote by diluting their votes—dilution being recognized to
> be an impairment of the right to vote.[34]

Again, failing to cite or advance any evidence of voter fraud, Judge Posner's argument falls on deaf ears. Without any reports, allegations, or statistics to affirm the existence of voter fraud, particularly, in-person fraud, his argument simply cannot move forward. After all, if the purpose of the law, as articulated by Judge Posner, is to "reduce voting fraud," yet it has *never* been proven by state supporters to exist, then what purpose does the law serve? Yet again, the court turns a blind eye to this reality and instead continues to praise the law on the grounds of preventing voting fraud. As mysteriously reasoned by the court, "on the other side of the balance is voting fraud, specifically the form of voting fraud in which a person shows up at the polls claiming to be someone else—someone who has left the district, or died, too recently to have been removed from the list of registered voters, or someone who has not voted yet on election day. Without requiring a photo ID, there is little if any chance of preventing this kind of fraud because busy poll workers are unlikely to scrutinize signatures carefully and argue with people who deny having forged someone else's signature."[35] Relying on speculation and exposing themselves to various fallacies, the court proceeded with this line of reasoning when upholding the merits of this law.

Now turning away from the facts of the case, the court took a turn for the worse, engaging in reasoning via speculation. In what continued to be a stretch of reasoning fueled by an absence of evidence, Judge Posner sought to provide us with both a reason as to why voter fraud does not exist within the context of the case before the court and in the state, along with a real scenario where the law's impact would be most beneficial. In his words:

> But the absence of prosecutions is explained by the endemic under-enforcement of minor criminal laws (minor as they appear to the public and prosecutors, at all events) and by the extreme difficulty of apprehending a voter impersonator. He enters the polling place, gives a name that is not his own, votes, and leaves. If later it is discovered that the name he gave is that of a dead person, no one at the polling place will remember the face of the person who gave that name, and if someone did remember it, what would he do with the information?[36]

If this line of reasoning is not peculiar enough, Judge Posner goes on to say that, "the plaintiffs argue that while vote fraud by impersonation may be a problem in other states, it is not in Indiana, because there are no reports of such fraud in that state. But that lacuna may reflect nothing more than the vagaries of journalists' and other investigators' choice of scandals to investigate."[37] To argue that the court went out on a limb to defend this law would be a grave understatement. In a case of such great public importance, the court failed to move beyond their apparent personal/political dispositions to consider the facts and context of the case before them.

While Judge Posner wrote on behalf of the court's majority, it was Judge Terence T. Evans who cast the court's lone dissenting opinion. Not convinced by the majority opinion, Judge Evans had stern words of criticism for his colleagues. "Let's not beat around the bush: the Indiana voter photo ID law is a not-too-thinly-veiled attempt to discourage election-day turnout by certain folks believed to skew Democratic," wrote Judge Evans.[38] His scathing critique of the majority opinion reflects what Judge Evans believed to be glaring dismissal of the facts. Mincing no words, Judge Evans opined:

> The fig leaf of respectability providing the motive behind this law is that it is necessary to prevent voter fraud—a person showing up at the polls pretending to be someone else. But where is the evidence of that kind of voter fraud in this record? Voting fraud is a crime (punishable by up to 3 years in prison and a fine of up to $10,000 in Indiana) and, at oral argument, the defenders of this law candidly acknowledged that no one—in the history of Indiana—had ever been charged with violating that law. Nationwide, a preliminary report to the U.S. Election Assistance Commission has found little evidence of the type of polling-place fraud that photo ID laws seek to stop. If that's the case, where is the justification for this law? Is it wise to use a sledgehammer to hit either a real or imaginary fly on a glass coffee table? I think not.[39]

Believing that the well has been poisoned by political and judicial impropriety, Judge Evans offered an alternative reading of the facts and context surrounding the plaintiffs' key claims of voter disenfranchisement. With no justification to support the so-called need for this change in the law, Judge Evans remains very concerned that these actions were derived with the intent to discriminate certain classes of citizens.

In perhaps what exists as one of Judge Evans's most memorable rejoinders to supporters who argue there will be no impact felt by low-income voters, given the allowances within the law, Judge Evans explains what he believes to be the "real problem." As seen through his eyes:

> The real problem is that this law will make it significantly more difficult for some eligible voters—I have no idea how many, but 4 percent is a number that has been bandied about—to vote. And this group is mostly comprised of people who are poor, elderly, minorities, disabled, or some combination thereof. I would suspect that few, if any, in this class have passports (which

cost in the neighborhood of $100), and most don't have drivers licenses (who needs a driver's license if you don't drive a car?) or state-issued ID cards which require valid (certified) birth certificates. And it's not particularly easy for a poor, elderly person who lives in South Bend, but was born in Arkansas, to get a certified copy of his birth certificate . . . And I recognize that there is, and perhaps there may always be, a fundamental tension between claims of voter fraud and fears of disenfranchisement. But Indiana's law, because it allows nothing except a passport or an Indiana ID card to prove that a potential voter is who he says he is, tips far too far in the wrong direction.[40]

This final grapple with what appears to be a lapse in judgment and denial of reality raises many concerns for the plaintiffs, as the court's majority opinion eagerly dismissed many substantial concerns. While it is true, in pursuant upon Article 1, Section 4 of the Constitution, that states can regulate the time, places, and manner in which elections are conducted, this does not dismiss the states' judicial responsibility to apply some form of a legal litmus test, especially pertaining to voting. For the plaintiffs, not much solace can be garnered from Judge Evans's lonely dissenting opinion, as judgment was rendered in favor of the defendants. Not convinced that the circuit court delivered an impartial judgment, especially amidst the absence of supporting evidence over voter fraud, upon appeal, the U.S. Supreme Court decided to add this case to its 2008 docket.

Indiana Voter Identification Law and the Supreme Court

Pursuant upon the previous lower court's decision to affirm the 2005 passage of an Indiana law requiring persons who vote in person to present photo identification, the Supreme Court did not stray far from that path. Understood by the Supreme Court in the context of whether or not the Indiana voter identification law presents voters with an "unduly burden" upon their right to vote, the Court upheld and expanded all previous decisions in favor of the state of Indiana. The Court's affirmation of the lower court's decision came as quite a surprise, as the Supreme Court, by a 6–3 margin, offered a peculiar rationale that turned a blind eye to evidence, or the lack thereof, and instead focused largely upon voter integrity and perceptions of voter fraud. Writing on behalf of the Court's majority, Justice John Paul Stevens relied upon the same shallow level of analysis exhibited in *Indiana Democratic Party v. Todd Rokita.*

The constitutional question at hand lends itself to considerable legal precedence, as the conflict between burdens imposed on voters versus state interests has been the cause of much controversy. In the 1966 case of *Harper v. Virginia Board of Elections,* the question before the Supreme Court pertained to the issuance of a $1.50 poll tax. Augmented by the claim that such a cost would promote civic responsibility by means of eliminating those voters who did not care enough about public affairs to pay the cost, the Supreme Court rejected this claim and invalidated the law in a manner of great importance to the case at hand. In the Court's dissent, it was affirmed that, "a state violates the Equal Protection Clause of the Fourteenth Amendment whenever it makes the affluence of the voter or payment of any fee an electoral standard."[41] Moreover, the Harper decision underscored, "that a state violates the Equal Protection Clause of the Fourteenth Amendment whenever it makes the affluence of the voter or payment of any fee an electoral standard. Voter qualifications have no relation to wealth nor to paying or not paying this or any other tax."[42] Most importantly, the Court established the understanding that, "however slight that burden may appear, as Harper demonstrates, it must be justified by relevant and legitimate state interests sufficiently weighty to justify the limitation."[43] As seen here, the Court held that it was unconstitutional to require the payment of *any* fee as an electoral standard; however, whether or not the Court saw a parallel to the case at hand that is part of the larger question. This point will become very significant soon, as the debate before us centers on competing interests over voter burdens and state interests.

The 1974 case of *Lubin v. Panish* is also relevant to the tensions at hand. In *Lubin,* as summarized by the Supreme Court, the "petitioner, an indigent, was denied nomination papers to file as a candidate for the position of County Supervisor in California because, although otherwise qualified, he was unable to pay the filing fee required of all candidates by a California statute."[44] In a unanimous decision, Chief Justice Warren Burger authored the Court's majority opinion that overturned the California law. In his decision, Chief Justice Burger opined that, "for me, the difficulty with the California election system is the absence of a realistic alternative access to the ballot for the candidate whose indigency renders it impossible for him to pay the prescribed filing fee . . . I would hold that the California election statutes are unconstitutional insofar as they presently deny access to the ballot. If § 18603 (b) were to be stricken, the Code, as before, would permit write-in access with no prior fee."[45] Tracing some of the landmark decisions pertaining to the right to vote is imperative if the grander context of ballot access is to be understood and accessed under the current conversation. As noticed thus far, and again in the two final examples ahead, the Court has been very clear in its approach toward providing access to all, regardless of socioeconomic status. When reflecting upon these past decisions, the "burden" upon voters becomes a concurrent theme that requires special attention to the legal details.

In the 1980 case of *Anderson v. Celebrezze,* the question before the court was whether or not Ohio's separate filling deadlines for independent candidates placed too "high of a burden [upon voters] to petition the government." In response, not only did the court find the law in violation of both the First and Fourteenth Amendments, but the court also affirmed that, "rather than applying any 'litmus test' that would neatly separate valid from invalid restrictions, we concluded that a court must identify and evaluate the interests put forward by the State as justifications for the burden imposed by its rule, and then make the 'hard judgment' that our adversary system demands."[46] And finally, in the 1992 case of *Burdick v. Takushi,* the Supreme Court had to determine whether or not Hawaii's prohibition on write-in voting unreasonably infringed upon its citizens' rights under the First and Fourteenth Amendments. As Justice Stevens recounts of the Court's actions, "we reaffirmed *Anderson's* requirement that a court evaluating a constitutional challenge to an election regulation weigh the asserted injury to the right to vote against the 'precise interests put forward by the State as justifications for the burden imposed by its rule.'"[47] As we continue to move through landmark decisions and the standards erected by the Court pertaining to the imposition of burdens placed upon voters, it is imperative to connect the context and rulings of these cases to the case before us, as our attention turns to now.

The Supreme Court, in deciding the merits of Indiana's new law, had much to consider. First, the Court must consider the decisions they reached in each of the aforementioned cases, as they established a legal precedence defining what qualifies as a reasonable burden that can be placed upon voters. Next, given the unique details and context of the case, the Court was also tasked with separating and analyzing what it believed to be the pressing legal questions of the case. Through the eyes of the Court, there were two pressing issues: (1) determining the validity of the state's interest in "deterring and detecting voter fraud" and (2) assessing the state's interest in "safeguarding voter confidence." As briefly noted before expounding upon both questions,

The first is the interest in deterring and detecting voter fraud. The State has a valid interest in participating in a nationwide effort to improve and modernize election procedures that have been criticized as antiquated and inefficient. The State also argues that it has a particular interest in preventing voter fraud in response to a problem that is in part the product of its own maladministration—namely, that Indiana's voter registration rolls include a large number of names of persons who are either deceased or no longer live in Indiana. Finally, the State relies on its interest in safeguarding voter confidence. Each of these interests merits separate comment.[48]

With the stage set, insofar as articulating how the court will proceed with evaluating the evidence before them, there appears to be no reason for alarm, as their stated objectives are lockstep with the questions raised by the plaintiffs. However, what remains most controversial and ambiguous is how the court will assess the lack of evidence pertaining to in-person voter fraud against the state's claim of wanting to deter fraud, as well as increase voter confidence. After all, through the eyes of the plaintiffs, with no evidence to uphold the claims of voter fraud, must the state first articulate and therefore provide evidence for a problem that actually exists in order to drastically change the law? Or, does state interest alone, absent of any articulable problem, rise to the level of meeting the legal sufficient condition?

The age-old saying "if it aint broke don't fix it" immediately comes to mind upon reviewing the facts of this case. As the state continued to fumble in explicating what broken mechanisms warrant the "fix" of a voter identification law, the state cited inflated voter rolls by more than 41 percent. To their defense, the state argued that in order to prevent individuals from voting twice, although no cases of such fraud have been reported, it is necessary for individuals to produce certain government-issued identification cards. In assessing the merits of this claim, the court explained, "even though Indiana's own negligence may have contributed to the serious inflation of its registration lists when SEA 483 was enacted, the fact of inflated voter rolls does provide a neutral and nondiscriminatory reason supporting the State's decision to require photo identification."[49] As opposed to asking identifying questions to voters, or even providing alternative forms of identification that fall outside the realm of government-issued photo identification, both the state and the court feel that Indiana's efforts are both "neutral" and "nondiscriminatory."

By no means does either the state or the court believe that requiring individuals to possess and produce government-issued photo identification places a "substantial burden on the right to vote," and thus the court quickly turned to uphold the law. In striking the final blow to the plaintiff's case, the court stated:

> But if a nondiscriminatory law is supported by valid neutral justifications, those justifications should not be disregarded simply because partisan interests may have provided one motivation for the votes of individual legislators. The state interests identified as justifications for SEA 483 are both neutral and sufficiently strong to require us to reject petitioners' facial attack on the statute. The application of the statute to the vast majority of Indiana voters is amply justified by the valid interest in protecting "the integrity and reliability of the electoral process."[50]

Hampered in the majority opinion for not demonstrating "that the proper remedy—even assuming an unjustified burden on some voters—would be to invalidate the entire statute," the plaintiff's arguments fell on deaf ears in the court's 6–3 decision. However, this was not to say that the court's three dissenting justices (Souter, Ginsburg, and Breyer) did not notice the shortcomings in the arguments advanced by both the state and their six colleagues.

In writing his dissenting opinion, Justice David Souter, who was joined by Justice Ruth Bader Ginsburg, offered a stark difference in constitutional interpretation in relation to state-imposed burdens on voters. Mincing no words, Justice Souter remarked:

> The statute is unconstitutional under the balancing standard of *Burdick v. Takushi*, 504 U.S. 428 (1992): a State may not burden the right to vote merely by invoking abstract interests, be they legitimate, see ante, at 7–13, or even compelling, but must make a particular, factual showing that threats to its interests outweigh the particular impediments it has imposed. The State has made no such justification here, and as to some aspects of its law, it has hardly even tried. I therefore respectfully dissent from the Court's judgment sustaining the statute.[51]

Informed by the belief that the court did not meticulously scrutinize a statute that possesses the ability to immediately disenfranchise those previously enfranchised, Justices Souter and Ginsburg were deeply troubled. For both justices, their dissent was largely influenced by assessing the level of burdens imposed by the state upon its citizens rather than analyzing the facts of the case. One major theme that reveals itself over the course of their dissenting opinion is a focus upon practical oversights made by the courts.

Given the wide reach and impact of the law in the question, the dissenting justices believed that the court must not disavow the multiple realities surrounding the context of the case.

Up first was the burden of traveling to a state branch of the BMV, the agency those without state-issued photo identification must visit in order to become compliant with the law. Upon further review of the practical/logistical details that escaped consideration by the court's majority, it is revealed that:

> The need to travel to a BMV branch will affect voters according to their circumstances, with the average person probably viewing it as nothing more than an inconvenience. Poor, old, and disabled voters who do not drive a car, however, may find the trip prohibitive, witness the fact that the BMV has far fewer license branches in each county than there are voting precincts The burden of traveling to a more distant BMV office rather than a conveniently located polling place is probably serious for many of the individuals who lack photo identification . . . According to a report published by Indiana's Department of Transportation in August 2007, 21 of Indiana's 92 counties have no public transportation system at all, 15 and as of 2000, nearly 1 in every 10 voters lived within 1 of these 21 counties.16 Among the counties with some public system, 21 provide service only within certain cities, and 32 others restrict public transportation to regional county service, leaving only 18 that offer countywide public transportation.[52]

While a reality to those voters who lack personal means of transportation, public access to these locations becomes paramount for compliance. Overlooked by the majority opinion and even by the state, what then becomes of the previously eligible voters who reside in parts of the state where (1) public transportation does not exist; and/or (2) countywide transportation does not serve areas with BMV offices? Additionally, the dissenting justices were not convinced with the law's allowance to cast provisional ballots for those considered "indigent." As they understand the law, "unlike the trip to the BMV (which, assuming things go smoothly, needs to be made only once every four years for renewal of non-driver photo identification, see id.), this one must be taken every time a poor person or religious objector wishes to vote, because the State does not allow an affidavit to count in successive elections . . . Forcing these people to travel to the county seat every time they try to vote is particularly onerous for the reason noted already."[53] But again, at no point throughout the lower court's decision, and even in the majority opinion, is there mention of this reality. If nothing else, to fully access and debate the degree to which a "severe burden" may or may not exist, there must be careful attention to the context surrounding the case. Strict scrutiny of the law must foster a dialogue that grapples with these tensions, as they are the lived experiences of those impacted by the law, because the provisional ballot allowance only causes more problems than it solves.

In casting a separate dissenting opinion, Justice Stephen Breyer offered an opinion that placed the Indiana law in an uncharted realm of its own. While Justice Breyer reached much of the same conclusions as Justices Souter and Ginsburg, he took his dissent one step further. With states like Georgia and Florida already invoking similar laws, there are stark differences in what qualifies as acceptable forms of identification when compared to Indiana. In Florida, for example, items like a debit or credit card, employee identification, and student identification and the like are permissible forms of identification. Moreover, the Florida law allows for provisional ballots to be counted if the state determines a match in signature from their voter registration form. In Georgia, documents like a paycheck stub, Social Security, Medicare, Medicaid statement, among others, serve as sufficient documentation. As Justice Breyer explains, "while Indiana allows only certain groups such as the elderly and disabled to vote by absentee ballot, in Georgia any voter may vote absentee without providing any excuse, and (except where required by federal law) need not present a photo ID in order to do so. Finally, neither Georgia nor Florida insists, as Indiana does, that indigent voters travel each election cycle to potentially distant places for the purposes of signing an indigency affidavit."[54] Here, Justice Breyer explains not only why he is not convinced nor believes this law is constitutional, but amidst the grander backdrop of voter identification laws in general, he notes that "the record nowhere provides a convincing reason why Indiana's photo ID requirement must impose greater burdens than those of other States."[55] He concluded that, "I need not determine the constitutionality of Florida's or Georgia's requirements (matters not before us), in order to conclude that Indiana's requirement imposes a significantly harsher, unjustified burden."[56]

League of Women Voters of Indiana v. Rokita

While this decision was hardly a victory for many critics, just one year following this decision, the League of Women Voters of both Indianapolis and Indiana filed suit; however, it was not on the grounds of disenfranchisement. Instead, the plaintiffs argued on the grounds that the law violates the Indiana Constitution, specifically, Article 2, Section 2, and

Article 1, Section 23. The Indiana Constitution, in Article 2, Section 2 provides that:

(a) A citizen of the United States, who is at least eighteen (18) years of age, and who has been a resident of a precinct thirty (30) days immediately preceding an election, may vote in that precinct at the election.

(b) A citizen may not be disenfranchised under (a), if the citizen is entitled to vote in a precinct under (c) or federal law.

(c) The General Assembly may provide that a citizen who ceases to be a resident of a precinct before an election may vote in a precinct where the citizen previously resided if, on the date of the election, the citizen's name appears on the registration rolls for the precinct.[57]

Not satisfied over the state's argument that free identification will be made available (to those who otherwise possess and do not need to purchase the needed documentation to qualify for the free ID), the League argued that the law posed a "new substantive qualification on the right to vote." Instead of advancing claims of voter disenfranchisement, the League argued that requiring photo identification was a substantive voting qualification that the Indiana legislature was prohibited from adding, according to Article 2, Section 2, of the Indiana Constitution. The court, by citing the aforementioned 2006 case of *Indiana Democratic Party v. Rokita*, dismissed the League's claim as the precedence had already been established that voter identification laws were "constitutionally valid."

While the Court of Appeals of Indiana eventually upheld the League's claim, affirming that the law violated the Equal Privileges and Immunities Clause of the Indiana Constitution, how the court articulated this disparity in their ruling provided very little substance for critics of the law. Upon the League's second and final challenge pertaining to Article 1, Section 23, of the Indiana Constitution, it is understood that the "General Assembly shall not grant to any citizen, or class of citizens, privileges or immunities which, upon the same terms, shall not equally belong to all citizens." Specifically, as the court explains, the League argues that the law violates Section 23 in three ways: "(1) the disparate treatment between mail-in absentee voters and in-person voters; (2) the disparate treatment between voters who reside at state licensed care facilities that by happenstance are polling places and elderly and disabled voters who do not reside at state licensed care facilities that also happen to be polling places; and (3) the requirements that an identification contain an expiration date and photograph is not reasonably related to the purpose of the statute."[58] As a result of the League's objection, the court agreed that not all voter qualifications were uniform, ultimately creating separate requirements for certain classes of people.

In declaring their judgment, the court invalidated the portion of the law that did not require nursing home residents or mail-in voters to follow the same procedures as those voting in person.

> We fail to see how the Voter I.D. Law's exception of those residing in state licensed care facilities, which happen to also be a polling place would be a uniform or impartial regulation. Furthermore, the Voter I.D. Law treats in-person voters disparate from mail-in voters, conferring partial treatment upon mail-in voters. It seems that the inconsistent and impartial treatment favoring voters who reside at state care facilities who also happen to be polling places could be excised from the Voter I.D. Law without destroying the primary objective of the Law. However, the same cannot be said for the inconsistent and partial treatment favoring absentee voters who choose to mail their votes without destroying the opportunity for mailing votes. There may be different ways in which the inconsistent and partial treatment of the Voter I.D. Law could be cured, but it is not our task to form suggestions for legislation . . . Therefore, we must reverse and remand, with instructions to the trial court that it enter an order declaring the Voter I.D. Law void.[59]

With the law struck down by the Indiana Court of Appeals, the case was appealed in 2010 to the Indiana Supreme Court. Upon appeal, the court responded in accordance with the court of appeals. In doing so, the Indiana Supreme Court noted that "here the plaintiffs seek a declaration that it is unconstitutional to require voters to identify themselves at the polls using a photo ID. This is relief to which the plaintiffs are not entitled. But in affirming the trial court, we do so without prejudice to future particularized as-applied claims. We affirm the judgment of the trial court granting the appellee's motion to dismiss and rejecting the plaintiffs' claims that the Indiana Voter ID Law contravenes Article 2, Section 2 or Article 1, Section 23 of the Indiana Constitution."[60]

Updates and Conclusion

The long road to the Supreme Court and the decision that was finally reached continues to place *Crawford v. Marion County* as one of the most notable landmark cases pertaining to voter identification laws. Specifically, this case will forever be known as the gateway decision that established the precedence needed to enact, without cause or evidence, voter identification laws. While decided in 2008, current cases continue to cite the majority opinion of this case as a means of establishing justification for enacting laws that continue to lack reported cases of actual voter fraud. Oddly enough, however, seven years after writing the opinion of the U.S. Court of Appeals for the Seventh Circuit, Judge Richard Posner released a series of statements and interviews reflecting upon his decision to uphold the Indiana law that shocked the legal/political world.

As the debate over voter identification laws continues, mirroring the pace of enactment by various states, Judge Richard Posner made a rare admission, admitting he was wrong to uphold Indiana's voter identification law. In Posner's new book, *Reflections on Judging*, he comes to grips with his past decision. According to the *New York Times*, when "asked whether the court had gotten its ruling wrong, Judge Posner responded: 'Yes. Absolutely'. Back in 2007, he said, 'there hadn't been that much activity in the way of voter identification', and 'we weren't really given strong indications that requiring additional voter identification would actually disenfranchise people entitled to vote'. The member of the three-judge panel who dissented from the majority decision, Terence T. Evans, 'was right', Judge Posner said."[61] Posner's reflection, not always welcomed, especially by proponents of such laws, must be taken within the context it was received. Upon reflecting over his past decisions, Posner, a Ronald Reagan-appointed conservative federal appeals judge, wishes he would have joined his dissenting colleague, Judge Terence Evans, by not only dissenting, but striking down the Indiana law altogether. Given the incredibly rare occurrence that a judge admits error in judgment, especially over such a pressing current controversy, it gives hope to those who believe, as Posner now does, that voter identification laws are largely politically motivated and absent of probable cause for enactment.

As suspected by the dissenting Judge Terence Evans, linking voter identification laws to race and political parties continues to consume much controversy and contemplation. While Judge Evans believed that the Indiana voter identification law was a ploy to skew Democratic voters, much resurgence around that tactic continues to consume much conversation today. Much like how gerrymandering in states like Texas continues to draw scornful eyes over how critics believe minority votes have become diluted, the same sentiment is felt in regard to voter identification laws. While states attempt to uphold their supposed neutral and nondiscriminatory rationale of deterring nonexistent cases of voter fraud and improving "voter confidence," many of the same arguments from the aforementioned series of court cases find themselves back in the public eye again. Could there be a link between increasing calls for voter identification laws and shifting racial demographics throughout the United States? Are increasing populations of immigrants from Latin America part of the campaign calculus behind widespread calls for voter identification laws and its popularity among Republican office holders and seekers? These questions, especially as they pertain to Pennsylvania, are the feature of our next chapter.

Notes

1. Martin DeAgostino, "New Senator's Bill Passes Senate; Legislation for Red-Light Cameras Get 31–17 Vote," *South Bend Tribune,* March 2, 2005, p. B1.

2. Martin DeAgostino, "One Compromised Reached; Middle Ground Found on Inspector General Bill, But Not Voter ID Measure," *South Bend Tribune,* March 15, 2005, p. B1.

3. Martin DeAgostino, "Senate OK's Voter ID Bill; Governor Likely to Sign Measure," *South Bend Tribune,* April 13, 2005, p. B1.

4. Public Law 109, 2005.

5. http://www.cnn.com/ELECTION/2004/pages/results/states/AZ/I/01/epolls.0.html.

6. Chandler Davidson, "The Historical Context of Voter Photo-ID Laws," *PS: Political Science and Politics,* 42:1, 2009, p. 93. Also, see Morgan Kousser, *The Shaping of Southern Politics: Suffrage Restriction and the Establishment of the One-Party South, 1880–1910* (New Haven: Yale University Press, 1974).

7. Ibid., 93.

8. *Indiana Democratic Party v. Todd Rokita.* 458 F. Supp. 2d 775; 2006 U.S. District.

9. Ibid.

10. Ibid.

11. Ibid.

12. Ibid.

13. Ibid.

14. Ibid.

15. Ibid.

16. Ibid.

17. Ibid.

18. Ibid.

19. Ibid.

20. Ibid.

21. Ibid.

22. Ibid.

23. Ibid.

24. Ibid.

25. Ibid.

26. Ibid.

27. Ibid.

28. Ibid.

29. Ibid.

30. *Crawford v. Marion County Election Board.* Nos. 06–2218, 06–2317.

31. Ibid.

32. Ibid.

33. *Burdick v. Takushi.* 504 U.S. 428, 433–34, 112 S.Ct. 2059, 119 L.Ed.2d 245 (1992).

34. *Crawford v. Marion County Election Board.* Nos. 06–2218, 06–2317.

35. Ibid.

36. Ibid.

37. Ibid.

38. Ibid.

39. Ibid.

40. Ibid.

41. *Harper v. Virginia Board of Elections,* 383 U.S. 663.

42. Ibid.

43. Ibid.

44. *Lubin v. Panish,* 415 U.S. 709 (1974).

45. Ibid.

46. *Anderson v. Celebrezze,* 460 US 780–1983.

47. *Burdick v. Takushi* (91–535), 504 U.S. 428 (1992).

48. *Crawford v. Marion County Election Board,* 553 U.S. 181 (2008).

49. Ibid.

50. Ibid.

51. Ibid.

52. Ibid.

53. Ibid.

54. Ibid.

55. Ibid.

56. Ibid.

57. Indiana Constitution Article 2, Section 2.

58. *League of Women Voters of Indiana v. Rokita.*

59. Ibid.

60. Ibid.

61. John Schwartz, "Judge in Landmark Case Disavows Support for Voter ID," *New York Times,* October 16, 2013, p. 16.

Chapter 4

Controversy in the Keystone State: A Pennsylvania Story

The 2008 Supreme Court case of *Crawford v. Marion County* paved the way for the continuation of voter identification laws across the country, as the Court rejected the claim that requiring voters to present photo identification did not rise to merits of an unconstitutional or unjust burden. With Indiana proving to be a legal and political model of success, at least for proponents of voter ID laws, Republican state officials in Pennsylvania sought to transplant and apply much of the same restrictions upon voters in their state in March of 2012. Following three days of debate, largely led by Democrats likening Pennsylvania's voter identification law with a new wave of Jim Crow, the Grand Old Party (GOP)-led state House of Representatives, passed the measure by a 104–88 vote, where it then advanced and passed the GOP-controlled Senate. As constructed in the Pennsylvania House of Representatives under House Bill 934, this law would require "proof of identification." The new law amended the Pennsylvania election code by adding numerous sections and subsections all pertaining to defining what does and does not qualify as acceptable forms of identification.

Each new section and subsection of the law went to great lengths to articulate acceptable documents and procedures for voting. Under Section 102, for instance, voters must show photo identification (either state or federally issued) that includes an expiration date that is either not expired or expired after the date of the most recent general election. Section 206 of the proposed law charged the secretary of the Commonwealth with "preparing and disseminating" information to the public regarding the new addendum under Section 102. Much like the Indiana law, Pennsylvania lawmakers in Section 206(b) directed the state Department of Transportation to, at no cost, provide any registered voter who has "made application therefor and has included with the completed application a signed affidavit stating that the elector is unable to obtain another form of photo identification . . . that the elector is unable to pay the required fee for the identification card and that elector is a registered elector."[1] Again, like Indiana, in order to qualify for the free identification card, voters must provide a social security card in addition to *one* of the following: certificate of U.S. citizenship, certificate of naturalization, birth certificate with raised seal *plus* two proofs of residency, such as lease agreement, current utility bills, mortgage documents, W-2 form, or tax records. In attempts to duck charges of disenfranchisement, the law also contained subsections pertaining to students, "other individuals," and those who are homeless. For college students, permitted documents include residence hall room assignment paperwork, one bill with their dorm room and address on it, along with bank statements, paystubs, and credit card bills. Those classified as "other individuals" are those without bills, leases, or mortgages in their name. Here, these individuals can bring the person they reside with along with that person's driver's license or photo identification along with one piece of official mail with their name and address. And finally, those who are homeless may use the address of a shelter as their residence, so long as they are accompanied by an employee from that shelter, who bears photo identification, and a letter on the shelter's letterhead indicating that the individual resides at the shelter in question.

In the case that a Pennsylvania-born registered voter does not have access to the certified copy of his or her birth certificate, the state will attempt, free of charge, to verify the voter's health records using state health records. Finally, like Indiana, Pennsylvania requires voters to provide proof of identification with an application for absentee ballots. With all these changes to state law, especially with no supporting evidence of voter fraud, nationwide attention consumed the state; however, this attention did not come amidst the initial debates over the law's purpose or goal. It was not until a leaked video of state Republican House Majority Leader Mike Turzai addressed a gathering of Pennsylvania Republicans, did the debate intensify. Discussing a list of party accomplishments, Turzai uttered the most memorable sound bite of the entire debate, "voter ID, which is going to allow Governor Romney to win the state of Pennsylvania: done." Needless to say, this caused much tension throughout the state and around the country, as the rationale given for the law's purpose, like Indiana, was to prevent (the currently nonexistent cases of) voter fraud, and not for political gain. Critics, largely Democrats, used Turzai's comment as evidence of the real motivation behind this and other laws like this to further advance their "I told you so" claims.

In order to better understand the multilayered fight over voter identification in Pennsylvania, we must first become familiar with a few facts.

First, with 67 counties in the state, granting the victorious presidential candidate with 20 electoral votes, how Pennsylvanians vote, matters. In 2008, then senator Barack Obama, running against Arizona Republican senator John McCain, carried the state by a 10 percent margin. However, in 2012, the landscape quickly changed. President Barack Obama, facing Governor Mitt Romney, only carried the state by a slim five percent margin, winning just over a dozen counties. This drastic shift exemplifies the state's "bell-wether" reputation, that is, how states like Missouri and Pennsylvania vote, so does the nation. Coupled with this tide change come shifting racial demographics as well. According to 2010 Census data, the state continues to undergo population growth, especially by those identified as "black or African American alone," and "persons of Hispanic or Latino origin." This data indicates a 12 percent gain in the state's African American population and just under an 83 percent gain in the state's Latino population. Needless to say, amidst controversies regarding immigration reform and claims that undocumented immigrants are committing in-person voter fraud in states like Florida, race too places a factor in this debate, whether stated by supporters or not.[2]

After signed into law by Pennsylvania Republican governor Tom Corbett on March 4, 2012, a lawsuit was filed on May 1, 2012, seeking a preliminary injunction, claiming the rights of many residents including the elderly, the poor, and people of color were disenfranchised by the law. Little did anyone know, however, that this case, *Applewhite v. the Commonwealth of Pennsylvania,* would develop into a series of interesting arguments and peculiar appeals, lasting over a year. To begin, we revisit the first trial held at the Commonwealth Court seeking a preliminary injunction against the state's voter identification law and the appeal it triggered. From there, we continue our analysis with the two final hearings and the eventual outcome it produced. Given the unique twists and turns throughout this series of litigation, especially given the precedence this case established, we place careful attention upon how state lawmakers argue the constitutional validity of the law and how they cast this law as *the* solution to their electoral troubles.

Applewhite v. the Commonwealth of Pennsylvania: Acts One and Two

Before the court was a request seeking preliminary injunctive relief against the enactment of the state's voter identification law. Enjoined by numerous "friends of the court," including the League of Women Voters and the National Association for the Advancement of Colored People (NAACP), the petitioners claimed their right to vote has been sustainably burdened in three respects. As court records recount, petitioners:

> Allege Act 18 unduly burdens the fundamental right to voter in violation of Article 1, Section 5 of the Pennsylvania Constitution, which states in part: "elections shall be free and equal." Second, petitioners avert Act 18 imposes burdens on the right to vote that do not bear upon all voters equally under similar circumstances in violation of the equal protection guarantees of Article 1, Sections 1 and 26 of the Pennsylvania Constitution. Third, they allege Act 18 imposes an additional qualification on the right to vote in violation of Article VII, Section 1 of the Pennsylvania Constitution.[3]

Here, petitioners steep their claims of unconstitutionality in the belief that the law creates unjust barriers and prevents equal access to the polls. Additionally, petitioners argue that despite the free photo identification offered by the state, it does not fully prevent disenfranchisement, should voters not possess all the needed documents. While it is true that the state can perform a free online scan of a registered voters health records to determine residency, the same cannot be said for those who were born outside the state, and thus those individuals would incur the cost of purchasing such documents in order to become compliant with the law. However, even with this clear and present disparity, presiding Judge Robert Simpson was not convinced that the specified burdens exist. In his words, "I am not convinced any qualified elector need be disenfranchised by Act 18 . . . I am not convinced any of the individual Petitioners or other witnesses will not have their votes counted in the general election."[4] More specifically, Judge Simpson noted, "petitioners did not establish that greater inquiry will occur from refusing to grant the injunction than from granting it," believing that the state has taken proper precautions to ensure equal access to the ballot.[5]

With several factors at play, Judge Simpson went to great, albeit deeply flawed, lengths to articulate his judicial rationale behind his ruling to uphold the law. Chief among his list was a quasi-procedural distinction, which he believed harmed the merit of the petitioners' suit. Believing this case was improperly introduced to the court, Simpson began deconstructing his ruling by means of distinguishing the difference between an "as applied" and "facial" challenge. Brought before the court as a facial challenge, the petitioners sought injunctive relief by means of arguing that Pennsylvania's voter identification law is *unconstitutional in all of its applications,* the very spirit of a facial challenge. More specifically, "a statute is facially unconstitutional only where no set of circumstances exist under which the statue would be valid," representing a very sweeping injunctive measure, resulting in the dismantling of an entire statute.[6] For the purposes of the case at hand, seeking a facial challenge is the first mistake Simpson outlines in his decision, as Simpson believes that an as-applied challenge would have been more fitting. An as-applied challenge, by contrast, has a more narrowly defined objective. An as-applied challenge "does not contend that a law is unconstitutional as written, but that its application to a particular person under particular circumstances deprived that person of a constitutional right."[7]

The legal distinction between a facial and as-applied challenge presents the question as to whether or not the law is wholly unconstitutional, or if parts of the law are both legal and salvageable. While many petitioners have argued that voter identification laws are unconstitutional in all of its applications, Judge Simpson believes otherwise. In his words, the "petitioners have not demonstrated that the proper remedy—even assuming an unjustified burden on some voters—would be to invalidate the entire statute."[8] Viewing the petitioners' challenge as an argument that only applies to a small population of the state, Judge Simpson notes, "the court must focus upon the impact of the law across the entire state, rather than specific individuals."[9] Judge Simpson minced no words when expressing his belief that an as-applied challenge was more suitable than the petitioner's facial challenge. To provide better specificity and transparency behind his ruling, Judge Simpson assessed many of the petitioners' claims, particularly those pertaining to the negative outcomes linked to the law's application. Referred to as "speculation about hypothetical or imaginary cases which have no place in a facial challenge," Judge Simpson dismisses a wide variety of the petitioners' claims. Of these claims, he dismisses:

(1) Possible inconsistencies as to which voters are indigent for purposes of counting provisional ballots for those who cannot obtain photo ID before or within six days after the general election
(2) Possible disruption at the polls caused by inadequate training of poll workers
(3) Possible failure of the vendor to implement the software changes before August 27, 2012, for the Department of State (DOS) photo IDs to be made available at PennDOT Drivers' License Centers
(4) Overworked DOS Help Desk workers causing delays for PennDOT-initiated inquiries regarding DOS photo IDs
(5) Possible failures of county election boards to have indigents' affirmations at polling locations on election day, thereby necessitating an additional trip to obtain the affirmation[10]

While many of the concerns raised above, along with others, are by no means unfounded, Judge Simpson takes solace in the belief that if any of these situations arise, they can be remedied individually. In short, Judge Simpson writes, "petitioners proved an as applied case, but they are seeking facial remedy. This legal disconnect is one of the reasons I determined that it is unlikely they will prevail on the merits."[11]

Next, Judge Simpson responds to the most controversial challenge against this and other voter identification laws, the accusation that these laws create an unnecessarily unjust and unwarranted burden upon the fundamental right to vote. Initially failing to address this accusation directly, Simpson instead spent considerable time advancing a "legislative authority" argument, one that asserts that state lawmakers have the right to regulate elections as they see fit. Relying upon Article VII, Section 1 ("qualifications of electors") of the state constitution, Simpson reminded the petitioners that, "every citizen . . . possessing the following qualifications, shall be entitled to vote at all elections subject, however, to such laws requiring and regulating the registration of electors as the General Assembly may enact."[12] Unfortunately, this line of reasoning begins a series of straw man and nonsequitur arguments, as the petitioners never questioned or filed suit specifically challenging lawmakers' ability to alter the law; instead, the challenge resides within the laws' discriminatory application and impact, hence the facial challenge before the court.

Continuing down this fallacious path, though, now in a far more bigoted fashion, Judge Simpson executed a sleight of hand maneuver that should have raised much concern, drawing from the decision reached in the notorious 1869 case of *Patterson v. Barlow*, a case that challenged the constitutionality of Pennsylvania's extraordinary procedures to establish voter eligibility. Specifically, the suit challenged the passage of a registry law that (1) only applied to residents of Philadelphia and (2) required said residents to undergo separate and additional hurdles to vote, causing grave inequities. In defense of upholding the law, the court contended that repealing the law "would be to place the vicious vagrant, the wandering Arabs, the Tartar hordes of our large cities, on a level with the virtuous and good man."[13] Said best by Jessie Allen, the Patterson decision, much like the Applewhite case, "shows that a majority of the Pennsylvania Supreme Court was once led to rationalize burdensome election procedures based on generalized and biased fears of fraudulent voting. That historic mistake should make the court hesitate to uphold another election law ostensibly aimed at preventing fraud when the state has offered no evidence that any such fraud has actually occurred."[14] Not disturbed by the context and outcome of this case, Simpson forged nonexisting parallels between the two cases at hand. Aside from further supporting his straw man argument over the legislature's right to regulate elections, Simpson turned to the Patterson decision to do what he initially chastised the petitioners for supposedly doing, engaging in "speculation about hypothetical or imaginary cases."

In his decision to cite the Patterson decision, Simpson exposes himself to well-founded criticism and controversy in how he forged nonexisting relationships and imaginary occurrences. For instance, Simpson quotes the Patterson decision, in part, noting, "the court stated the legislature possess a 'wide field' for the exercise of its discretion in the framing of facts to meet changed conditions and to provide new remedies for such abuses as may arise from time to time."[15] Yet, with no evidence of in-person voter fraud, what abuses is the court referencing? Why even reference a court decision whose foundation was supported by disenfranchisement? Again, with the petitioners in the Applewhite case seeking injunctive relief over the application and impact of Pennsylvania's voter identification law, the same relief sought and denied in the Patterson decision represents a dismal failure in strict scrutiny. While Simpson's rationale is bereft of the legal history surrounding the Patterson decision, it becomes increasingly difficult to read and believe that this case received unbiased treatment.

The further we dive into the case before us, the more we learn about and question the arguments and actions of the Pennsylvania court system. Simpson, in citing the 2000 case of *Mixon v. Commonwealth,* a case that challenged the exclusion of convicted felons from the state's definition of "qualified absentee electors" on the grounds of its disparate impact on African American Pennsylvanians, again, dodges the question directly. While the petitioners in this case argued that the state lacked a compelling reason to disenfranchise felons, citing the discriminatory impact of the application of the law, the court repeated an earlier move: upholding the legislatures authority to regulate elections. Explaining that the state legislature can pass laws as it pleases, so long as they are constitutional, the petitioners were simply informed that they were not "qualified electors" under state law. Noting specifically, "legislation may be enacted which regulates the exercise of the elective franchise, and does not amount to a denial of the franchise itself."[16] The bizarre nature of the state court's handling of legal challenges over disparate impact created by various statutes runs rampant throughout Simpson's upholding of Pennsylvania's voter identification law. For instance, when Simpson cited the 1868 case of *McCafferty v. Guyer,* a case challenging a law that expressively disenfranchised those registered as military dissenters, many questions quickly began to arise.

In many ways, the McCafferty case is very similar to the Applewhite case, in that both claim state law interferes with their fundamental right to vote. In previous cases of this nature, the court has favorably sided with the state legislature, asserting their right to regulate elections accordingly; however, the inclusion of the McCafferty decision is a game changer. In the court's decision to overturn the law, they note, "a right conferred by the Constitution is beyond the reach of legislative interference . . . it is in the nature of a constitutional grant of power or of privileges that it cannot be taken away by any authority known to the government."[17] Understanding that such language can be easily interpreted and applied in favor of the plaintiffs in the Applewhite case, Judge Simpson instead opines that, "unlike the statute at issue in McCafferty, which expressly disenfranchised certain otherwise qualified voters, however, Act 18 does not attempt to alter or amend the Pennsylvania Constitution's substantive voter qualifications, but rather is merely an election regulation to verify a voter's identity."[18] While Simpson agrees that "expressive" disenfranchisement is unconstitutional, so long as disenfranchisement is achieved through veiled means or language, like Act 18, then it is permissible. While it might not be legal for me to name/target my political adversaries by racial, ethnic, or socioeconomic group, I can, however, use common traits like lacking certain photo identification and land perfectly within the boundaries of the law. Shamefully, this appears to be the route Simpson took in this case.

Recalling the comments made by state Republican House Majority Leader Michael Turzai about securing a voter identification law to allow Governor Mitt Romney to carry Pennsylvania, Simpson quickly revisits this watershed moment. Noting that this political episode was the single contributing event that supported allegations of discriminatory partisan intent/motivation, Simpson disappointedly avers:

> Ultimately, however, I determined that this evidence did not invalidate the interests supporting Act 18 . . . I declined to infer that other members of the General Assembly shared the boastful views of Representative Turzai without proof that other members were present at the time the statement was made. Also, the statements were made away from the chamber floor.[19]

The statement in question, recorded at a gathering of Pennsylvania Republicans, according to Simpson, does not indicate anything less than a compelling state interest. As seen through Simpson's eyes, "the Commonwealth's asserted interest in protecting public confidence in elections is a relevant and legitimate state interest sufficiently weighty to justify the burden." Never mind the unsubstantiated claims made by the state over the existence of in-person voter fraud. Never mind Michael Turzai's fairly targeted message, and let us too disregard that it remains irrelevant if other members of the General Assembly were present during that gathering or not. Ironically, court documents indicate no attempt was made to discover if other legislators were present, ultimately invalidating Judge Simpson's "concern."

Finally, before he denied injunctive relief, Judge Simpson discussed his belief that greater injury would be caused not by the law itself, but by granting an injunction *against* the law. According to Simpson, granting an injunction at this point would interfere with the:

> August mailing by DOS of informational packets to all poll workers across the Commonwealth; with the August educational conference hosted by DOS for all judges of elections; with the August software installation for the new DOS IDs; with other steps to make the DOS IDs available through designated PennDOT sites beginning in late August; with the extensive television advertising/web/automated phone calls/mobile billboard campaign to begin after Labor Day; and with the DOS mailing to approximately 5.9 million households, representing every household in the Commonwealth . . . I questioned Jonathan Marks, the Commissioner of the Bureau of Commissions, Elections and Legislation with DOS, about the effect of a preliminary injunction and the appeal process on the ability of DOS to implement Act 18. While his response in the transcript was equivocal, everyone in the courtroom could see his reaction: alarm, concern, and anxiety, at the prospect of an injunction. His demeanor tells the story.[20]

In what amounts to quite a bizarre rationale, largely absent of any judicial scrutiny pertaining to the charges brought against the Commonwealth, Judge Simpson instead places greater concern in both process and procedure. While rejecting on all grounds the petitioners' arguments over the immediate creation of voter disenfranchisement at the hands of Act 18, stating, "they [the petitioners] have failed to persuade me," Judge Simpson's ruling, by no means, is impartial. For example, while not persuaded by the petitioners' arguments/evidence and overall concerns over disenfranchisement, Judge Simpson ironically found judicial solace in the "alarm, concern, and anxiety" exhibited by Jonathan Marks, the commissioner of the Bureau of Commissions, Elections' and Legislation. Absent of fact, we note the lack of emotional appeal Judge Simpson cites as a chief factor in siding with Marks's testimony and thus denied a preliminary injunction.

Pursuant upon many false assumptions, straw man arguments, forged legal relationships, and questionable intent, do we arrive at this decision. Not convinced their case was free of politically motivated bias from the bench, the petitioners sought an immediate appeal. Upon the single-judge order to deny preliminary injunctive relief, the state supreme court decided to hear the case. Before the court were serious questions pertaining to (1) whether or not the state's voter identification law violated the "free and equal" access clause of the state constitution; and (2) whether or not the law curbs "liberal access" to the identification cards needed to vote. These questions before the court stemmed directly from many of the concerns the petitioners initially made over implementation.

With the initial assurances and allowances from state lawmakers that those without the newly required identification cards can receive them for "free," lawmakers asserted this argument against claims of disenfranchisement. However, upon closer inspection, implementation of the law did not proceed as promised by lawmakers, causing much concern for dissenters of the law. For example, as court documents show, "the Department of State has realized, and the Commonwealth parties have candidly conceded, that the law is not being implemented according to its term," further adding, "the reason why PennDOT will not implement the law as written is that the Section 1510(b) driver's license equivalent is a secure form of identification, which may be used for example, to board commercial aircraft."[21] From this testimony, it appears that the initial implementation concerns raised by the petitioners were well founded, even if the judge dismissed them as hypothetical and imaginary. However, more disturbing is testimony from a deputy secretary for PennDOT on the topics of free and equal access to the ballot and liberal access to identification cards, stating, "at the end of the day there will be people who will not be able to qualify for a driver's license or a PennDOT ID card," impairing otherwise qualified and eligible electors from voting.[22]

While the lower court believed that if any imperfections resulting from implementation would arise, they could easily be remedied on a case by case basis, the state supreme court uncovered evidence contrary to this flimsy assumption. Given the state's difficulty with issuing nonsecure identification cards, "preparations for the issuances of Department of State identification cards were still underway as of the time of the evidentiary hearing in the Commonwealth Court in this case, and the cards were not slated to be made available until approximately two months before the November election," barring no delays.[23] Moreover, those applying for this nonsecure card may still undergo the same application process for a secure card, calling into question the law's liberal access requirement. Pursuant upon this evidence, the petitioners assert that the only way to disrupt such gross discrepancies is by means of enjoining the law's implementation. More specifically, petitioners continue to advance the argument that a number of voters will be disenfranchised by this law, noting:

> Given their personal circumstances and the limitations associated with the infrastructure through which the Commonwealth is issuing identification cards—these voters will not have had an adequate opportunity to become educated about the Law's requirements and obtain the necessary identification cards.[24]

In addition to the great haste in which state lawmakers sought implementation, despite candid testimony over the law's incongruences, the court found more than enough reason to be alarmed. For instance, the court agreed that while the number of individuals who would be affected by this law is still debatable, "there is little disagreement with the Appellants' observation that the population involved includes members of some of the most vulnerable segments of our society." Not swayed by the predictive judgment made by the lower court, the state supreme court continued to chisel away at the previous ruling.

Here, the greatest challenge before the court exists within the parameters of a bait and switch, meaning, while the law states one thing, implementation has introduced another. Upon the court's review of this argument, "we find that the disconnect between what the law prescribes and how it is being implemented has created a number of conceptual difficulties in addressing the legal issues raised."[25] Acknowledging the rather ambitious efforts undertaken by state lawmakers with respect to this law, the court refers to this entire rollout as "an implementation process which has by no means been seamless in light of the serious operational constraints faced by the executive branch," later adding, "given this state of affairs, we are not satisfied with a mere predictive judgment based primarily on the assurances of government officials."[26] Not falling for simple assurances by state officials, the court takes a direct jab at the lower court's rationale, even revisiting Judge Simpson's controversial claims over the use of a facial rather than an as-applied challenge. As seen through the court's eyes, "we agree with Appellants' essential position that if a statute violates constitutional norms in the short term, a facial challenge may be sustainable even though the statute might validly be enforced at some time in the future," quite contrary to the lower court's invalidation of their challenge.[27]

Not convinced by much of the lower court's decision, the state supreme court minced no words arguing they were still not convinced there will be no voter disenfranchisement arising from the implementation of the law. Accordingly, the court sent specific instructions back to the lower court, urging them to (1) make a present assessment of the actual availability of the alternate identification cards and (2) consider whether procedures being used for deployment of the cards comport with the requirement of liberal access.[28] And in this manner, the state supreme court vacated the previous lower court decision and returned the matter back to the lower court for further proceedings, predicated upon the instructions provided and evidenced uncovered.

Act Three: Back to the Lower Court We Go

With marching orders in hand, Judge Simpson presided over another hearing along with several phone conferences in order to obtain updates and to gather additional evidence. First on the list was assessing liberal access insofar as determining whether the changes to the law violate this requirement. With testimony obtained from both the Deputy Secretary for Transportation and Deputy Secretary for the Commonwealth, the court was again assured that changes in implementation would eliminate previous tensions. Chiefly, the elimination of requiring two proofs of residency along with the once previous necessity for a second trip to a drivers' licensing center were championed as two pivotal improvements to ease access. While state officials believed these new and improved procedures would curb criticism and allegations of disenfranchisement, Judge Simpson, under great pressure from the state supreme court, was not as easily swayed this time.

Immediately noticing that the testimony and policy evidence presented by state officials were similar in scope to what the state supreme court previously chastised, Simpson was forced to go further in his analysis and not solely rely upon "assurances of government officials." While acknowledging that these structural changes will likely place the state in a "better position moving forward," Simpson offered a more thorough and thoughtful read of the situation, explaining:

> The proposed changes are to occur about five weeks before the general election, and I question whether sufficient time now remains to attain the goal

of liberal access. Third, the proposed changes are accompanied by candid admissions by government officials that any new deployment will reveal unforeseen problems, which impede implementation. These admissions were corroborated by anecdotal evidence offered by Petitioners regarding the initial rollout of the DOS ID's in August. For these reasons, I cannot conclude the proposed changes cure the deficiency in liberal access identified by the Supreme Court.[29]

In what amounts to quite an about-face from his previous judgment, Simpson applies a stricter level of scrutiny when assessing the ever-changing details of the state's voter identification law. Poised to proceed with great haste, state officials were otherwise convinced that, despite the possibility of other unforeseen tensions that could arise and with only five weeks to educate the public before Election Day, the rollout would not violate liberal access. At moments like this, one begins to seriously question the motives of state officials, noting that they have failed to produce any evidence of in-person voter fraud, have failed to specifically name any particular threat facing the ballot box, and have otherwise failed to sustain the burden of proof that such change is actually needed. Never mind, of course, the fairly politically charged comments made by state Republican House Majority Leader Michael Turzai about securing a voter identification law to allow Governor Mitt Romney to win Pennsylvania. Instead, we are left with numerous empty assurances, straw man and nonsequitur arguments, ultimately leading us to the legal challenges before us now.

Upon dismissing the state's claims over improved access to the ballot, Judge Simpson quickly turned to his final task, reassessing the evidence pertaining to the issuance of a preliminary injunction. Understanding that the lengthy legal precedence involving preliminary injunctions require courts to narrowly tailor a remedy that abates the harm, Judge Simpson was charged with the task of identifying and removing the harm. First, Judge Simpson rejected the request from petitioners to enjoin all outreach and educational programs, not convinced that even with the constant changes in the law that this would lead to confusion among the voting public. Next, Simpson rejected the "underlying assertion that the offending activity is the request to produce photo ID," not convinced this was the specific harm. Instead, Simpson directed his attention to what he believed was the "salient offending conduct," voter disenfranchisement.[30] As of now, two observations should be noted. First, when Simpson was initially presented with allegations over disenfranchisement in the initial challenge, he asserted and upheld legislative privilege, meaning that lawmakers enjoy the right to regulate elections as they see fit. However, in the appeal before us now, Simpson was faced with either rejecting his previous judicial rationale or endorsing the possibility of abuse of legislative discretion. Next, if Simpson decided to execute an about-face, how would he now attempt to grapple with his past decision by means of identifying the "salient offending conduct?"

Now ready to revisit his past decision, Simpson calls attention to what he believes was the most egregious/disenfranchising factor, provisional ballots. Upon "careful review" of the state election code, Simpson points to both preexisting and amended language regarding how/why provisional ballots are not counted. To rid the law of its discriminatory impact, Simpson believes that the problem stems from how provisional ballots are counted, otherwise ignoring the photo identification aspect that is central to the law. Nonetheless, Simpson points to two sections of the law he feels must be stricken, as they state that a provisional ballot shall not be counted if:

> In the case of a provisional ballot that was cast under subsection (a.2)(1)(i), within six calendar days following the election, the elector fails to appear before the county board of elections to execute an affirmation or the county board of elections does not receive an electronic facsimile or paper copy of an affirmation affirming, under penalty of perjury, that the elector is the same individual who personally appeared before the district election board on the day of the election and cast a provisional ballot and that the elector is indigent and unable to obtain proof of identification without the payment of a fee; or
>
> In the case of a provisional ballot that was cast under subsection (a.2)(1)(ii), within six calendar days following the election, the elector fails to appear before the county board of elections to present proof of identification and execute an affirmation or the county board of election does not receive an electronic, facsimile or paper copy of the proof of identification and an affirmation affirming, under penalty of perjury, that the elector is the same individual who personally appeared before the district election board on the day of the election and cast a provisional ballot.[31]

Initially introduced before the court as evidence of disenfranchisement, Judge Simpson finally comes around to realize the disparate impact this portion of the law places upon various demographics, most notably, those financially compromised and those with mobility restrictions. Interestingly enough, Judge Simpson rejected petitioners' request to enjoin the law's requirement that election officials request that in-person voters present photo identification, citing that the "General Assembly's express intent that during the transition period a request for photo ID be made even though the vote will be counted regardless of compliance with the request."[32] Aside from the obvious questions pertaining to locating the purpose of asking electors for such identification if it is not required, one is also left to question Simpson's predictive judgment that such incongruence in the law will not lead to possible disenfranchisement.

Failing to reach the opinion that requesting or otherwise requiring photo identification when no exigency exists to support its presence, Simpson rejects the argument that the offending activity in need of remedy resides in the overall spirit of the law. Nonetheless, Judge Simpson executes a noticeable shift in attitude by ordering a narrowly tailored preliminary injunction limited to the 2012 general election. While a representation of progress from Simpson's initial decision, the petitioners were still not convinced that voter disenfranchisement had been completely ridded, as the ruling still upheld the laws most controversial aspect, photo identification. This final vestige of discrimination would undergo one more round of judicial scrutiny, as petitioners sought full relief of the law.

Liberal Access and Equal Protection: Our Final Act

In our final act, petitioners bring three points of challenge against all aspects of the law, specifically targeting accessibility and implementation in attempts to dismantle the law entirely. Count one of the petitioners' amended petition cites two failures pertaining to liberal access. First, as initially challenged, petitioners allege that the law fails to comport with liberal access by means of its various layers of demands for electors to receive photo identification, and second, petitioners argue that the Pennsylvania DOS does not possess the authority to issue photo identification, hence challenging its reliability and validity. Because the court has already ruled that the law does not comport with liberal access, especially for: (1) those born out of state, (2) those who never possessed a state driver's license or other state photo identification, and (3) those with financial and mobility challenges, the court turned its attention to the second allegation instead.

This allegation over the Pennsylvania DOS's authority to issue photo identification charges that state law possesses no language directing DOS to issue "free" photo identification. Instead, as the court identified, DOS has other specific duties; however, none of them involves issuing photo identification. Further articulating this incongruence, the court reminds the state legislature that the DOS can only: (1) create and collect the photo identification application form; (2) develop and change the criteria for issuing the

DOS ID; (3) dictate criteria to PennDOT; (4) decide to whom DOS IDs are issued; and (5) advertise the DOS ID. Through the court's eyes, there are several variables conspicuously missing that warrant a legislative/legal challenge to the agency's authority. By contrast, "DOS is *not* authorized to create the identification to be issued at no cost to any registered elector . . . This Court agrees with Petitioners that DOS lacks the requisite authority to issue the DOS ID to fulfill Penn DOT's duties under the Voter ID law," acknowledged the court.[33] More directly, writes the court:

> That DOS began issuing the DOS ID, in coordination with PennDOT, does not legitimize. Use of the issuance powers conferred in Section 2(b) of the Voter ID Law does not empower DOS beyond its legislative parameters, which are confined to education. By disregarding its statutory delegation, DOS over-stepped legislative constraints. As an unauthorized substitute for the Penn-DOT Voting ID, the DOS ID and accompanying process is *ultra vires* and invalid.[34]

By means of invalidating the process and dismantling the legislative mechanism and authority to continue issuing photo identification, the court sought to clarify and settle the issue once and for all. Because the issuance of photo identification cards runs concurrent with other issues, like disenfranchised voters and the impact therein, instead of issuing their decree and moving onward toward the remaining allegations, the court provided additional analysis responding directly to claims made by lawmakers.

At the very beginning of this legal saga, petitioners charged that a significant number of otherwise qualified voters would be disenfranchised should this law be implemented. Prepared for this claim, as it is a fairly concurrent argument from dissenters of voter identification laws, the state promised "free" photo identification for those lacking it and heavily downplayed the number of residents negatively impacted by the law. With no consensus over specifically how many individuals lacked such identification, the state supreme court found various strains of discrimination in the law's implementation and ordered the lower court to remove the law to prevent discrimination. While the lower court found discriminatory impact regarding the casting of provisional ballots, the court upheld all aspects of the law's photo identification provisions. However, in order for such a provision to withstand challenge, the state must satisfy the burden of proof that voter disenfranchisement was a major side effect of the law. Upon further review, using figures from both 2012 and 2013, the court revealed:

> Specifically, DOS's 2012 Database Match showed approximately 759,000 registered electors did not have PennDOT Secure ID (representing 9% of all

registered electors), *plus* another almost 575,000 whose ID would be invalid (based on expiration date) on Election Day in 2012. The total from the 2012 Database Match exceeds 1.3 million lacking a PennDOT Secure ID . . . The evidence establishes that this need is largely unmet, and that alternate IDs are incapable of filling it. In contrast to the hundreds of thousands who lack compliant photo ID, only 17,000 photo IDs for voting purposes have been issued.[35]

With such damning evidence, and with no rebuttal to the large number of residents lacking identification, the court grew very weary of the state's hurried efforts toward implementation. Mincing no words, the court declares that "the DOS ID does not remedy or excuse PennDOT's refusal to follow statutory mandates, and fails to satisfy liberal access. For all the foregoing reasons, Petitioners' requested relief is granted as to Count I."[36]

Next, the court had to consider the second charge before them, whether or not the state's voter identification law violates the right to vote as established by the state constitution. Under state law, petitioners must be able to clearly articulate how a law "clearly, palpably, and plainly violates the Constitution," if the requested relief is to be granted.[37] Taking into consideration both the text of the law and context of the case, the court accepted the facial challenge brought in front of them, as the case involved more than "mere speculation." Recognizing the right to vote as "fundamental," the court weighed in heavily on this charge, specifically analyzing how burdensome obtaining photo identification under the law is. In their scathing critique, the court opines that:

The Voter ID Law does not provide a non-burdensome means of obtaining compliant photo ID . . . Like a house of cards, everything rises and falls upon the legitimacy of the DOS ID. As analyzed above, the DOS ID is an unauthorized agency creation, and is difficult to obtain. Thus, the Voter ID Law does not contain photo ID to qualified electors. Accordingly, the Voter ID Law is facially unconstitutional.[38]

Further adding, "in the majority of its applications, the Voter ID Law renders Pennsylvania's fundamental right to vote so difficult to exercise as to cause de facto disenfranchisement."[39] While state lawmakers cited what they believed were three compelling state interests (integrity, reliability, and public confidence in the electoral process), such vague and otherwise unsubstantiated claims did not sit well with the court. In response to the widespread allegation of rampant in-person voter fraud, the court simply noted, "in the full trail on the merits, Respondents again wholly failed to show any evidence of in-person voter fraud," leading the court to further question the need for photo identification.[40]

As seen through the court's eyes, simply listing Pennsylvania's so-called compelling state interest in implementing a voter identification law, without evidence, is baseless and fails to shoulder any burden of proof. On the contrary, the court opines, "Respondents' witnesses testified as to their confidence in the integrity of the elections held to date, in which the photo ID requirement was not enforced. Thus, Respondents did not establish the compelling nature of government interest."[41] To no surprise, we continue to see evidence that bespeaks testimony and vice versa, causing considerable harm to the state's defense. With no evidence of in-person voter fraud or waning voter confidence in the electoral process, this made the court's job of accessing the state's narrowly tailored remedy of producing photo identification a lot easier. Said best by the court:

> Respondents also failed to establish a nexus between photo identification—showing voters are who they say they are, and the integrity of elections—when prior elections accepted a number of types of proof to verify identity. The burdens the Voter ID Law entails are unnecessary and not narrowly tailored to serve a compelling state interest.[42]

Again, upon questioning the compelling state interest with implementing this law, we continue to find mere speculation, absent of fact or evidence. While denying allegations of political motivation as the catalyst behind the law's creation, it is quite difficult to believe otherwise when no evidence exists to support the state's counterclaim over voter integrity. With no problem identified, it then becomes increasingly difficult for state lawmakers to argue that their "solution," a voter identification law, is narrowly tailored to remedy a nonexistent harm. In this light, more questions begin to surface from the court.

Dumbfounded by the severe degree of burden placed upon electors, along with the existence of a "solution" that solves no identified problem, the court then inquired as to why some forms of photo identification were deemed permissible while others were restricted. Again, while the previous lower court did not believe that electors faced unreasonable burdens to vote by means of producing some forms of photo identification over others, this now became weighed by the court to determine the existence of unreasonable voting restrictions. For instance, the law excluded items like employee IDs for school districts, welfare cards, bus passes containing a picture, gun permits, student identification cards, retired military and veteran's identification cards along with out-of-state driver's license. While driver's licenses issued from other states are valid to drive in Pennsylvania, they are otherwise invalid to vote. In regards to college students and university-issued photo identification cards, the state deems such identification invalid because it contains no expiration date. To remedy this, DOS simply urged colleges and universities to incorporate this change on student identification cards, without providing any funds or administrative assistance. The court notes that institutions like Pennsylvania State University only issue expiration stickers to new students, not the entire student body, creating a tremendous disparity and otherwise questionable exercise of legislative authority.

Because college students are not the only class of people who oftentimes possess photo identification absent of expiration dates, the court then turned to residents of health care facilities. According to court documents, "respondents' witnesses admit they have not tracked the number of care facilities that issue photo ID. In fact, Respondents admitted the majority of care facilities do not issue photo IDs," again, further questioning the so-called "problem" this "solution" addresses.[43] Said decisively by the court:

> To the extent the Voter ID Law requires photo ID to identify in-person voters at the polls, there is no reasonable basis for the ID to contain an expiration date. The photo on an expired ID would allow a poll worker to verify identification and ensure voters are who they are, so the expiration date seems obviously unnecessarily restrictive. The Voter ID Law as written suggests a legislative disconnect from reality.[44]

With no rationale as to how or why expiration dates assist or are fundamentally necessary to vote, the court had no other option but to deem this restriction as "unreasonable and unconnected to any legitimate state purpose." Because the law disenfranchises so many and fails to provide a safety net to ensure enfranchisement, the court enjoined enforcement of the photo identification provision, declaring this provision unconstitutional. Accordingly, the court sided with the petitioners' request for relief pertaining to Count II, leaving one final challenge to be considered by the court.

In the third and final count before the court, petitioners claimed that the state voter identification law violates the right to equal protection to all. Spending very little time on this allegation, the court maintained that "this Court agrees the statute allows for differences among classes of voters based upon difficulty in obtaining compliant ID and likelihood of possessing compliant ID, this does not in itself constitute disparate treatment," as the petitioners needed to establish that the law was enacted in part due to its adverse effects on certain groups.[45] Presented with no purposeful evidence of discrimination, the court denied the petitioners' relief.

In the court's final verdict, the court asserted that voting laws are to ensure that elections are both free and fair, noting that the voter identification does not attend to this goal. Citing previously mentioned evidence about the number of individuals who would be disenfranchised and the great injury that would overall result from this law, the court declared the photo identification provision and related implementation invalid, thus dismantling the spirit of the law.

Conclusion

This four-part saga that to date has dismantled Pennsylvania's voter identification law may not indicate total finality. Upon receiving the court's ruling, Pennsylvania Republican governor Tom Corbett released a statement indicating that while the state will not pursue an appeal, they have not ruled out other avenues. In his statement, Governor Corbett understood the ruling to mean that, "it is clear that the requirement of photo identification is constitutionally permissible. However, the court also made clear that in order for a voter identification law to be found constitutional, changes must be made to address accessibility to photo identification."[46] Seemingly learning nothing from the ruling, Corbett concluded with the argument that "a photo identification requirement is a sensible and reasonable measure for the Commonwealth to reassure the public that everyone who votes is registered and eligible to cast a ballot."[47] While many dissenters of the law, like state Democratic House Minority Leader Frank Dermody, believe that "the governor finally opened his eyes and saw the light," we are not entirely convinced this is a settled matter.[48]

Through the governor's eyes, the sole issue thwarting the law's constitutionality is liberal access. While the court agreed that the hurdles electors must overcome in order to receive permissible forms of photo identification subjected them to significant undue burdens, there still exist varying schools of thought surrounding its purpose and goals. For instance, while the governor insists that the law's purpose is to reassure the public that "everyone who votes is registered and eligible to cast a ballot," this fraudulent rationale, as the court clearly explained, is simply without merit. If re-pursued under the same rationale, this might indicate to the court that such an effort to reinstate the law might be tainted with abuse of legislative authority by means of partisan interest. With no exigency found by the court, along with many cited failures by the state to distribute identification, educate the public, and to execute the law as written, such hasty action still has many dissenters asking, "why?" Why present a "solution" to a "problem" that does not exist? Why adopt a rhetorical platform that disseminates the claim that in-person voter fraud exists, while failing to produce such evidence in court? And finally, why pursue such a law now?

Questions like these along with others continue to baffle many dissenters of the law, not only in Pennsylvania, but across the country. In what follows in our next chapter, we turn our attention to the fight over voter identification laws in a state notorious for executing maneuvers of intentional racial discrimination at the ballot box. Next, we visit the Lone Star state of Texas.

Notes

1. Pennsylvania House Bill 934 (2011).
2. Hans Von Spakovsky, "The Threat of Non-Citizen Voting," *The Heritage Foundation*, http://www.heritage.org/research/reports/2008/07/the-threat-of-non-citizen-voting (accessed July 18, 2014).
3. *Applewhite v. Commonwealth of Pennsylvania*, 330 M.D. 2012.
4. Ibid.
5. Ibid.
6. Ibid.
7. *United States v. Marcavage*, 609 F.3d 264, 273 (3d Cir. 2010).
8. *Applewhite v. Commonwealth of Pennsylvania*, 330 M.D. 2012.
9. Ibid.
10. Ibid.
11. Ibid.
12. Ibid.
13. *Patterson v. Barlow*, 60 Pa. 54, 1869.
14. Jessie Allen, "Look at the History of Voter ID: A Case Cited to Support Pennsylvania's New Voter ID Law Instead Calls It into Question," *Pittsburg Post-Gazette*, September 11, 2012, www.post-gazette.com/Op-Ed/2012/09/11/Look-at-the-history-of-voter-ID-A-case-cited-to-support-Pennsylvania-s-new-voter-ID-law-instead-calls-it-into-question/stories/201209110190#ixzz26AVgDxOl (accessed August 2, 2014).
15. *Applewhite v. Commonwealth of Pennsylvania*, 330 M.D. 2012.
16. *Winston v. Moore*, 244 Pa. 447, 454, 1914.
17. *McCafferty v. Guyer*, 59 Pa. 109, 1868.
18. *Applewhite v. Commonwealth of Pennsylvania*, 330 M.D. 2012.
19. Ibid.

20. Ibid.

21. *Applewhite v. Commonwealth of Pennsylvania,* 71 MAP, 2012.

22. Ibid.

23. Ibid.

24. Ibid.

25. Ibid.

26. Ibid.

27. Ibid.

28. Ibid.

29. Ibid.

30. Ibid.

31. Election Code, 25 P.S. §3050(a.2).

32. *Applewhite v. Commonwealth of Pennsylvania,* 71 MAP, 2012.

33. Ibid.

34. Ibid.

35. Ibid.

36. Ibid.

37. See: *Pennsylvanians Against Gambling Expansion Fund, Inc. v. Com.,* 583 Pa. 275, 2005.

38. *Applewhite v. Commonwealth of Pennsylvania,* 71 MAP, 2012.

39. Ibid.

40. Ibid.

41. Ibid.

42. Ibid.

43. Ibid.

44. Ibid.

45. Ibid.

46. "Governor Corbett Issues Statement on Recent Commonwealth Court Ruling on Voter ID," May 8, 2014, http://www.pa.gov/Pages/NewsDetails.aspx?agency= Governors%20Office&item=15598#.U8f8YZRdXng (accessed July 17, 2014).

47. Ibid.

48. Kate Giammarise, "Corbett Won't Contest Voter ID Ruling; But He Hints at Push for New Legislation," *Pittsburgh Post-Gazette,* May 9, 2014, A1.

Chapter 5

In Defense of Voter ID: *Texas v. Holder* and *Shelby v. Holder*

Recent trends in voter identification laws, led largely by partisan fervor from state Republican lawmakers, continue to cause much confusion and constitutional controversy. Across the country, proponents of voter identification continue to repeat the phrase "voter fraud" in hopes to convince both the people and the courts that their efforts to "secure" the ballot box is a compelling state interest. In states like Texas and elsewhere throughout the South, not everyone is convinced that voter fraud actually exists, let alone as a widespread problem. Nonetheless, as the chief claim in defense of voter identification laws continues to circulate the airwaves and dominate the campaign trails, this championing has captured the attention of many media outlets and policy centers that began their own investigation into this so-called problem.

As more interest began to shift toward possible alterations to voting procedures, impacting who can and cannot vote, investigative research began to paint a contrasting picture of what the laws' proponents have argued. In Texas, the *Dallas Morning News,* upon receiving data from the state's attorney general's office spanning 2004–2012, reported that former attorney general and GOP Governor Greg Abbott, "who's making his defense of the state's voter ID law a centerpiece of his campaign for governor, has pursued 66 people on charges of voting irregularities since 2004. Only four cases involved someone illegally casting a ballot at a polling place where a picture ID would have prevented it."[1] Of these 66 cases, it is imperative to note that 11 of them were dismissed or the defendants were acquitted. Additionally, "in most cases, voter-fraud violations in Texas have involved mail-in ballots. A few involved felons who aren't allowed to vote. Some involved an election official engaged in illegal behavior. But none of those would have been stopped by the photo ID requirement."[2] Despite claims by proponents that voter identification laws do not target any particular group, the *Dallas Morning News*' report uncovered that, "although most of Abbott's prosecutions were against blacks or Hispanics, he rejects Democratic claims that the photo ID requirement targets minority voters."[3]

Ironically enough, much of the landmark cases pertaining to voter rights grew out of policy disputes in Texas. In order to better understand the current controversies at hand, it is only fitting to begin this chapter by revisiting the past. Known best as the "Texas primary cases," we begin by briefly revisiting *Nixon v. Herndon* (1927), *Nixon v. Condon* (1932), *Grovey v. Townsend* (1935), and *Smith v. Allwright* (1944). With the legal precedence analyzed, we then move toward the 2012 case of *Texas v. Holder* followed by the 2013 Supreme Court case, *Shelby County v. Holder*.

What's Old Is New Again

Beginning their legacy of targeted disenfranchisement in 1902, the Texas legislature passed a law requiring a poll tax aimed at curbing African American and Mexican participation. After years of declining voter participation due to the law's impact, Texas lawmakers sought out political maneuvers aimed at insulating one-party control. In 1923, under the inconspicuous name of Article 3093a, this law held that, "in no event shall a negro be eligible to participate in a Democratic Party primary election held in the State of Texas."[4] In an attempt to ensure a Southern white male power base, this statute's intent was to create a sustainable source of untethered access to powerbrokers who only answer to and represent a fraction of the otherwise eligible constituency. Then came Dr. L.A. Nixon, an African American physician from El Paso, Texas, who challenged the law's constitutionality, as he was denied from voting by magistrates who cited Article 3093a as their defense.

In what would later become the 1927 landmark case of *Nixon v. Herndon*, Dr. Nixon sought an injunction against the Texas law, citing the safeguards guaranteed under both the Fourteenth and Fifteenth Amendments of the Constitution. Because Nixon initially sought injunctive relief in a federal district court who dismissed the case, he later appealed to the Supreme Court, who agreed to hear it. Under the auspices of Chief Justice William Taft, it was Justice Oliver Wendell Holmes who wrote the unanimous majority opinion. In what amounts to a very brief, yet historic decision, Justice Holmes did not take long to invalidate the law. While Dr. Nixon cited the Fourteenth and Fifteenth Amendments as contrary to the spirit of the law, Justice Holmes found it unnecessary to consider the Fifteenth, arguing instead:

> It seems to us hard to imagine a more direct and obvious infringement of the Fourteenth. That Amendment, while it applies to all, was passed, as we know, with a special intent to protect the blacks from discrimination against them. That Amendment "not only gave citizenship and the privileges of citizenship to persons of color, but it denied to any State the power to withhold from them the equal protection of the laws . . . What is this but declaring that the law in the States shall be the same for the black as for the white; that all persons, whether colored or white, shall stand equal before the laws of the States, and, in regard to the colored race, for whose protection the amendment was primarily designed, that no discrimination shall be made against them by law because of their color?" The statute of Texas in the teeth of the prohibitions referred to assumes to forbid negroes to take part in a primary election the importance of which we have indicated, discriminating against them by the distinction of color alone. States may do a good deal of classifying that it is difficult to believe rational, but there are limits, and it is too clear for extended argument that color cannot be made the basis of a statutory classification affecting the right set up in this case.[5]

In just one move, Justice Holmes vacated the standing of the Texas law, siding with the plaintiff. The blatant violation to the Equal Protection clause of the Fourteenth Amendment that Holmes cites, however, would not be a loud enough message for Texas lawmakers, as Dr. Nixon's victory was very short lived.

Determined to treat access to the ballot like a country club membership, Texas lawmakers quickly enacted a new provision that allowed political parties to determine who can and cannot vote in their primaries. Creating what was commonly referred to as an "all-White primary," the executive committee of the Texas Democratic Party adopted a resolution to counter the unfavorable decision reached in *Nixon v. Herndon*. As the resolution read,

> All white democrats who are qualified under the Constitution and laws of Texas and who subscribe to the statutory pledge provided in Article 3110, Revised Civil Statutes of Texas, and none other, be allowed to participate in the primary elections to be held July 28, 1928, and August 25, 1928.

Again denied the right to vote as a result of this resolution, Dr. L.A. Nixon sought injunctive relief against Texas's new provision, resulting in the 1932

Supreme Court case of *Nixon v. Condon*. In defense of this new provision, state officials of the Texas Democratic Party insisted that Nixon's challenge was without merit, because the state Democratic Party argued it was "merely a voluntary association" that has the power to pick and choose its membership qualifications. With this rationale, party officials argued that the equal protection clause was null, likening their membership process to most "voluntary organizations," understanding that not everyone can join. This claim to exclusivity raised many questions, namely, if equal protection applied to so-called voluntary organizations not associated with the state.

Before the court, there were questions over constitutional exclusion in the face of voluntary organizations. Said best, the court had to determine, "whether in given circumstances parties or their committees are agencies of government within the Fourteenth or the Fifteenth Amendment," later noting, "the test is whether they are to be classified as representatives of the State to such an extent and in such a sense that the great restraints of the Constitution set limits to their actions."[6] Decided by a narrow 5–4 margin in Nixon's favor, it was Justice Benjamin Cardozo who offered the court's majority opinion. In his words:

> The very fact that such legislation was thought necessary is a token that the committees were without inherent power . . . The pith of the matter is simply this, that, when those agencies are invested with an authority independent of the will of the association in whose name they undertake to speak, they become to that extent the organs of the State itself, the repositories of official power. They are then the governmental instruments whereby parties are organized and regulated to the end that government itself may be established or continued. What they do in that relation, they must do in submission to the mandates of equality and liberty that bind officials everywhere . . . With the problem thus laid bare and its essentials exposed to view, the case is seen to be ruled by *Nixon v. Herndon*, supra. Delegates of the State's power have discharged their official functions in such a way as to discriminate invidiously between white citizens and black. The Fourteenth Amendment, adopted as it was with special solicitude for the equal protection of members of the Negro race, lays a duty upon the court to level by its judgment these barriers of color. The judgment below is reversed, and the cause remanded for further proceedings in conformity with this opinion.[7]

At least from the standpoint of the court's majority, the inconsistent treatment between African American electors and others stands in direct contradiction to the intent and spirit of the Fourteenth Amendment. Additionally, the claim to exclusivity made by the defendants was denied in part on the merits that the executive committee existed as a governing arm of the party, not excluded from upholding the safeguards of the Constitution. However, in the court's dissenting opinion written by Justice James McReynolds,

> The plaintiff's petition does not attempt to show what powers the Democratic Party had entrusted to its state Executive Committee. It says nothing of the duties of the committee as a party organ; no allegation denies that, under approved riles and resolutions, it may determine and announce qualifications for party membership.[8]

Later adding that, "the Committee's resolution must be accepted as the voice of the party," Texas Democratic Party officials, not pleased by the court's majority opinion, took solace in Justice McReynolds' words.

Because the key weakness of the judicial branch is the power to enforce its own rulings, the Texas Democratic Party responded to the court's decision by amending and extending their discriminatory impact. Upon revision, the Texas Democratic Party barred African Americans, Mexican Americans, and other people of color from participation in the party's nomination conventions as well. Specifically, the Texas legislature gave the executive committee the power to prescribe the qualifications of its members for voting and other purposes. In the second of four court decisions typically referred to as the "Texas primary cases," the 1935 case of *Grovey v. Townsend* involved R.R. Grovey, an African American Texas resident who sued the state's Democratic Party for denying him the right to vote. Specifically, Grovey challenged the adoption of a May 1932 resolution, adopted by the state Democratic convention, maintaining that, "be it resolved, that all white citizens of the State of Texas who are qualified to vote under the Constitution and laws of the state shall be eligible to membership in the Democratic party and as such entitled to participate in its deliberations."[9] With the newly granted powers from the state, the Democratic Party argued that (1) their actions to establish membership criterion by means of their executive committee was acting in accordance with *Nixon v. Condon;* and (2) as a private organization, they had the right to deny membership, even along the lines of race. State Democratic officials, who undoubtedly were enjoying the political spoils attributed from maintaining the Solid South, were anxious to defend their practices.

In the court's rather appalling decision to deny injunctive relief and to uphold the all-white Texas primaries, much of the court's rationale derived from the distinction articulated between state versus private actions. Specifically, the court believed that voting in the primary was a private political party function, not a state function, as the plaintiff asserted. On this matter, the court affirmed that:

> While it is true that Texas has by its laws elaborately provided for the expression of party preference as to nominees, has required that preference to be expressed in a certain form of voting, and has attempted in minute detail to protect the suffrage of the members of the organization against fraud, it is equally true that the primary is a party primary; the expenses of it are not borne by the state, but by members of the party seeking nomination; the ballots are furnished not by the state, but by the agencies of the party; the votes are counted and the returns made by instrumentalities created by the party; and the state recognizes the state convention as the organ of the party for the declaration of principles and the formulation of policies.[10]

While it is true that the state cannot prescribe or limit the membership of a political party, this does not include non-state-controlled organizations, like the Democratic Party of Texas. As seen here, the court sees no relationship between voter participation in the primary and actions by or pertaining to the state. Because of the mutual exclusivity established by the court, this continued along the lines of race as well. With respect to racial exclusion, the court opined that Grovey confused "the privilege of membership in a party with the right to vote for one who is to hold a public office. With the former the state needs have no concern, with the latter it is bound to concern itself, for the general election is a function of the state government and discrimination by the state as respects participation by negroes on account of their race or color is prohibited by the Federal Constitution."[11] And with that demarcation, the court unanimously upheld Texas's white-only primaries.

It would not be for nearly another 10 years until the deathblow would come to the retrogressive politics of Texas's all-white primary. In the 1944 case, *Smith v. Allwright,* an African American Harris County voter, Lonnie Smith, who, like Nixon and Grovey, challenged the authority of the state Democratic Party to include only white electors in their membership. For the court, the issue had to be decisively resolved as to whether or not it was constitutionally permissible for the state Democratic Party to establish its own internal rules that permit only white electors to participate in the party's nomination conventions as well as primaries and efficiently disenfranchising all nonwhite voters. The plaintiff, Lonnie Smith, was represented by soon to be Supreme Court justice, Thurgood Marshall. Writing on behalf of the court's majority, Justice Stanley Reed expressed immediate frustration with Texas Democratic lawmakers, noting, "the right of a Negro to vote in the Texas primary has been considered heretofore by this Court," highlighting the court's rulings in cases like *Nixon v. Herndon* and *Nixon v. Condon*. While the state held firm to the belief that its voluntary organization status lent them the power to determine its own membership criterion, the court understood the law differently. Because the membership criterion barred people of color from participation in nominating conventions and voting in primaries, Justice Reed argued that the organizational structure and overall statutory system maintained by the state Democratic Party was subjected to constitutional oversight. In Justice Reed's words, "we think this statutory system for the selection of party nominees for inclusion on the general election ballot makes the party, which is required to follow these legislative directions, an agency of the state in so far as it determines the participants in a primary election," that the statutory system in question be subjected to tests that determine the "character of discrimination."[12]

Under the illusion that the case before the court was a matter of no concern to the state Democratic Party, given their alleged voluntary status, Justice Reed quickly corrected the state's judicial rationale. Speaking more directly to their membership qualifications, Reed affirmed that:

> But when, as here, that privilege is also the essential qualification for voting in a primary to select nominees for a general election, the state makes the action of the party the action of the state. In reaching this conclusion, we are not unmindful of the desirability of continuity of decision in constitutional questions. Here, we are applying . . . the well-established principle of the Fifteenth Amendment, forbidding the abridgement by a state of a citizen's right to vote.[13]

In just that manner, the Supreme Court rid the practice of all-white primaries, ending a 21-year struggle. While on face value, this series of legislative and judicial jousting might appear to have resolved voter disenfranchisement by race, equal or liberal access to the polls would be a battle only born anew in the face of voter identification laws. Like old wine in a new jug, the recent clashes over voter identification laws contain elements from previous struggles for equality. Not too far removed from the aforementioned court cases, we now turn our attention, yet again, to Texas, in the 2012 Supreme Court case, *Texas v. Holder*.

The Great Texas Shootout: *Texas v. Holder*

The politics of representation has an undeniable link to voting. Casting a ballot signifies an endorsement of numerous political variables, whether they are social, political, economic, cultural, or otherwise. Because the ballot has an immediate and direct impact on state, local, and federal power dynamics, voting has always been at the center of much debate. Recent trends in voter identification laws, led largely by partisan fervor from state Republican lawmakers, continue to cause much confusion and constitutional controversy. At the heart of this case was the 2011 passage of Senate Bill 14 (SB 14), Texas's voter identification law.

Pursuant upon greatly exaggerated claims of widespread voter fraud, Texas lawmaker's ascended upon a partisan-driven initiative to secure SB 14. Passing in the state senate by a 19 to 11 margin, with Democrats representing all 11 nay notes, and passing in the state house by a 101 to 48 margin, with Democrats representing 47 nay votes, the bill immediately moved to Governor Rick Perry's desk where it was signed into law. With highly suspect claims and scant evidence given in defense of this measure, SB 14 followed in pursuit of the efforts established in Pennsylvania. Under Section 63.0101, lawmakers defined the terms of "qualified" voters by means of identifying the acceptable forms of identification, setting off a firestorm of criticism. To qualify to vote, Texas voters now needed:

A driver's license, election certificate, or personal identification card issued to the person by the Department of Public Safety that has not expired or that expired no earlier than 60 days before the date of presentation; A United States military identification card that contains the person's photograph that has not expired or that expired no earlier than 60 days before the date of presentation; United States citizenship certificate issued to the person that contains the person's photograph; a United States passport issued to the person that has not expired or that expired no earlier than 60 days before the date of presentation; or a license to carry a concealed handgun.[14]

These forms of identification exhibit the extremes Texas lawmakers sought, as earlier versions of the bill included more accessible forms of identification. Stricken from previous versions of the bill included items such as mail from a government entity, a current utility bill, bank statement, government check, paycheck, or other government document that shows the name and address of the voter.[15] Not even photo identification generated by colleges and universities rose to the merits of consideration, thus further increasing the number of disenfranchised Texans. Additionally, votes by mail, no longer called absentee voting in Texas, are exempted from providing such identification. Granted the feasibility of doing so would render difficulties, but if the desire was to rid fraudulent votes from being tallied, and half of the 66 cases of voter fraud cited by the state's attorney general arose from mail-in ballots, one would think this is where you would focus your efforts.

Immediately following the passage of this bill, Texas lawmakers sought federal preclearance, an action required under Section 5 of the Voting Rights Act (VRA) that requires covered jurisdictions to undergo administrative review in order to ensure that the proposed law has neither a discriminatory purpose nor effect. In a highly publicized exchange, U.S. attorney general Eric Holder took aim at Texas lawmakers in an address to the members of the National Association for the Advancement of Colored People (NAACP) in Houston, Texas. Likening the law to a poll tax, Holder remarked, "many of those without IDs would have to travel great distances to get them, and some would struggle to pay for the documents they might need to obtain them. We call those poll taxes."[16] Later adding, "the arc of American history has always moved toward expanding the electorate. It is what made this nation exceptional" he said, "We will simply not allow this era to be the beginning of the reversal of that historic progress. I will not allow that to happen."[17]

Upon receipt of Texas's application for federal preclearance, Eric Holder and the U.S. Department of Justice (DOJ) denied the state's request. In the denial letter written by Assistant Attorney General Thomas Perez, the DOJ found many issues when considering the state's request for preclearance. Accordingly, any changes to voting procedures by those states housed under federal preclearance jurisdiction will be accessed against the benchmark practice to determine whether they would "lead to a retrogression in the position of racial minorities with respect to their effective exercise of the electoral franchise."[18] Not convinced that SB 14 adheres to this standard, Perez studied the data sets concerning those registered voters without a driver's license or personal identification card issued by the Texas Department of Public Safety (DPS) and noted the following:

The September data indicate that 60,892 (4.7%) of the state's registered voters do not have such identification; this population consists of 174,866 voters (29.0% of the 603,892 voters) who are Hispanic and 429,026 voters (71.0%) who are non-Hispanic. The January data indicate that 795,955 (6.2%) of the state's registered voters do not have such identification; this population consists of 304,389 voters (38.2%) who are Hispanic and 491, 566 voters (61.8%) who are non-Hispanic. The state has not provided an explanation for the disparate results . . . Starting our analysis with the September data set, 6.3 percent of Hispanic registered voters do not have the forms of identification described above, but only 4.3percent of non-Hispanic registered voters are similarly situated. Therefore, a Hispanic voter is 46.5 percent more likely than a non-Hispanic voter to lack these forms of identification. In addition, although Hispanic voters represent only 21.8 percent of the registered voters in the state, Hispanic voters represent fully 29.0 percent of the registered voters without such identification.[19]

This discovery of evidence pertaining to the immediate creation of an underclass of otherwise qualified voters did not sit well with Justice Department officials, causing great concern. Continuing down this path, according to "the state's own data, a Hispanic registered voter is at least 46.5 percent, and potentially 120 percent, more likely than a non-Hispanic registered voter to lack the required identification," said Xochitl Hinojosa, a Justice Department spokeswoman.[20] With no explanation about these staggering statistics from Texas lawmakers, Justice Department equated this lack of response as a silent acknowledgment of the data.

The burden of proof placed upon the state of Texas to illustrate that the impact of the law possesses no discriminatory effect left much to be desired. As the DOJ continued its investigation using the data provided by state officials, far too many disparities and unanswered questions arose. As observed by Perez:

The state has provided no data on whether African American or Asian registered voters are also disproportionately affected by S.B. 14 . . . The state has produced no data showing what percent of registered voters lack a driver's license or personal identification card issued by DPS, but do possess another allowable form of photographic identification. Nor has the state provided any data on the demographic makeup of such voters.[21]

With more questions than answers arising from the DOJ's analysis, nothing favorable developed from the standpoint of state lawmakers. As the evidence began to paint a startling reality of immediate disenfranchisement for an estimated 603,892 to 795,955 Texans upon the law's enactment, this caused tremendous doubt for DOJ officials. After incurring delays caused by the state's failure to submit sufficient information, the DOJ was convinced that this law would "lead to a retrogression in the position of racial minorities with respect to their effective exercise of the electoral franchise," as the sheer number of residents without photo identification did not meet the federal standard for preclearance.

Not pleased with the DOJ's denial, Texas lawmakers appealed this decision and appeared before a three-judge district court, resulting in the 2012 case, *State of Texas v. Eric Holder*. Joining the DOJ were the Texas NAACP, the Mexican American Legislative Caucus of the Texas House of Representatives, along with other parties to the case whose aim was to assist in arguing that Texas's voter identification would be detrimental to many otherwise qualified voters.

Faced with the task of proving that the voter identification law in question "neither has the purpose nor will have the effect of denying or abridging the right to vote on account of race, color," or "membership in a language minority group," Texas lawmakers had many obstacles in their path. Because SB 14 represented such a grave departure from past election procedures, the court found it necessary to compare the proposed changes against the current procedures for voting. Prior to the passage of SB 14, Texas election code stated that any Texan who wished to vote must file a registration application, whereupon approval, the applicant receives a "voter registration certificate" either in person or by mail. This certificate contains no photograph of the voter, yet instead, it includes information like name, gender, year of birth, along with a unique voter ID number. Voters must present this certificate at the polls in order to receive an in-person ballot. Additionally, Texas election code recognized eight broad categories of acceptable forms of identification, some containing a photograph of the voter, some not. The range of these items included expired and nonexpired driver's licenses, birth certificates, utility bills, and passports. This flexibility in acceptability provided for a wider range of individuals to participate. However, if declaratory judgment were granted for Texas, not only would the range of identification decrease, voters could no longer use their voter registration certificate or photo identification that has expired more than 60 days before the date of presentation at the polls.

Should previously qualified voters not possess or not be able to obtain the new forms of identification needed to vote, SB 14 provides a "free" election identification certificate that can only be obtained by visiting a state DPS office. Despite presented as free, the court, in their presentation of facts, object that, "not only will prospective voters have to expend time and resources traveling to a DPS office, but once there they will have to verify their identity by providing . . . (1) one piece of primary identification; (2) two pieces of secondary identification; or (3) one piece of secondary identification plus two pieces of supporting identification in order to receive an EIC."[22] State election code defines secondary identification as either an original or a certified copy of a birth certificate; a court order indicating an official change of name and/or gender; or proof of U.S. citizenship or naturalization papers without an identifiable photo. Additionally, supporting identification would then change to include school records, social security cards, pilot's licenses, and out-of-state driver's license. With the past and the proposed election procedures juxtaposed, the court was able to gather a clearer understanding of the degree to which changes would occur.

By no stretch of the imagination was this trial speedy, as the court cited the state of Texas on numerous occasions with delaying progress. Whether by means of submitting late evidence or by simply not submitting the requested data whatsoever, the court expressed its frustration with Texas's lackadaisical handling of the case. In their words, "our efforts to accelerate this litigation, however, were often undermined by Texas's failure to act with diligence or a proper sense of urgency . . . Texas repeatedly ignored or violated directives and orders of this Court that were designed to expedite discovery," including the failure to deliver its voter registry, DPS ID, and license-to-carry databases until 35 days *after* the deadline.[23] Despite these impediments, the court proceeded as best it could, even if it meant not having all the requested records from the state of Texas. Understanding that a ruling must come sooner, rather than later, given the goal of Texas to implement the law before the next election cycle, the court proceeded to assess Texas's two chief claims argued in defense of the law.

First before the court was the argument from Texas that applying the preclearance condition to SB 14 was inappropriate because such photo identification laws can never "deny" or "abridge the right to vote." As seen by state officials, "voter ID requirements are, at worst, a minor inconvenience," arguing that, "would be voters who refuse to countenance minor inconveniences, like registration requirements, have *chosen* not to vote." Continuing in a similar rhetorical fashion, state officials argued that voters "who opt to go without photo ID and decline to obtain one prior to the election have eschewed their right to vote," concluding that voting is a choice, while the proposed law can hardly be considered a denial or abridgment by the state.[24] In response, the court was stunned that Texas exempted itself and voter identification laws overall from Section 5 preclearance. Not convinced that Texas followed the spirit of the preclearance doctrine, the court reminded Texas that they bear the burden of proof to establish that any change to voting laws, whether small or large, must illustrate that they do not "worsen the position of minority voters compared to the general populace."[25] To this end, the court opined, "our rejection of Texas's unqualified assertion that laws are immune from Section 5 so long as they can be tied to voter choice should come as no surprise, for another . . . court recently rejected a similar argument advanced by none other than the state of Texas."[26] To conclude their response to Texas's first argument, the court minced no words in saying, "we decline Texas's recycled invitation to collapse the entire retrogression analysis into a question of voter choice."[27]

Now before the court was Texas's second argument, advancing the claim that if the court upheld Indiana's photo identification law, ruling that it only imposed a "limited burden" upon voters, Texas should be allowed to proceed in the same manner. Contending that there are more similarities than differences between the two laws, Texas argued that their preclearance decision should be granted on account of the precedence set in the 2008 case of *Crawford v. Marion County.* Here again, the court found fault with this reasoning, arguing that *Crawford,* while pertaining to voter identification, is largely irrelevant to the context of the case before them. Though not covered by Section 5 of the VRA, the *Crawford* case presented another set of challenges not applicable to the case at hand. For instance, in *Crawford,* the plaintiffs were faced with the burden of proving that the law was invalid in all its form, thus the basis of a facial challenge. Here, however, because Section 5 applies to Texas, the state bears the burden of proving that any change in voting procedures would not "deny or abridge the right to vote." Additionally, because a facial challenge was pursued in the *Crawford* case, a challenge that took into consideration the effect of the law on *all* Indiana voters, the Texas case pertains only to certain subsets of voters, chiefly, racial and language minorities.

While Texas specifically cites Indiana and Georgia, two states that have passed voter identification laws, the court continues to show how the many differences in the proposed changes to Texas election code that invalidates their comparison. While Georgia allows voters to use any expired photo ID at the polls and Indiana allows the use of any photo ID that has expired after the most recent general election, Texas prohibits the use of photo ID that expired more than 60 days before voting. Next, the court considered the comparative burdens imposed on voters in each state, arguing that the burden is significantly steeper under SB 14. Citing various examples, the court reasoned that under SB 14, applicants would pay at least $22 for a certified copy of birth certificate, whereas by contrast, Georgia accepts 24 categories, including student identification, Medicare or Medicaid statement, and school transcript, all of which are not permissible under SB 14. Moreover, the court considered the cost of transportation incurred by those Texas voters without photo identification who, in turn, must appear at a DPS office in order to complete an application. Through the court's eyes, "the United States submitted unrebutted evidence showing that 81 Texas counties have no DPS office, and 34 additional counties have DPS offices open two days per week or less. This means that in at least one-third of Texas's counties, would-be voters will have to travel out-of-county merely to apply for an EIC, Georgia and Indiana face no such burdens."[28] As seen here, the comparative approach undertaken by Texas did nothing to advance their preclearance argument, only worsening their case.

In defense of SB 14, Texas argued that Texans across the board, whether they are African American, Latino, white, or otherwise, possessed photo identification at roughly the same rate, thus invalidating the DOJ's claim of retrogression. On the other hand, the DOJ argued quite the opposite, with both sides providing statistical analyses arguing their angle. Unfortunately for both, the court found both studies unreliable and dismissed them. Nonetheless, pursuant upon the sequence of arguments and evidence provided by Texas in defense of their preclearance request, the court concluded this declaratory request in memorable fashion. "Because all of Texas's evidence on retrogression is some combination of invalid, irrelevant, and unreliable, we have little trouble concluding that Texas has failed to carry its burden of proof."[29]

In much of the same contentious manner this case entered the court, it exited much in the same manner. While the U.S. District Court's ruling prevented Texas from implementing SB 14, it would not be long until the VRA, namely, Sections 5 and 4(b) along with voter identification laws would get another day in court. In the landmark 2013 Supreme Court case of *Shelby County v. Holder*, a new trail was forged that altered the political and judicial landscape as we know it. In the final section of this chapter, we attend to this case and the judicial and political repercussions therein.

Goodbye Section 5: *Shelby County v. Holder*

Known also as the "Fannie Lou Hamer, Rosa Parks, and Coretta Scott King Voting Rights Act Reauthorization and Amendments Act of 2006," the House of Representatives both introduced and passed the measure where the Senate quickly followed suit. Of great importance to this conversation are the policy "findings" that were included in the passage of this act. Of these axioms, Congress found the following:

(1) Significant progress has been made in eliminating first-generation barriers experienced by minority voters, including increased numbers of registered minority voters, minority voter turnout, and minority representation in Congress, State legislatures, and local elected offices. This progress is the direct result of the VRA of 1965.

(2) However, vestiges of discrimination in voting continue to exist as demonstrated by second-generation barriers constructed to prevent minority voters from fully participating in the electoral process.

(3) The continued evidence of racially polarized voting in each of the jurisdictions covered by the expiring provisions of the VRA of 1965 demonstrates that racial and language minorities remain politically vulnerable, warranting the continued protection of the VRA of 1965.

(4) Evidence of continued discrimination includes—

(A) the hundreds of objections interposed, requests for more information submitted followed by voting changes withdrawn from consideration by jurisdictions covered by the VRA of 1965, and Section 5 enforcement actions undertaken by the DOJ in covered jurisdictions since 1982 that prevented election practices, such as annexation, at-large voting, and the use of multimember districts, from being enacted to dilute minority voting strength;

(B) the number of requests for declaratory judgments denied by the U.S. District Court for the District of Columbia;

(C) the continued filing of Section 2 cases that originated in covered jurisdictions; and

(D) the litigation pursued by the DOJ since 1982 to enforce Sections 4(e), 4(f)(4), and 203 of such Act to ensure that all language minority citizens have full access to the political process.[30]

Here, this bipartisan piece of legislation directly and specifically acknowledged the continuing challenges faced by "minority voters." By no means does this language give the impression that voter protection via federal oversight is no longer needed; in fact, many of the same tactics aimed at disenfranchisement continue, yet under a different mask. Additionally, as the bill makes quite clear, "despite the progress made by minorities under the VRA of 1965, the evidence before Congress reveals that 40 years has not been a sufficient amount of time to eliminate the vestiges of discrimination," understanding that not only is this reauthorization needed, but that the nation still harbors countervailing sentiments. Even with Congress's findings, this was not enough to satisfy those jurisdictions covered under the VRA who were not convinced over the extent of Congress's findings and thus decided to file suit.

The U.S. District Court along with the U.S. Court of Appeals for Washington, D.C., both upheld Congress's 2006 reauthorization, explaining that the evidence obtained from the Congressional record suitably meets all constitutional burdens to justify the continuance of the law. Nonetheless, in 2013, the Supreme Court decided to grant *certiorari* and hear the case. Before the Court was a lawsuit against the attorney general led by Shelby County, Alabama, a covered jurisdiction, like Texas, that needs federal approval in order to enact changes to any of its voting procedures. Shelby County sued on the basis that the preclearance requirement and its formula is facially unconstitutional, thus arguing for a permanent injunction against its enforcement. Specifically, the Court was called upon to decide whether or not Congress's 2006 reauthorization of the VRA, chiefly Sections 5 and 4(b), exceeded its authority under the Fifteenth Amendment, thus violating both the Tenth Amendment and Article IV of the Constitution. In other words, the Supreme Court had to determine whether this action of Congress exceeded their authority under the Fourteenth and Fifteenth Amendments.

Given the possible effect the Supreme Court's decision would have upon voting rights in the United States, there were many concerned parties on both sides of the aisle. During oral arguments, however, advocates of the VRA were stunned to learn of Justice Antonin Scalia's remarks that Section 5, as reauthorized by Congress, constituted a "racial entitlement," expressing his belief that our country's actions and attitudes about race have evolved far beyond the need for Section 5. Drawing immediate condemnation from civil rights advocates and others, *Shelby County v. Holder* promised to be a decision for the ages.

With the aforementioned chief question before the court, Shelby County, along with many of the amicus briefs filed on its behalf, extended their argument with the addition of three claims. First, *Shelby* and its allies raised the issue of double standards, the very same argument that *Texas* sought just one year ago. *Shelby* held that other states, including some covered under Section 5, received preclearance to enact the same laws *Shelby* attempted to pass, yet *Shelby* was denied preclearance by the DOJ. Citing the DOJ's request for supplemental information before considering *Shelby*'s request, *Shelby* noted that other covered states like Arizona and Georgia, were not required to do so, claiming there is not only a double standard, but also severe ambiguity in understanding the DOJ's standards for pre-clearance. Next, *Shelby* and many of its amici advanced a state sovereignty claim that believes that while the historically granted power for states to regulate their own elections is not absolute, those states housed under Section 5 infringes upon this sovereignty, creating different classes/categories of states. Additionally, the preclearance formula itself, Section 4(b), relies upon antiquated data from a previous time in U.S. history that is no longer relevant, raising the concern that covered states are being punished for past actions. Combined, the aggressive nature of Sections 5 and 4(b) have outlived their use, failing to make evidentiary based claims supported by current conditions.

In one of the Supreme Court's most controversial decisions, Chief Justice John Roberts delivered the slim 5–4 majority opinion, followed by the dissenting opinion offered by Justice Ruth Bader Ginsburg. With much attention directed at the court, Chief Justice Roberts interpreted and consolidated the questions before the justices into one. As Chief Justice Roberts explained, "the question is whether the Act's extraordinary measures, including its disparate treatment of the States, continue to satisfy constitutional requirements. As we put it a short time ago, the Act imposes current burdens and must be justified by current needs."[31] On trial here is temporality, as you will notice the frequent amount of times the word "current" is used throughout this decision when assessing the justifications leveled by the DOJ and its supporters. If the DOJ were to be victorious, they must rejoin Shelby County's claim that their data, like that used by Congress in 2006, reflects current conditions, as opposed to the past. Whether or not the court's majority accepts that the current formula addresses the "denial or abridgement to vote on account of race or color," thus leading to disparate treatment of the states, will now receive its days in court.[32]

In his analysis of state sovereignty against the demands of the VRA, Chief Justice Roberts addressed his concerns directly. While leaving little room for ambiguity, Roberts left plenty of room for controversy in his assessment. Agreeing that states retain their sovereignty under the Constitution, citing the court's opinion in the 2009 case of *Northwest Austin Municipal Utility District v. Holder* that there exists a "fundamental principle of equal sovereignty among the states," Roberts believed that the VRA "sharply departs" from these principles.[33] Through his eyes, the VRA "suspends all changes to state election law—however innocuous—until they have been precleared by federal authorities in Washington, D. C. . . . And despite the tradition of equal sovereignty, the Act applies to only nine States (and several additional counties). While one State waits months or years and expends funds to implement a validly enacted law, its neighbor can typically put the same law into effect immediately, through the normal legislative process."[34] Here, the emphasis is placed upon procedural variances, underscoring Shelby County's claim of double standards and state sovereignty. This claim would only gain more footing with Roberts, as he considered whether or not the context of racial discrimination used to uphold these measures in the past is still needed today. This would prove to be the most controversial aspect of the court's majority opinion.

In this regard, Chief Justice Roberts sought to apply his understanding of race and politics in the United States, first noting that the actions of the past were, despite claims of double standards, fully warranted. Citing voter registration data by race prior to the passage of the VRA, there was no argument that disparities existed, that they were encouraged by certain political behaviors whereas the coverage formula made sense. Explaining that Congress found two patterns pertaining to voter discrimination; "the use of tests and devices for voter registration," and "a voting rate in the 1964 presidential election was at least 12 points below the national average." Later adding, it too was understood that, "tests and devices are relevant to voting discrimination because of their long history as a tool for perpetuating the evil," and that a "low voting rate is pertinent for the obvious reason that widespread disenfranchisement must inevitably affect the number of actual voters."[35] Congress's and the court's previous rationale become important to understand for two reasons. First, if the court was to uphold the VRA, it would need to acknowledge that much of the same patterns of discrimination exists today with respect to voter identification laws, or second, that these tests and devices are not relevant to voting discrimination, citing nuances like "compelling state interests," the absence of racial discrimination/disparities in voting procedures, among others.

Unfortunately, for dissenters of voter identification laws, Chief Justice Roberts's arguments fall short in many regards. Relying upon empirical data, though failing to provide much needed context, Roberts takes selective solace in the findings of Congress upon its 2006 reauthorization of the VRA. As Roberts cites in this opinion, "significant progress has been made in eliminating first-generation barriers experienced by minority voters, including increased numbers of registered voters, minority voter turnout, and minority representation in Congress, State legislatures and local elected offices."[36] The findings of Congress, as he cites, do not exist in a vacuum, though he fails to acknowledge that. Instead, these findings are in reference to previous intentionally discriminatory barriers placed on voting, such as literacy exams and poll taxes. Even with these exams, whether you passed the literacy exam and/or paid the tax, white primaries became another wave of intentional discrimination. While these "first-generation barriers" have been eradicated, it says nothing about second-generation barriers like voter identification laws. In many respects, Roberts raises a moot point that he otherwise attempts to pass off as evidence to dismantle the VRA. Cherry-picking again, Roberts cites the House report pertaining to the VRA that elaborated that, "the number of African Americans who are registered and who turn out to cast ballots has increased significantly over the last 40 years, particularly since 1982."[37] What are missing here are two facts; one is common sense while the other is more statistical. First, it only makes sense that once the courts began to uphold equal protection, striking down white primaries for instances, that more African Americans and others would exercise their right to vote. Once the courts imparted what African Americans and others already knew, that is, they have a protected and fundamental right to vote, an increase in participation rates are to be expected.

Next, Roberts's use of statistical evidence lacks serious empirical context to help explain the rise in registered African American voters and those elected to office. Drawing from data compiled by the U.S. Census Bureau in their "50th Anniversary of the Civil Rights Act," the Census Bureau cross compared multiple variables pertaining to race between 1964 and 2013, the exact time period Roberts performed his statistical analysis. In accordance with this data, several interesting facts emerge. First, between 1964 and 2013, the "total estimated black population" has doubled, from 20.6 million to more than 42.6 million. The percentage of African Americans living in "the South" between 1960 and 2010 has decreased from 59.9 to 56.5 percent, noting that this geographical area continues to have the largest concentration of African Americans in the country. This data too indicates that the high school graduation rate between 1964 and 2012 has more than tripled; however, the percentage of African Americans who voted in the 1964 presidential election (58.5%), compared to those who voter in the 2012 presidential election only rose by 3.5 percent.[38] Additionally, there have been only 105 African Americans elected to the House of Representatives between 1950 and present, according to the Office of the Historian and the Clerk of the House's Office of Art and Archives. On the Senate side, the numbers are much slimmer, counting a total of seven, since the election of 1967 of Massachusetts Republican Edward Brooke.[39] On the state level, only eight African Americans have been elected as governor, as tabulated by the National Governors Association.[40] These facts must be understood within the context of this case if we are to fully and accurately juxtapose past and present developments in voter participation and representation by race.

Content nonetheless that the vestiges of disenfranchisement have largely subsided, especially upon presenting data that African Americans voter turnout is on par with white voters in five of the covered six states, Roberts believed that now was the time to switch legal gears. Convinced that the coverage formula used under Section 4 is outmoded, Chief Justice Roberts audaciously claims that while states in 1965 could be divided in two groups, those with and those without voting tests and devices, "today the nation is no longer divided along those lines, yet the Voting Rights Act continues to treat it as if it were."[41] Failing to recognize the evidence and concerns over the retrogressive impact voter identifications laws place upon various racial, socioeconomic, and ability groups, along with how these laws amount to voting "tests and devices," once harshly condemned by Congress and the courts,[42] Roberts continues to understand race and politics from a statistical standpoint absent of content. From his perspective, so long as African Americans are being elected to office, continue to register to vote, and vote, voter identification laws represent no threat to this progress.

To assist his argument in defense of this line of justification, Roberts advanced the Fifteenth Amendment. In his eyes, this amendment "commands that the right to vote shall be not denied nor abridged on account of race or color, and it gives Congress the power to enforce that command. The Amendment is not designed to punish for the past; its purpose is to ensure a better future."[43] With no direction as to how one can interpret voter identification laws as a means of ensuring the future, Roberts also cited Congressional failure to update the coverage formula of the VRA as to why the court granted Shelby County's request for facial relief. "Its failure to act leaves us today with no choice but to declare §4(b) unconstitutional. The formula in that section can no longer be used as a basis for subjecting jurisdictions to preclearance," ultimately striking down Sections 4(b) and 5.

Given the court's close 5–4 decision, the court's dissenting opinion is just as important to discuss. Offered by Justice Ruth Bader Ginsburg, on behalf of herself along with Justices Stephen Breyer, Sonia Sotomayor, and Elena Kagan, she rejoins Chief Justice Roberts's argument.

A Matter of Differing Opinions

Spending considerable time reflecting upon past political and legal allowances that encouraged the formation of discursive disenfranchisement, ironically including the aforementioned "Texas primary" cases, Justice Ginsburg argued that a different question should have been considered before the court. For her, the question should have been whether or not it is the court or Congress who is charged with the obligation of enforcing "the post-Civil War Amendments by appropriate legislation," explaining that the 2006 reauthorization received overwhelming bipartisan support in both chambers of Congress, whereupon presented evidence, Congress felt the VRA was still necessary. Contrary to Chief Justice Roberts's belief that the VRA has reached its goals of political parity between African Americans and whites, Justice Ginsburg was of the belief that, "continuance would facilitate completion of the impressive gains thus far made; and second, continuance would guard against back-sliding. Those assessments were well within Congress' province to make and should elicit this Court's unstinting approbation."[44] Understanding that the VRA could safeguard against other barriers aimed at diluting minority participation and influence, like racial gerrymandering and the incorporation of at-large voting over district voting, Justice Ginsburg was not as easily swayed by the empty numbers Chief Justice Roberts presented as evidence of parity.

Justice Ginsburg's dissenting opinion finds much fault in the slight-of-hand maneuvers entered in the court's majority opinion. As we previously illustrated Roberts's cherry-picking habits, Justice Ginsburg noted this characteristic as well. Citing from the same Congressional findings surrounding the 2006 reauthorization that Roberts drew upon to argue that Section 4(b) and thus Section 5 no longer apply, Ginsburg brings the House report full circle. According to these findings, "second generation barriers constructed to prevent minority voters from fully participating in the electoral process continued to exist, as well as racially polarized voting in the covered jurisdictions, which increased the political vulnerability of racial and language minorities in those jurisdictions," leading Congress to conclude that, "evidence of continued discrimination . . . clearly show the continued need for Federal oversight."[45] Although it was based upon these findings that Congress reauthorized the VRA, Chief Justice Roberts's account of this report would lead you to believe otherwise. Moreover, it was precisely this schism that lead Ginsburg to believe that the court should have accepted the findings of a bipartisan Congress and have not intervened. Nonetheless, the question became whether or not Congress had the authority under the Constitution to act in the manner it did.

Justice Ginsburg's dissenting opinion seized the moment to discuss the counter reality of voter discrimination otherwise glossed over by Roberts. In quite the stunning comparison between data sets, Ginsburg entered into evidence compelling examples that she believed authorized Congress to act in the manner it did while rejecting Shelby County's facial challenge. For instance, between 1982 and 2006, the DOJ blocked the passage of 700 changes in voting procedures that were deemed retrogressive; successfully enforcing over 100 actions to enforce preclearance requirements; and more than 800 proposed changes to voter procedures were either altered or withdrawn since the last reauthorization 1982.[46] With just this addition of this data alone, one can easily suggest that Congress acted in good faith with sufficient evidence acknowledging that our nation has not fully ridded itself of politically and racially motivated maneuvers, like Roberts leads you to believe.

Leading up to the 2006 reauthorization, Justice Ginsburg highlighted some of the attempted measures that were blocked by the VRA, as a means of opining the continual importance of the law. As stated in the Congressional record:

- In 1995, Mississippi sought to reenact a dual voter registration system, "which was initially enacted in 1892 to disenfranchise Black voters," and for that reason, was struck down by a federal court in 1987.
- Following the 2000 census, the City of Albany, Georgia, proposed a redistricting plan that DOJ found to be "designed with the purpose to limit and retrogress the increased black voting strength . . . in the city as a whole."
- In 2001, the mayor and all-white five-member Board of Aldermen of Kilmichael, Mississippi, abruptly canceled the town's election after "an unprecedented number" of African-American candidates announced they were running for office. DOJ required an election, and the town elected its first black mayor and three black aldermen.
- In 2006, this Court found that Texas' attempt to redraw a congressional district to reduce the strength of Latino voters bore "the mark of intentional discrimination that could give rise to an equal protection violation," and ordered the district redrawn in compliance with the VRA. *League of United Latin American Citizens v. Perry*, 548 U.S. 399, 440 (2006). In response, Texas sought

to undermine this Court's order by curtailing early voting in the district, but was blocked by an action to enforce the §5 preclearance requirement.

- In 2003, after African-Americans won a majority of the seats on the school board for the first time in history, Charleston County, South Carolina, proposed an at-large voting mechanism for the board. The proposal, made without consulting any of the African-American members of the school board, was found to be an "exact replica" of an earlier voting scheme that, a federal court had determined, violated the VRA. DOJ invoked §5 to block the proposal.
- In 1993, the City of Millen, Georgia, proposed to delay the election in a majority-black district by two years, leaving that district without representation on the city council while the neighboring majority white district would have three representatives. DOJ blocked the proposal. The county then sought to move a polling place from a predominantly black neighborhood in the city to an inaccessible location in a predominantly white neighborhood outside city limits.
- In 2004, Waller County, Texas, threatened to prosecute two black students after they announced their intention to run for office. The county then attempted to reduce the availability of early voting in that election at polling places near a historically black university.
- In 1990, Dallas County, Alabama, whose county seat is the City of Selma, sought to purge its voter rolls of many black voters. DOJ rejected the purge as discriminatory, noting that it would have disqualified many citizens from voting "simply because they failed to pick up or return a voter update form, when there was no valid requirement that they do so."[47]

Examples like these, along with many others, were entered as evidence, justifying the continuation of the VRA. Had observers of the court not read the dissenting opinion or the legislative record, they would have no knowledge of this counterreality that shows that preclearance has not outlived its functionality.

Not persuaded by the temporal argument advanced and accepted by the court's majority, Ginsburg continued to dilute Roberts's naïve beliefs about racial equity. Now addressing the coverage formula that Roberts criticized as using past actions to punish current and future developments, Ginsburg argued that the punishment fits both the past and present crime. While the covered jurisdictions account for less than 25 percent of the country's population, it ironically accounted for 56 percent of successful litigation since 1982.[48] Explained by Ginsburg, "the evidence before Congress . . . indicated that voting in the covered jurisdictions was more racially polarized than elsewhere in the country. While racially polarized voting alone does not signal a constitutional violation, it is a factor that increases the vulnerability of racial minorities to discriminatory changes in voting law."[49] Throughout much of Roberts's opinion, insightful context and content was conveniently and continually absent, causing many questions to arise about the degree of objectivity he and the court's majority took in arriving at their decision.

Reading the majority opinion alone leaves many questions unanswered and much skepticism in the air. Never did Roberts address many of the facts surrounding preclearance status, including, whether or not the designation of "covered jurisdiction" is permanent or not. Given that one of the chief claims advanced by Shelby County pertained to their status as a covered jurisdiction, Congress's "bailout mechanism" should have been discussed, yet it too was absent. As explained by Ginsburg:

> Congress was satisfied that the VRA's bailout mechanism provided an effective means of adjusting the VRA's coverage over time. H.R. Rep. No. 109–478, at 25 (the success of bailout "illustrates that: (1) covered status is neither permanent nor over-broad; and (2) covered status has been and continues to be within the control of the jurisdiction such that those jurisdictions that have a genuinely clean record and want to terminate coverage have the ability to do so"). Nearly 200 jurisdictions have successfully bailed out of the preclearance requirement, and DOJ has consented to every bailout application filed by an eligible jurisdiction since the current bailout procedure became effective in 1984. The bail-in mechanism has also worked. Several jurisdictions have been subject to federal preclearance by court orders, including the States of New Mexico and Arkansas.[50]

Later remarking that, "this experience exposes the inaccuracy of the Court's portrayal of the Act as static, unchanged since 1965," she accurately captured the level of frustration Ginsburg's opinion sought to express.[51] Additionally, "even while subject to the restraining effect of §5, Alabama was found to have denied or abridged voting rights on account of race or color more frequently than nearly all other States in the Union."[52] Ginsberg asserted that Alabama's sorry history of Section 2 violations alone "provides sufficient justification for Congress' determination in 2006 that the State should remain subject to §5's preclearance requirement."[53] Given Roberts's belief that Section 4(b) does not respond to "current conditions," Ginsburg sought to prove otherwise.

In typical fashion, Justice Ginsburg leaves little to wonder in her closing thoughts. Not convinced that the problems of the past have stayed in the past, not convinced that Section 4(b) does not address current conditions, and not convinced with the selective inclusion and glaring omission of content and data within Chief Justice Roberts's opinion, Ginsburg leaves us with this. "Leaping to resolve Shelby County's facial challenge without considering whether application of the VRA to Shelby County is constitutional, or even addressing the VRA's severability provision, the Court's opinion can hardly be described as an exemplar of restrained and moderate decision making. Quite the opposite. Hubris is a fit word for today's demolition of the VRA."[54]

Conclusion

Since the removal of key provisions within the VRA, the influx of voter identification laws began to flood state legislatures. Immediately upon release of the court's decision, lawmakers in Texas quickly enforced SB 14, under the direction of the former state's attorney general, Greg Abbot. Without the existence of preclearance, previously covered jurisdictions can do as they please, even if it includes purposely incorporating alterations to voting procedures that possess a disparate impact upon certain demographics. While the DOJ can still bring suit against a state, they must now prove discriminatory intent, a task extremely difficult to argue, especially in light of how the courts have treated "compelling state interests," like voter confidence as a justifiable rationale.

In situations like this, the task falls back upon the shoulders of Congress to rectify. However, much like comprehensive immigration reform, a new VRA is not on the horizon anytime soon. While a bipartisan bill, introduced by Representatives Jim Sensenbrenner (R-WI), John Conyers (D-MI), and Senator Patrick Leahy (D-VT), was introduced in the House of Representatives in mid-January of 2014, the bill has yet to come up for a vote on the House floor. To date, this represents Congress's progress toward fully restoring the VRA.

Notes

1. Wayne Slater, "Few Texas Voter-Fraud Cases Would Have Been Prevented by Photo ID Law, Review Shows," *Dallas News*, September 8, 2013, http://www.dallas news.com/news/politics/headlines/20130908-few-texas-voter-fraud-cases-would-have-been-prevented-by-photo-id-law-review-shows.ece (accessed July 30, 2014).

2. Ibid.

3. Ibid.

4. *Nixon v. Herndon,* 273 U.S. 536 (1927).

5. Ibid.

6. *Nixon v. Condon,* 286 U.S. 73 (1932).

7. Ibid.

8. Ibid.

9. *Grovey v. Townsend,* 295 U.S. 45 (1935).

10. Ibid.

11. Ibid.

12. *Smith v. Allwright,* 321 U.S. 649 (1944).

13. Ibid.

14. Texas Senate Bill 14, 2011.

15. Ibid.

16. Joe Holley, "Holder Calls Texas Voter ID Law a Poll Tax," *Houston Chronicle,* July 10, 2012, http://www.chron.com/news/houston-texas/article/Holder-calls-Texas-voter-ID-law-a-poll-tax-3697707.php#photo-3179975 (accessed July 30, 2014).

17. Ibid.

18. See *Beer* v. *United States,* 425 U.S. 130 (1976).

19. Thomas Perez, "United States Department of Justice, Civil Rights Division," March 12, 2012, http://s3.amazonaws.com/static.texastribune.org/media/documents/2011–2775_ltr.pdf (accessed July 30, 2014).

20. Julian Aguilar, "Feds Reject Texas Voter ID Law," *Texas Tribune,* March 12, 2012, http://www.texastribune.org/2012/03/12/feds-reject-texas-voter-id-law (accessed March 12, 2012).

21. Perez, "United States Department of Justice, Civil Rights Division."

22. *Texas v. Holder,* 1:12-cv-00128.

23. Ibid.

24. Ibid.

25. Ibid.

26. Ibid.

27. Ibid.

28. Ibid.

29. Ibid.

30. Public Law 109–246, 109th Congress, 2006.

31. *Shelby County v. Holder,* 570 U.S.___(2013).

32. See: 42 U.S.C. §1973(a).

33. *Northwest Austin Municipal Utility District No. 1 v. Holder,* 557 U.S. 193 (2009).

34. *Shelby County v. Holder,* 570 U.S.___(2013).

35. Ibid.

36. Ibid.

37. Ibid.

38. Special Edition, "50th Anniversary of the Civil Rights Act: July 2," United States Census Bureau, http://www.census.gov/newsroom/releases/archives/facts_for_features_special_editions/cb14-ff17.html.

39. "Breaking New Ground—African American Senators. United States Senate," http://www.senate.gov/pagelayout/history/h_multi_sections_and_teasers/Photo_Exhibit_African_American_Senators.htm.

40. "Former Governor's Bios," *National Governors Association,* http://www.nga.org/cms/FormerGovBios?begincac77e09-db17–41cb-9de0–687b843338d0=25&endcac77e09-db17–41cb-9de0–687b843338d0=49&pagesizecac77e09-db17–41cb-9de0–687b843338d0=25&higherOfficesServed=&lastName=&sex=Any&honors=&submit=Search&college=&state=Any&inOffice=Any&party=&race=Any&biography=&birthState=Any&religion=&militaryService=&nbrterms=Any&firstName=&warsServed=&.

41. *Shelby County v. Holder,* 570 U.S.___(2013).

42. See: *South Carolina v. Katzenbach,* 383 U.S. 301 (1966).

43. *Shelby County v. Holder,* 570 U.S.___(2013).

44. Ibid.

45. Ibid.

46. Ibid.

47. Ibid.

48. Ibid.

49. Ibid.

50. Ibid.

51. Ibid.

52. Ibid.

53. Ibid.

54. Ibid.

Chapter 6

Conclusion: Current Trends in Voter ID Laws and Felon Disenfranchisement

This book has focused on the modern attack on the right to vote in the United States. Despite declarations that the country had entered a period of post-racialism with the ascendancy of President Barack Obama, efforts to reduce the effectiveness of voting by people of color have been heightened. Our findings reveal that historically, episodes of African American social inclusion and political success have typically been followed by systematic legal and extralegal efforts to erode such progress and reassert white supremacy. In the 21st century, the nation once again finds itself in a situation in which the right to vote is manipulated by those seeking to acquire and maintain political power.

The first chapter focused on the right to vote, particularly the acquisition of the right to vote, and the Voting Rights Act of 1965. Considerable attention was given to the constitutional safeguards against racial disenfranchisement provided under the act, especially Section 5 and the recently overturned constitutional guidance it provided to freeze election practices or procedures in certain states until they have been subjected to federal review. In Chapter 2, we investigated the laws that currently exist at the state level throughout the United States, which restrict the voting rights of convicted felons, and assessed the impact on individuals' right to exercise enfranchisement. Chapter 3 addresses the much neglected 2005 landmark Indiana voter identification law, and the fallout it produced in the 2008 Supreme Court case, *Crawford v. Marion County Election Board*. While dissenters in this case pointed out that voter identification laws were merely a thinly veiled attempt to disenfranchise low-income Democratic voters, supporters of the law defended it as legal assurance against voter fraud. Chapter 4 focuses on Pennsylvania, which also insisted upon the passage of a voter identification policy that only later was exposed as part of a plan to facilitate a state electoral victory for presidential candidate Mitt Romney. Chapter 5 analyzes and discusses two of the most recent and controversial court cases, *Texas v. Holder* and *Shelby v. Holder,* which demonstrate the linkages of past voter disenfranchisement efforts with those of the present. With respect to Texas the rather pressing matter that the Latino population is increasing rapidly and is outpacing whites in some places will continue into the future. Consistent with this trend we have argued that shifting racial demographics and political power balances matter and not necessarily "voter fraud." Finally, we focus on the latest developments in voter identification laws giving specific attention to states that have enacted voter identification legislation following the landmark *Shelby v. Holder* decision. Also provided is a brief epilogue on the growth of majority–minority areas throughout the United States.

In the introduction to this book, we point out that as of September 2014, 31 of 34 states had already passed laws requiring voters to show some form of identification at the polls. We pointed out further that while two at that point had been struck down, one is scheduled to go into effect in 2016. The remaining 19 states employ additional methods of voter verification, including checking a voter's signature against information on file. As bills pertaining to the creation of voter identification laws continue to surface across the country, it is evident that this legislative and legal struggle is far from over.

Contemporary developments reflect an ongoing incremental and evolutionary process—one that only stubbornly advances the process of social change in regard to voting as the nation becomes increasingly diverse and multicultural. While there is an interest in bringing about broad inclusion, the focal point of this protracted struggle for enfranchisement has been on the acquisition of black voting rights, and more importantly, the wherewithal of group members to cast their ballot without fear of reprisal or doubts about it being counted. These same principles obviously apply not just to African Americans and whites, but also to Latinos, Asians, and others who hold membership in racial, ethnic, and identity groups in the United States, who are citizens and therefore have the right to vote. The application of the fundamental principal of "one person, one vote" was a critical objective of the Civil Rights Movement, which eroded Jim Crow segregation and the politics of exclusion. The contemporary contours of the struggle to achieve and maintain the right to vote are built on the past successful struggles of African Americans and women, which stand as models for contemporary protest politics. Ironically, however, voting rights in the United States continue to be threatened by and subjected to changes that undermine the hard-won achievements of the 1965 Voting Rights Act.

We remain steadfast in our conviction that race not only matters in these debates, but also that the relationship between race and the current attack on voting rights is consistent with the historic pattern initiated with the decline of the first Reconstruction. Our primary goals in this work have been to highlight the past and present underpinning racial dimensions involved throughout the political legacy of the struggle for voting rights. We have also sought to demonstrate how historical experience is essential for understanding current patterns, practices, and controversies concerning the voting rights of African Americans, Latinos, people of color, and the poor, including the homeless. Charges of voter fraud aimed at the black and immigrant communities have been demonstrated to be largely false, with the reference to "immigrants" virtually serving as a surrogate term for "Latinos" or "Hispanics," regardless of official citizenship status. These dynamics demonstrate that race is alive and well in the struggle to obtain and/ or maintain the right to vote. Our focus on the centrality of race as a factor in the political behavior and rhetoric associated with the ongoing debate over voting rights in the United States consequently has not been in vain.

Thus, we want to turn our attention to some of the most recent important developments on the voting rights horizon that portend the status of voting rights for African Americans, Latinos, and other groups whose voting rights have traditionally been targeted for suppression. Moreover, in light of the bitterly partisan nature of the voting rights skirmish, we assess the nature and depth of recent developments that suggest that cracks may be appearing in the wall of U.S. political partisanship in regard to perhaps the most cherished of citizenship rights—the right to vote. Finally, we offer some concluding remarks about the future of U.S. democracy and the evolution of an increasingly diverse society within this framework.

Recent Developments

Registration and Voting

The U.S. Supreme Court's ruling in *Shelby v. Holder* has had an important effect on the behavior of many of the 15 states, which had been covered under Section 5 of the Voting Rights Act. However, there are states such as Ohio and Wisconsin, which were not covered by Section 5 that respectively have reduced the opportunity for early voting and imposed wide-ranging restrictions. There have been some recent developments, which for many may be a signal of alarm; however, others may breathe a sigh of relief.

Among the states challenged in the voting rights battle is Texas. Once the Supreme Court struck down Section 5, Texas moved immediately to enforce its voter identification law, which had been in place since 2003. Specifically, the state moved forward with a plan that had previously been ruled under Section 5 to be discriminatory toward African American and Hispanic voters. Texas also began implementation of its plan to change election district boundaries. The Supreme Court allowed Texas to use its voter identification law in an upcoming election, despite the ruling by a federal court that the Texas law was a violation of both the U.S. Constitution and the Voting Rights Act and that the state was engaged in deliberate racial discrimination in voting. Previously, the trial court had barred Texas from using its law. However, early October 2014, the U.S. Court of Appeals for the Fifth Circuit reversed the decision of the trial court, and the law's challengers went to the Supreme Court where as expected, the Court sided with Texas. Justice Ruth Bader Ginsberg was joined in her dissent by Justices Elena Kagan and Sonia Sotomayor. The Supreme Court's order was consistent with some of its other recent orders indicating that lower courts should not change the election procedure rules shortly before the start of voting.[1]

The state of North Carolina is among those that have imposed new voting restrictions, and in this case, they happen to be among the harshest in the country. Following the Supreme Court's ruling, which overturned Section 4 of the Voting Rights Act, the North Carolina Senate crafted legislation that repealed virtually every electoral reform that had encouraged citizens to vote in 2008 and 2012. Key provisions of this bill imposed strict photo identification requirements, shortened the early voting period by a week, eliminated same-day voter registration, and eliminated preregistration for 16- and 17-year-olds. North Carolina was able to make these changes, as they no longer had to comply with Section 5. This change in effect, transferred the burden of proof from the state to citizens, primarily African Americans in the case of North Carolina, who now were being called to demonstrate that they were being discriminated against racially.[2] Various parts of the North Carolina voting law were challenged during summer 2014. A district court refused to issue a preliminary injunction for the Justice Department, North Carolina National Association for the Advancement of Colored People (NAACP), American Civil Liberties Union (ACLU), and other groups. However, on October 1, 2014, the Fourth Circuit reinstated same-day registration and out-of-precinct voting. Two days before the voter registration deadline in North Carolina, on October 8, 2014, with Justices Ginsberg and Sotomayor dissenting, the U.S. Supreme Court overruled the decision of the Fourth Circuit Court of appeals in time for the midterms. The court's action was projected to have a devastating effect on the 2014 midterm elections since during the early voting period in 2012, almost 100,000 voters employed same-day registration during the early voting period; among these voters there were twice as many blacks as whites. Moreover, in 2012, approximately 7,500 citizens voted in the right county; however, they did so in the wrong precinct.[3] It is important to note that states that use same-day voter registration have been shown to have the highest voter turnout in the country. For example, during 2012, the average voter turnout was more than 10 percentage points higher in same-day registration states than in other states. The merits of the case are scheduled for a full trial in July 2015.[4]

Although not covered by Section 5, the state of Wisconsin is among those that have taken action to tighten voter requirements. A 2011 law requires voters to present a photo identification at the polls. Due to early problems, a state court blocked the use of the law. In early 2014, a federal district court judge ruled the law unconstitutional based on its disproportionate impact on African American and Latino voters. It was pointed out that the rationale that voters were impersonating others was virtually without basis. In October 2014, a three-judge panel of the Seventh Circuit Court of Appeals overturned that decision partially based on last-minute changes made by state officials to reduce the burden on voters without the proper identification. The full appeals court then deadlocked 5–5 on whether to reconsider the issue, thereby keeping the photo-ID rule in place. The ACLU and the Advancement Project, a civil rights group, contend that the law jeopardizes the votes of some 300,000 residents who lack the proper ID—particularly racial minorities, seniors, students, and people with disabilities. Along with consideration of the situation in Texas, the Supreme Court could take up the case of Wisconsin.[5]

In 2011, Arkansas also implemented a voter identification law. However, in May 2014, a judge ruled the law unconstitutional, although he suspended his ruling allowing the identification requirement to remain in effect.[6] Nonetheless, the Arkansas Supreme Court found that requiring voters to present a photo identification imposed a new qualification for voting, in violation of the state's constitution.[7]

Ohio passed legislation in 2011 to reduce its early voting period, only to have it overturned by a lower court, which was eventually blocked by the

U.S. Supreme Court. The upshot of the ruling is that early voting would begin one week later instead of on September 30, 2014. In addition, the decision eliminated early voting during evening hours and on Sunday, October 26, 2014. Early voting in Ohio did remain in place during the weekend prior to the 2014 midterm election. While the state of Ohio maintains that it provides more opportunities for early voting than other states, those opposed to the law point out that the early-voting cuts would likely do the most harm to minority voters.[8]

One final pending case involves Arizona and Kansas, which maintain that voters should have to demonstrate proof of citizenship in order to register to vote. Kansas adopted more stringent citizenship requirements when its legislature passed the Secure and Fair Elections Law of 2011, known as the SAFE Act. The act required people registering to vote after January 1, 2013, to produce the additional documents to prove their citizenship. Arizona has also passed legislation requiring those registering to vote to provide additional proof of citizenship. Last year, however, the U.S. Supreme Court struck down a law requiring state officials to reject federal voter registration forms due to lack of proof of citizenship. In the aftermath of the Court's decision, Arizona signed on to the Kansas lawsuit to force the federal government to modify its registration form to reflect that requirement. The case is currently before a federal appeals court (a decision could come before the November 4, 2014, midterm elections). If the court does not render its ruling by then, Arizona and Kansas voters who used the federal registration form, but did not demonstrate proof of citizenship will be barred from voting in state and local elections.[9] Thus, the Supreme Court has shown a reluctance to allow implementation of major voting changes just prior to the occurrence of an election. While such reluctance may be encouraging, the Court has yet to rule on the constitutionality of these laws. Its action on this matter is expected to take place following the 2014 midterm elections in 2015.

Felon Voting Rights

Over the past 15 years, advocacy groups such as the Brennan Center for Justice and the Sentencing Project have lobbied state and federal officials to restore the voting rights of ex-felons. The Sentencing Project reports that 23 states have made changes to their laws and/or policies on felon disenfranchisement since 1997 resulting in a simpler process for ex-felons to pursue to get their voting rights restored. However, while some states have minimized the complications of restoring voting rights in some instances making it automatic, others have made their felony disenfranchisement policies even harsher. For example, Connecticut passed a law in 2001 that restored voting rights to felons serving probation, while in 2002 the Kansas legislature enacted legislation to include felons serving probation on that state's list of those disenfranchised. At the same time, policies can change from one administration to the next. For example, in 2005 then Iowa governor Tom Vilsack restored voting rights to ex-felons by executive order, only to be rescinded in 2011 by Governor Terry Branstad. Florida provides yet another example of the tenuous nature of executive action when it comes to felon disenfranchisement. In 2007, Florida's Office of Executive Clemency in 2007, headed by then governor Charlie Crist, amended the state's policies to automatically approve the restoration of voting rights to most of those convicted of nonviolent offenses. However, this policy was changed four years later in 2011, when the office, then headed by Governor Rick Scott, ruled that those seeking restoration of their voting rights had to wait at least five years following the completion of their sentence before applying.[10]

When it comes to registration and voting generally, and specifically in reference to felon disenfranchisement, we continue to believe that historical conditions combine with race and partisanship in the contemporary era in a manner that is ultimately quite disruptive to democratic practice. Since political parties will do what is in their best interest electorally when it comes to determining how strict to make felon disenfranchisement laws, and given the current makeup of the disenfranchised, it would behoove Republicans to assume a policy stance that would result in the relaxation of harsh penalties. Republican senator Rand Paul of Kentucky appears to be among the first of those to break away from the pack, notwithstanding there are Democrats who like their Republican counterparts, oppose the relaxation of the collateral consequences associated with felon or ex-felon status. During June 2014, Senator Paul introduced legislation to restore voting rights to nonviolent felons. He has also expressed an interest in sentencing reform, ways to help former felons reenter the job market, the elimination of disparities in sentencing for powder and crack cocaine, and the reclassification of certain drug offenses from felonies to misdemeanors.[11]

Recalcitrant states driven by the pressures of political partisanship continue to exercise power over felon disenfranchisement, even though some maintain there is constitutional justification for federal standards and oversight. Over the past century, there have been few legal challenges to state's disenfranchisement laws. Since passage of the 1965 Voting Rights Act, two significant cases have been argued before the U.S. Supreme Court: *Richardson v. Ramirez*, 418 U.S. 24 [1974] and *Hunter v. Underwood*, 471 U.S. 222 [1985]. In *Richardson*, the Supreme Court upheld the constitutionality of state disenfranchisement policies, except those explicitly racially biased. *Hunter v. Underwood* resulted in the Court's decision to permit states broad flexibility in developing disenfranchisement laws.[12] This ruling essentially reinforced the national hodgepodge of state-level felon disenfranchisement policies that are discriminatory against African Americans, Latinos, and other people of color and dismantling to the causes of democracy and social justice. It may be that federal oversight of the issue is inevitable. Along with minimizing state-level partisanship, the imposition of federal guidance can yield national consistency, uniformity of practice, and voting rights stability for felons and ex-felons.

The Future of Voting Rights: The Demise of Partisanship?

What does the future hold for voting rights and U.S. democracy? While the past few decades have yielded the repeal of some of the restrictions on voting associated with felony disenfranchisement, the nullification of Section 4 of the Voting Rights Act appears to balk at any semblance of progress in the area of voting rights. In this context, questions pertaining to the role that political partisanship has played are salient. By definition, U.S. democracy is nonpartisan. In other words, both Democrats and Republicans who are legitimately competing for power have conceded to the ideal that the United States ought to be based on the principles of democracy. However, the major political parties each have their own political interests and will do what is necessary to obtain power and articulate these interests. For example, when it comes to redistricting both Democrats and Republicans like the idea of concentrating Congressional districts with blacks, Hispanics, and other minorities because they each benefit: Democrats benefit by winning at least one Congressional seat, while Republicans benefit from whiter, therefore more Republican voters. Thinking of this sort, however, assumes that Republicans will continue to operate as they have in the past. However, nothing may be further from the truth. Partisanship has been shown to be associated with the harshness of felon disenfranchisement policies. One study reported the following: "Comparing final votes on rights-relaxation bills with the partisan breakdown of each legislative chamber, we see that while sponsors of such measures have almost been universally Democrats, final votes have ranged from almost perfectly partisan to unanimous."[13] This finding suggests that Republicans, like Democrats, might also see a silver lining in the issue of voting rights expansion. Alec C. Ewald acknowledges that Republicans in particular may see that they can benefit from embracing felon disenfranchisement reform. He writes:

> But there is also another dimension to the partisan landscape. Far from avoiding or suppressing debate, many Republicans appear to believe the issue is a political winner for them, precisely because they share the belief that former inmates are likely Democratic voters. Republicans seek to embed in public discourse the assumption that felons support Democratic politicians-and vice-versa. For Republicans, felony disenfranchisement offers a chance not only to capitalize on the "negative political leverage" possessed by criminal offenders in contemporary American politics, but also to describe Democrats as cravenly seeking partisan gain in the guise of high-minded rhetoric.[14]

Perhaps Kentucky's Republican senator Rand Paul understands the partisan dynamics of voting rights better than others in his political party do. In June of 2014, he introduced legislation to restore voting rights to nonviolent felons in national elections. Parallel to the Democrats' position, Paul asserts that justice calls him to the task, while acknowledging that he also has political motives. Senator Ben Cardin of Maryland, who has been a supporter of voting rights for ex-convicts regardless of their crime, has pointed out that "the effort is a 'breakthrough' toward a compromise, even with sticking points," while Nicole Austin-Hillery of the Brennan Center for Justice has stated, "This is going to help change the national conversation."[15] The reality, however, is that such a breakthrough has yet to occur, and whether or not it will likely depends on the nation's treatment of the issue of race and the attendant issue of diversity—especially recognition that it remains fundamentally important to for the society to strive to achieve an equitable distribution of social resources, including the right to vote.

It is crucial to recognize that the restrictive voting policies put into practice in the United States have a real impact on national elections. One day following the November 4, 2014, midterm elections, the Brennan Center for Justice made a preliminary assessment of the impact of new voting restrictions on the election. They concluded that "in several key races, the margin of victory came very close to the likely margin of disenfranchisement."[16]

One key to understanding race and voting rights rests with the dynamics at play in the political environment, including the evolutionary nature of the major political parties in the United States. During Reconstruction, the

Republican Party was at the forefront of eradicating slavery. Indeed, they were a leading voice in the call to punish Southern states for slavery and in promoting the ideal that all freed men were created equally. In the contemporary period, however, the party appears to have performed an about-face. Republicans have behaved and are largely seen as opponents of civil rights. Given this, African Americans remain voters who lean toward casting the lot of their ballots to Democratic Party candidates. Republicans' resistance to progressive immigration policies, as well as their views on crime and justice continues to undermine their political relations with not only African Americans, but also increasingly other citizens of color.

Appropriately, there have been calls among African American leaders to return to the early mantra of the Congressional Black Caucus (CBC). At the time of its founding, with only nine members, the Democratic Select Committee, forerunner of the CBC, was under considerable pressure to mobilize and activate many newly enfranchised constituents. William Clay of Missouri advanced the idea that "Black people have no permanent friends, no permanent enemies . . . just permanent interests." In the early years of its existence, this theme was a signal to the colleagues of CBC members and the nation that the organization would be an independent voice in Congress. The theme was intended to send the signal that neither of the major political parties would find the black vote to be a permanent fixture. Moreover, the slogan signified that the African American community would operate in a self-interested fashion, thereby resisting the historical temptation of being permanently tied to one political party or the other. If such an independent political stance was ever to come to fruition as the harness of the black vote, it would likely confound analysts and those campaigning for political office by challenging the notion that race could be applied as a modern-day means test of political partisanship.[17]

Since the Senator Clay's mantra would make clear that the African American vote is no longer wedded to the Democratic Party, perhaps Republican Party candidates would be better incentivized to campaign among African American constituents in the hope of attracting their electoral support. However, the assertion of independence in the electoral arena is important not only for African Americans, but for people of color in general, especially in the present era of franchise restriction. Multiracial coalitions in combination with reduced partisanship can create an extraordinary opportunity to establish conditions that will lead ultimately to strengthening and ensuring the persistence of U.S. democracy for the generations of the foreseeable future. Before this approach can proceed, however, it is crucial that the intersection of interests of African Americans, Latinos, and other people of color be carefully charted to demonstrate mutual benefit and gain. However, it remains to be seen if the temptations of U.S. politics can be overcome. If not, the contracted electorate will likely impede, if not eventually reverse the long pattern of voting rights extension in the United States. The only way to improve matters is by changing the laws that currently undermine democracy and the franchise. Not to do so will guarantee the continuation of extant patterns of racial and partisan conflict in the electoral arena.

Notes

1. Richard L. Hasen, "Dawn Patrol," *New York Times,* October 18, 2014, http://www.slate.com/articles/news_and_politics/jurisprudence/2014/10/ginsburg_s_dissent_in_texas_voter_id_law_supreme_court_order.html (accessed November 5, 2014). Also see Alan Liptak, "Supreme Court Allows Texas to Use Strict Voter ID Law in Coming Election," *New York Times,* October 18, 2014, http://www.nytimes.com/2014/10/19/us/supreme-court-upholds-texas-voter-id-law.html?ref=politics&_r=0 (accessed November 5, 2014).

2. Brennan Center for Justice at New York University School of Law, North Carolina, *NAACP v. McCrory* (Amicus Brief), October 1, 2014, http://www.brennancenter.org/legal-work/north-carolina-naacp-v-mccrory-amicus-brief (accessed November 2, 2014). Also see Ari Berman, "North Carolina Will Determine the Future of the Voting Rights Act," *The Nation,* July 10, 2014, http://www.thenation.com/blog/180608/north-carolina-will-determine-future-voting-rights-act (accessed November 5, 2014).

3. Ari Berman, "The Supreme Court Approves the Country's Worst Voting Restrictions in North Carolina," *The Nation,* October 8, 2014, http://www.thenation.com/blog/181925/supreme-court-approves-countrys-worst-voting-restrictions-north-carolina (accessed November 6, 2014).

4. No author, "What is Same Day Registration? Where is it Available?" *Demos,* March 1, 2013, http://www.demos.org/publication/what-same-day-registration-where-it-available (accessed November 1, 2014).

5. Richard Wolf, "Supreme Court Blacks Wisconsin's Voter ID Law," *USA Today,* October 9, 2014, http://www.usatoday.com/story/news/politics/2014/10/09/supreme-court-wisconsin-voter-id/16985963/ (accessed November 1, 2014).

6. Tierney Sneed, "Voting Rights Battles Rock Lead—Up to Elections," *U.S. News & World Report,* October 17, 2014, http://www.usnews.com/news/articles/2014/10/17/voting-law-challenges-in-wisconsin-arkansas-texas-and-elsewhere-roil-election-lead-up (accessed November 2, 2014).

7. Pam Fessler, "Recent Rulings Alter Voting Laws Ahead of November Election," *It's All Politics: Political News from NPR,* October 16, 2014, http://www.npr.org/blogs/itsallpolitics/2014/10/16/356710120/recent-rulings-alter-voting-laws-ahead-of-november-election (accessed November 6, 2014).

8. Ibid.

9. Alan Gomez, "Kansas, Arizona Win Citizenship Ruling," *USA Today,* March 17, 2014, http://www.usatoday.com/story/news/nation/2014/03/19/immigration-proof-of-citizenship-kansas-arizona/6614245/ (accessed November 6, 2013).

10. The Sentencing Project, "Felony Disenfranchisement Laws in the United States, 2014," April, http://sentencingproject.org/doc/publications/fd_Felony%20Disenfranchisement%20Laws%20in%20the%20US.pdf (accessed October 12, 2014).

11. Burgess Everett, "Rand Paul Seeks to Expand Voting Rights to Some Ex-Cons," *Politico,* July 22, 2014, 1–3, http://www.politico.com/story/2014/06/rand-paul-voting-rights-ex-felons-108156.html (accessed August 20, 2014).

12. William W. Lyles, "Challenges to Felon Disenfranchisement Laws: Past, Present and Future," *Alabama Law Review* 58, no. 3 (2007): 615, http://www.sentencingproject.org/doc/publications/fd_research_liles.pdf (accessed November 21, 2014).

13. Alec C. Ewald, "Criminal Disenfranchisement and the Challenge of American Federalism," *Publius: The Journal of Federalism,* 39, no. 3 (2009): 534.

14. Ibid., 535.

15. Everett, "Rand Paul Seeks to Expand Voting Rights to Some Ex-Cons, Politico."

16. Wendy R. Weiser, "How Much of a Difference Did new voting Restrictions Make in Yesterday's Close Races?" November 5, 2014, Brennan Center for Justice at New York University School of Law, http://www.brennancenter.org/print/12822 (accessed November 5, 2014).

17. Creation and Evolution of the Congressional Black Caucus, History, Art, and Archives, United States House of Representatives, http://history.house.gov/Exhibitions-and-Publications/BAIC/Historical-Essays/Permanent-Interest/Congressional-Black-Caucus/ (accessed October 23, 2014).

Epilogue: A Note on Majority–Minority Growth

Majority–minority[1] refers to any area, whether it is a county, city, or state where one or more racial and/or ethnic minorities are the statistical majority. To achieve this status, the "non-Hispanic white" population must be less than 50 percent. Data from the 2010 Census shows how shifting demographics continue to alter the social, cultural, economic, and political landscape of the United States. Resulting from variables like immigration and birthrates, states like Texas, New Mexico, and California are already known to be majority–minority states; however, this trend continues to experience rapid growth. As reported by the Census Bureau, "50.4 percent of our nation's population younger than age 1 were minorities as of July 1, 2011. This is up from 49.5% from the 2010 Census taken April 1, 2010."[2] Aside from the three aforementioned states, Hawaii (77.1%) and the District of Columbia (64.7%) are also majority–minority, whereas to date, no other state had a majority–minority population greater than 46.4 percent. Moreover, 2014 was the first year that the percentage of minority public school student enrollment overtook the percentage of white public school student enrollment.[3]

As various projections continue to illustrate that the nonwhite population could find itself as a statistical minority by 2050, this shifting trend is worth careful attention. As it is widely known, eight of the fifteen most rapidly growing cities are in Texas, where both Houston and San Antonio are firmly majority–minority, while Austin and Dallas-Fort Worth are quickly gaining ground. Interestingly enough, the number of Latinos counted in the 2010 Census was nearly 1 million more than expected, according to an analysis by the Pew Hispanic Center. Additionally, "the 2010 Census count of Hispanics was 50,478,000, compared with 49,522,000 Hispanics in the bureau's own estimates. The count was 1.9% higher than the estimated population. In 32 states, the 2010 Census count of Hispanics was at least

2% higher than the estimates; in nine states, it was at least 2% lower than the estimates. In the nine remaining states and the District of Columbia, the difference was less than 2% in either direction."[4]

The rapid growth of nonwhites throughout the United States not only makes statistical impacts, but these impacts carry political potentiality. Drawn from the November 2014 midterm election, Democrats continue to have an edge among Latino and African American voters. For instance, Latino voters, who comprised 8 percent of the voters this year, favored Democrats by garnering 62 percent of the vote, while African Americans favored Democrats by garnering 89 percent of the vote.[5] While exit polling data for all states was not available during the writing of this book, it is worth mentioning that in the Texas Senate race, there was a statistical deviation. In his bid for reelection, incumbent Republican senator John Cornyn and his Democratic challenger David Alameel nearly split the Latino vote; however, the edge went to the victor, John Cornyn. In the race for Texas governor, while Democrat Wendy Davis won 55 percent of the Latino vote, she was defeated by Republican challenger Greg Abbot.[6] While Democratic candidates won a bulk of Latino votes, Republican candidates continue to make slight, but noticeable gains in this area. Additionally, available exit poll data shows that while Republicans won most state races, they did so despite losing the Latino vote, especially in states like Florida.

Despite President Barack Obama's executive action delay on deportations, at the time this book was written, it was too soon to say what sway this move may have for Democratic candidates. Nonetheless, as Republicans have gained control of both chambers of Congress, yet at the same time eyeing their prospects for 2016, the actions produced in the years ahead could either help or harm the Grand Old Party (GOP), as the balance of power is anybody's contest. While many state legislatures are enjoying a Republican majority for now, nothing lasts forever, especially as highly polarized debates over immigration reform, voter identification laws, and job creation continues.

The once familiar version of the "Solid South" continues to loosen its grip, as shifting demographics are altering the political landscape in many areas. To date, we know that a record 25.2 million Latinos were eligible to vote during the 2014 midterm elections, making up, for the first time, 11 percent of all eligible voters nationwide.[7] Combine this with the latest trends showing that roughly 57 percent of the nation's African American residents now live in the South, the highest number in five decades. As the nation's largest "minority" groups continue to have a growing presence in certain regions of the country, we expect to see this translate into a shift of political power at all levels of government, assuming voter turnout rates mirror this rate of growth.

Notes

1. It is also common to find the term "minority–majority" used interchangeably to refer to the same population shift.

2. "Most Children Younger Than Age 1 are Minorities," United States Census Bureau, May 17, 2012, https://www.census.gov/newsroom/releases/archives/population/cb12-90.html (accessed November 21, 2014).

3. Jens Krogstad and Richard Fry, "Dept. of Ed. Projects Public Schools Will Be 'Majority-Minority' This Fall," Pew Research, August 18, 2014, http://www.pewresearch.org/fact-tank/2014/08/18/u-s-public-schools-expected-to-be-majority-minority-starting-this-fall/.

4. Jeffrey Passel and D'Vera Cohn, "How Many Hispanics? Comparing New Census Counts with the Latest Census Estimates," Pew Hispanic Center, March 15, 2011, http://www.pewhispanic.org/files/reports/139.pdf.

5. Jens Krogstad and Mark Lopez, "Hispanic Voters in the 2014 Election," Pew Hispanic Center, November 7, 2014, http://www.pewhispanic.org/2014/11/07/hispanic-voters-in-the-2014-election/.

6. Ibid.

7. Mark Lopez, Jens Krogstad, Eileen Patten, and Ana Gonzalez-Barrera, "Latino Voters and the 2014 Midterm Election," Pew Hispanic Center, October 16, 2014, http://www.pewhispanic.org/2014/10/16/latino-voters-and-the-2014-midterm-elections/.

Appendix: Current Voter ID Policy Snippets

This final chapter seeks to provide an even more in-depth look into the laws governing voter identification, as we provide excerpts of current laws from the states of North Carolina, Ohio, and Texas. We have selected these states due to their recent actions to curb early voting, shorten or eliminate same-day voting, along with other actions that extend our initial understanding of these laws, their intent, and so-called concerns.

North Carolina House Bill 589

AN ACT TO RESTORE CONFIDENCE IN GOVERNMENT BY ESTABLISHING THE VOTER INFORMATION VERIFICATION ACT TO PROMOTE THE ELECTORAL PROCESS THROUGH EDUCATION AND INCREASED REGISTRATION OF VOTERS AND BY REQUIRING VOTERS TO PROVIDE PHOTO IDENTIFICATION BEFORE VOTING TO PROTECT THE RIGHT OF EACH REGISTERED VOTER TO CAST A SECURE VOTE WITH REASONABLE SECURITY MEASURES THAT CONFIRM VOTER IDENTITY AS ACCURATELY AS POSSIBLE WITHOUT RESTRICTION, AND TO FURTHER REFORM THE ELECTION LAWS.

PART 1. SHORT TITLE SECTION 1.1. Parts 1 through 6 of this act shall be known and cited as the Voter Information Verification Act.

PART 2. PHOTO IDENTIFICATION SECTION 2.1. Article 14A of Chapter 163 of the General Statutes is amended by adding a new section to read: "§ 163–166.13. Photo identification requirement for voting in person.

  (a) Every qualified voter voting in person in accordance with this Article, G.S. 163–227.2, or G.S. 163–182.1A shall present photo identification bearing any reasonable resemblance to that voter to a local election official at the voting place before voting, except as follows:

(1) For a registered voter voting curbside, that voter shall present identification under G.S. 163–166.9.

(2) For a registered voter who has a sincerely held religious objection to being photographed and has filed a declaration in accordance with G.S. 163–82.7A at least 25 days before the election in which that voter is voting in person, that voter shall not be required to provide photo identification.

(3) For a registered voter who is a victim of a natural disaster occurring within 60 days before election day that resulted in a disaster declaration by the President of the United States or the Governor of this State who declares the lack of photo identification due to the natural disaster on a form provided by the State Board, that voter shall not be required to provide photo identification in any county subject to such declaration. The form shall be available from the State Board of Elections, from each county board of elections in a county subject to the disaster declaration, and at each polling place and one-stop early voting site in that county. The voter shall submit the completed form at the time of voting.

(b) Any voter who complies with subsection (a) of this section shall be permitted to vote.

(c) Any voter who does not comply with subsection (a) of this section shall be permitted to vote a provisional official ballot which shall be counted in accordance with G.S. 163–182.1A.

(d) The local election official to whom the photo identification is presented shall determine if the photo identification bears any reasonable resemblance to the voter presenting the photo identification. If it is determined that the photo identification does not bear any reasonable resemblance to the voter, the local election official shall comply with G.S. 163–166.14.

(e) As used in this section, 'photo identification' means any one of the following that contains a photograph of the registered voter. In addition, the photo identification shall have a printed expiration date and shall be unexpired, provided that any voter having attained the age of 70 years at the time of presentation at the voting place shall be permitted to present an expired form of any of the following that was unexpired on the voter's 70th birthday. Notwithstanding the previous sentence, in the case of identification under subdivisions (4) through (6) of this subsection, if it does not contain a printed expiration date, it shall be acceptable if it has a printed issuance date that is not more than eight years before it is presented for voting:

(1) A North Carolina driver's license issued under Article 2 of Chapter 20 of the General Statutes, including a learner's permit or a provisional license.

(2) A special identification card for non-operators issued under G.S. 20–37.7.

(3) A United States passport.

(4) A United States military identification card, except there is no requirement that it have a printed expiration or issuance date.

(5) A Veterans Identification Card issued by the United States Department of Veterans Affairs for use at Veterans Administration medical facilities, except there is no requirement that it have a printed expiration or issuance date.

(6) A tribal enrollment card issued by a federally recognized tribe.

(7) A tribal enrollment card issued by a tribe recognized by this State under Chapter 71A of the General Statutes, provided that card meets all of the following criteria:

Is issued in accordance with a process approved by the State Board of Elections that requires an application and proof of identity equivalent to the requirements for issuance of a special identification card by the Division of Motor Vehicles under G.S. 20–7 and G.S. 20–37.7.

Is signed by an elected official of the tribe.

(8) A driver's license or non-operators identification card issued by another state, the District of Columbia, or a territory or commonwealth of the United States, but only if the voter's voter registration was within 90 days of the election."

SECTION 2.2. Article 14A of Chapter 163 of the General Statutes is amended by adding a new section to read:

"§ 163–166.14. Evaluation of determination of non-reasonable resemblance of photo identification.

(a) Any local election official that determines the photo identification presented by a voter in accordance with G.S. 163–166.13 does not bear any reasonable resemblance to that voter shall notify the judges of election of the determination.

(b) When notified under subsection (a) of this section, the judges of election present shall review the photo identification presented and the voter to determine if the photo identification bears any reasonable resemblance to that voter. The judges of election present may consider information presented by the voter in addition to the photo identification and shall construe all evidence presented in a light most favorable to the voter.

(c) A voter subject to subsections (a) and (b) of this section shall be permitted to vote unless the judges of election present unanimously agree that the photo identification presented does not bear any reasonable resemblance to that voter. The failure of the judges of election present to unanimously agree that photo identification presented by a voter does not bear any reasonable resemblance to that voter shall be dispositive of any challenges that may otherwise be made under G.S. 163–85(c)(10).

(d) A voter subject to subsections (a) and (b) of this section shall be permitted to vote a provisional ballot in accordance with G.S. 163–88.1 if the judges of election present unanimously agree that the photo identification presented does not bear any reasonable resemblance to that voter.

(e) At any time a voter presents photo identification to a local election official other than on election day, the county board of elections shall have available to the local election official judges of election for the review required under subsection (b) of this section, appointed with the same qualifications as is in Article 5 of this Chapter, except that the individuals (i) may reside anywhere in the county or (ii) be an employee of the county or the State. Neither the local election official nor the judges of election may be a county board member. The county board is not required to have the same judges of election available throughout the time period a voter may present photo identification other than on election day but shall have at least two judges, who are not of the same political party affiliation, available at all times during that period.

(f) Any local or State employee appointed to serve as a judge of election may hold that office in addition to the number permitted by G.S. 128–1.1.

(g) The county board of elections shall cause to be made a record of all voters subject to subsection (c) of this section. The record shall include all of the following:

(1) The name and address of the voter. (2) The name of the local election official under subsection (a) of this section. (3) The names and a record of how each judge of election voted under subsection (b) of this section. (4) The date of the determinations under subsections (a) and (b) of this section. (5) A brief description of the photo identification presented by the voter.

(h) For purposes of this section, the term 'judges of election' shall have the following meanings:
   (1) On election day, the chief judge and judges of election as appointed under Article 5 of this Chapter.
   (2) Any time other than on election day, the individuals appointed under subsection (e) of this section.

(i) The State Board shall adopt rules for the administration of this section."

SECTION 2.8. Article 15A of Chapter 163 of the General Statutes is amended by adding a new section to read:

"§ 163–182.1A. Counting of provisional official ballots cast due to failure to provide photo identification when voting in person.

(a) Unless disqualified for some other reason provided by law, the county board of elections shall find that a voter's provisional official ballot cast as a result of failing to present photo identification when voting in person in accordance with G.S. 163–166.13 is valid and direct that the provisional ballot be opened and counted in accordance with this Chapter if the voter complies with this section.

(b) A voter who casts a provisional official ballot wholly or partly as a result of failing to present photo identification when voting in person in accordance with G.S. 163–166.13 may comply with this section by appearing in person at the county board of elections and doing one of the following:

   (1) Presenting photo identification as defined in G.S. 163–166.13(e) that bears any reasonable resemblance to the voter. The local election official to whom the photo identification is presented shall determine if the photo identification bears any reasonable resemblance to that voter. If not, that local election official shall comply with G.S. 163–166.14.

   (2) Presenting any of the documents listed in G.S. 163–166.12(a)(2) and declaring that the voter has a sincerely held religious objection to being photographed. That voter shall also be offered an opportunity to execute a declaration under G.S. 163–82.7A for future elections.

(c) All identification under subsection (b) of this section shall be presented to the county board of elections not later than 12:00 noon the day prior to the time set for the convening of the election canvass pursuant to G.S. 163–182.5.

(d) If the county board of elections determines that a voter has also cast a provisional official ballot for a cause other than the voter's failure to provide photo identification in accordance with G.S. 163–166.13, the county board shall do all of the following:

   (1) Note on the envelope containing the provisional official ballot that the voter has complied with the proof of identification requirement.

   (2) Proceed to determine any other reasons for which the provisional official ballot was cast provisionally before ruling on the validity of the voter's provisional official ballot."

PART 3. IMPLEMENTATION SECTION 3.1. G.S. 20–37.7(d) reads as rewritten:

(d) Expiration and Fee.—A special identification card issued to a person for the first time under this section expires when a driver's license issued on the same day to that person would expire. A special identification card renewed under this section expires when a driver's license renewed by the card holder on the same day would expire.

The fee for a special identification card is the same as the fee set in G.S. 20–14 for a duplicate license. The fee does not apply to a special identification card issued to a resident of this State as follows:

(1) The applicant is legally blind. (2) The applicant is at least 70 years old. (3) The applicant is homeless, has been issued a drivers license but the driver's license is cancelled under G.S. 20–15, in accordance with G.S. 20–9(e) and (g), as a result of a physical or mental disability or disease. (4) The applicant is homeless. To obtain a special identification card without paying a fee, a homeless person must present a letter to the Division from the director of a facility that provides care or shelter to homeless persons verifying that the person is homeless. (5) The applicant is registered to vote in this State and does not have photo identification acceptable under G.S. 163–166.13. To obtain a special identification card without paying a fee, a registered voter shall sign a declaration stating the registered voter is registered and does not have other photo identification acceptable under G.S. 163–166.13. The Division shall verify that voter registration prior to issuing the special identification card. Any declaration shall prominently include the penalty under G.S. 163–275(13) for falsely making the declaration.

The applicant is appearing before the Division for the purpose of registering to vote in accordance with G.S. 163–82.19 and does not have other photo identification acceptable under G.S. 163–166.13. To obtain a special identification card without paying a fee, that applicant shall sign a declaration stating that applicant is registering to vote and does not have other photo identification acceptable under G.S. 163–166.13. Any declaration shall prominently include the penalty under G.S. 163–275(13) for falsely making the declaration.

SECTION 3.2. G.S. 130A–93.1 is amended by adding a new subsection to read: "(c) Upon verification of voter registration, the State Registrar shall not charge any fee under subsection (a) of this section to a registered voter who signs a declaration stating the registered voter is registered to vote in this State and does not have a certified copy of that registered voter's birth certificate or marriage license necessary to obtain photo identification acceptable under G.S. 163–166.13. Any declaration shall prominently include the penalty under G.S. 163–275(13) for falsely or fraudulently making the declaration." SECTION 3.3. G.S. 161–10(a)(8) reads as rewritten: (8) Certified Copies of Birth and Death Certificates and Marriage Licenses.— For furnishing a certified copy of a death or birth certificate or marriage license ten dollars ($10.00). Provided however, a Register of Deeds, in accordance with G.S. 130A–93, may issue without charge a certified Birth

Certificate to any person over the age of 62 years. Provided, however, upon verification of voter registration, a register of deeds, in accordance with G.S. 130A-93, shall issue without charge a certified copy of a birth certificate or a certified copy of a marriage license to any registered voter who declares the registered voter is registered to vote in this State and does not have a certified copy of that registered voter's birth certificate or marriage license necessary to obtain photo identification acceptable under G.S. 163-166.13. Any declaration shall prominently include the penalty under G.S. 163-275(13) for falsely or fraudulently making the declaration.

SECTION 3.4. G.S. 163-275(13) reads as rewritten: (13) For any person falsely to make or present any certificate or other paper to qualify any person fraudulently as a voter, or to attempt thereby to secure to any person the privilege of voting; voting, including declarations made under this Chapter, G.S. 20-37.7(d)(5), 20-37.7(d)(6), 130A-93.1(c), and 161-10(a)(8).

Excerpt II

PART 5. REGISTRATION AND EDUCATION SECTION 5.1. G.S. 163-82.22 reads as rewritten:

§ 163-82.22. Voter registration at public libraries and public agencies. (a) Every library covered by G.S. 153A-272 shall make available to the public the application forms described in G.S. 163-82.3, and shall keep a sufficient supply of the forms so that they are always available. Every library covered by G.S. 153A-272 shall designate at least one employee to assist voter registration applicants in completing the form during all times that the library is open.(b) If approved by the State Board of Elections, the county board of elections, and the county board of commissioners, a county may offer voter registration in accordance with this section through the following additional public offices: Senior centers or facilities operated by the county. Parks and recreation services operated by the county.

SECTION 5.2. The State Board of Elections shall disseminate information about photo identification requirements for voting, provide information on how to obtain photo identification appropriate for voting, and assist any registered voter without photo identification appropriate for voting with obtaining such photo identification. Information may be distributed through public service announcements, print, radio, television, online, and social media. The State Board shall work with public agencies, private partners, and nonprofits to identify voters without photo identification appropriate for voting and assist those voters in securing the photo identification appropriate for voting. All outreach efforts to notify voters of the photo identification requirements shall be accessible to the elderly and persons with disabilities. The State Board of Elections shall work with county boards of elections in those counties where there is no Division of Motor Vehicles driver's license office open five days a week to (i) widely communicate information about the availability and schedules of Division of Motor Vehicles mobile units and (ii) provide volunteers to assist voters with obtaining photo identification through mobile units.

PART 16. ELIMINATE SAME-DAY VOTER REGISTRATION

SECTION 16.1. The subsections of G.S. 163–82.6A, other than subsection (e), are repealed.

PART 18. LIST MAINTENANCE/INTERSTATE AGREEMENTS TO IMPROVE VOTER ROLLS

SECTION 18.1. G.S. 163–82.14(a) reads as rewritten: "(a) Uniform Program.—The State Board of Elections shall adopt a uniform program that makes a diligent effort not less than twice each year:

(1) To remove the names of ineligible voters from the official lists of eligible voters, and

(2) To update the addresses and other necessary data of persons who remain on the official lists of eligible voters.

That program shall be nondiscriminatory and shall comply with the provisions of the Voting Rights Act of 1965, as amended, and with the provisions of the National Voter Registration Act. The State Board of Elections, in addition to the methods set forth in this section, may use other methods toward the ends set forth in subdivisions (1) and (2) of this subsection, including address-updating services provided by the Postal Service and entering into data sharing agreements with other states to cross-check information on voter registration and voting records. Any data sharing agreement shall require the other state or states to comply with G.S. 163–82.10 and G.S. 163–82.10B. Each county board of elections shall conduct systematic efforts to remove names from its list of registered voters in accordance with this section and with the program adopted by the State Board. The county boards of elections shall complete their list maintenance mailing program by April 15 of every odd-numbered year, unless the State Board of Elections approves a different date for the county."

SECTION 18.2. The State Board of Elections shall actively seek ways to share and cross-check information on voting records and voter registration with other states to improve the accuracy of voter registration lists, using resources such as the Electronic Registration Information Center and by entering into interstate compacts for this purpose.

PART 25. EARLY VOTING SITES WITHIN A COUNTY SECTION 25.1. G.S. 163–227.2(b) and (g) read as rewritten:

§ 163–227.2. Alternate procedures for requesting application for absentee ballot; "one-stop" voting procedure in board office.

(b) Not earlier than the second Thursday before an election, in which absentee ballots are authorized, in which a voter seeks to vote and not later than 1:00 P.M. on the last Saturday before that election, the voter shall appear in person only at the office of the county board of elections, provided in subsection (g) of this section. A county board of elections shall conduct one-stop voting on the last Saturday before the election until 1:00 P.M. That voter shall enter the voting enclosure at the board office through the appropriate entrance and shall at once state his or her name and place of residence to an authorized member or employee of the board. In a primary election, the voter shall also state the political party with which the voter affiliates and in whose primary the voter desires to vote, or if the voter is an unaffiliated voter permitted to vote in the primary of a particular party under G.S. 163–119, the voter shall state the name of the authorizing political party in whose primary he wishes to vote. The board member or employee to whom the voter gives this information shall announce the name and residence of the voter in a distinct tone of voice. After examining the registration records, an employee of the board shall state whether the person seeking to vote is duly registered. If the voter is found to be registered that voter may request that the authorized member or employee of the board furnish the voter with an application form as specified in G.S. 163–227. The voter shall complete the application in the presence of the authorized member or employee of the board, and shall deliver the application to that person.

(g) Notwithstanding any other provision of this section, a county board of elections by unanimous vote of all its members may provide for one or more sites in that county for absentee ballots to be applied for and cast under this section. Every individual staffing any of those sites shall be a member or full-time employee of the county board of elections or an employee of the county board of elections whom the board has given training equivalent to that given a full-time employee. Those sites must be approved by the State Board of Elections as part of a Plan for Implementation approved by both the county board of elections and by the State Board of Elections which shall also provide adequate security of the ballots and provisions to avoid allowing persons to vote who have already voted. The Plan for Implementation shall include a provision for the presence of political party observers at each one-stop site equivalent to the provisions in G.S. 163–45 for party observers at voting places on Election Day. A county board of elections may propose in its Plan not to offer one-stop voting at the county board of elections office; the State Board may approve that proposal in a Plan only if the Plan includes at least one site reasonably proximate to the county board of elections office and the State Board finds that the sites in the Plan as a whole provide adequate coverage of the county's electorate. If a county board of elections has considered a proposed Plan or Plans for Implementation and has been unable to reach unanimity in favor of a Plan, a member or members of that county board of elections may petition the State Board of Elections to adopt a plan for it. If petitioned, the State Board may also receive and consider alternative petitions from another member or members of that county board. The State Board of Elections may adopt a Plan for that county. The State Board, in that plan, shall take into consideration factors including geographic, demographic, and partisan interests of that county. Any plan adopted by either the county board of elections or the State Board of Elections under this subsection shall provide for the same days of operation and same number of hours of operation on each day for all sites in that county for that election. The requirement of the previous sentence does not apply to the county board of elections office itself nor, if one-stop voting is not conducted at the county board of elections office, to the reasonably proximate alternate site approved under this subsection.

SECTION 30.4. G.S. 163–166.7(c) reads as rewritten: "(c) The State Board of Elections shall promulgate rules for the process of voting. Those rules shall emphasize the appearance as well as the reality of dignity, good order, impartiality, and the convenience and privacy of the voter. Those rules, at a minimum, shall include procedures to ensure that all the following occur:

(1) The voting system remains secure throughout the period voting is being conducted.
(2) Only properly voted official ballots are introduced into the voting system.
(3) Except as provided by G.S. 163–166.9, no official ballots leave the voting enclosure during the time voting is being conducted there. The rules shall also provide that during that time no one shall remove from the voting enclosure any paper record or copy of an individually voted ballot or of any other device or item whose removal from the voting enclosure could permit compromise of the integrity of either the machine count or the paper record.

(4) All improperly voted official ballots are returned to the precinct officials and marked as spoiled.

(5) Voters leave the voting place promptly after voting.

(6) Voters not clearly eligible to vote in the precinct but who seek to vote there are given proper assistance in voting a provisional official ballot or guidance to another voting place where they are eligible to vote.

(7) Information gleaned through the voting process that would be helpful to the accurate maintenance of the voter registration records is recorded and delivered to the county board of elections.

(8) The registration records are kept secure. The State Board of Elections shall permit the use of electronic registration records in the voting place in lieu of or in addition to a paper pollbook or other registration record.

(9) Party observers are given access as provided by G.S. 163–45 to current information about which voters have voted.

(10) The voter, before voting, shall sign that voter's name on the poll book, other voting record, or voter authorization document. If the voter is unable to sign, a precinct official shall enter the person's name on the same document before the voter votes."

PART 33. REGULATE EXTENSION OF CLOSE OF POLLS SECTION 33.1. G.S. 163–166.01 reads as rewritten:

§ 163–166.01. Hours for voting. In every election, the voting place shall be open at 6:30 A.M. and shall be closed at 7:30 P.M. If the polls are delayed in opening for more than 15 minutes, or are interrupted for more than 15 minutes after opening, the State Board of Elections may extend the closing time by an equal number of minutes. As authorized by law, the State Board of Elections shall be available either in person or by teleconference on the day of election to approve any such extension. If any voter is in line to vote at the time the polls are closed, that voter shall be permitted to vote. No voter shall be permitted to vote who arrives at the voting place after the closing of the polls.

Any voter who votes after the statutory poll closing time of 7:30 P.M. by virtue of a federal or State court order or any other lawful order, including an order of a county board of elections, shall be allowed to vote, under the provisions of that order, only by using a provisional official ballot. Any special provisional official ballots cast under this section shall be separated, counted, and held apart from other provisional ballots cast by other voters not under the effect of the order extending the closing time of the voting place. If the court order has not been reversed or stayed by the time of the county canvass, the total for that category of provisional ballots shall be added to the official canvass.

PART 39. EXPEDITE VOTER LIST MAINTENANCE SECTION 39.1.(a) G.S. 163–33 reads as rewritten:

> § 163–33. Powers and duties of county boards of elections. The county boards of elections within their respective jurisdictions shall exercise all powers granted to such boards in this Chapter, and they shall perform all the duties imposed upon them by law, which shall include the following:
> (14) To make forms available for near relatives or personal representatives of a deceased voter's estate to provide signed statements of the status of a deceased voter to return to the board of elections of the county in which the deceased voter was registered. Forms may be provided, upon request, to any of the following: near relatives, personal representatives of a deceased voter's estate, funeral directors, or funeral service licensees.

SECTION 39.1.(b) G.S. 163–82.14(b) reads as rewritten: (b) Death.— The Department of Health and Human Services shall furnish free of charge

> To the State Board of Elections every month, in a format prescribed by the State Board of Elections, the names of deceased persons who were residents of the State. The State Board of Elections shall distribute every month to each county board of elections the names on that list of deceased persons who were residents of that county. The Department of Health and Human Services shall base each list upon information supplied by death certifications it received during the preceding month. Upon the receipt of those names, each county board of elections shall remove from its voter registration records any person the list shows to be dead. Each county board of elections shall also remove from its voter registration records a person identified as deceased by a signed statement of a near relative or personal representative of the estate of the deceased voter. The county board need not send any notice to the address of the person so removed.

SECTION 39.2. Article 13A of Chapter 90 of the General Statutes is amended by adding a new section to read:

§ 90–210.25C. Notification forms for deceased voters. (a) At the time funeral arrangements are made, a funeral director or funeral service licensee is encouraged to make available to near relatives of the deceased a form upon which the near relative may report the status of the deceased voter to the board of elections of the county in which the deceased was a registered voter.

(b) A funeral director or funeral service licensee may obtain forms for reporting the status of deceased voters from the county board of elections.

PART 49. VOTING IN INCORRECT PRECINCT SECTION 49.1. G.S. 163–55 reads as rewritten:

§ 163–55. Qualifications to vote; exclusion from electoral franchise. (a) Residence Period for State Elections.—Every person born in the United States, and every person who has been naturalized, and who shall have resided in the State of North Carolina and in precinct in which the person offers to vote for 30 days next preceding an election, shall, if otherwise qualified as prescribed in this Chapter, be qualified to vote in the precinct in which the person resides. Removal from one precinct to another in this State shall not operate to deprive any person of the right to vote in the precinct from which he the person has removed until 30 days after the person's removal.

Ohio Senate Bill 238 (2014)

AN ACT to amend sections 3509.01 and 3511.10 of the Revised Code to reduce the days for absent voting.

Be it enacted by the General Assembly of the State of Ohio:

SECTION 1. That sections 3509.01 and 3511.10 of the Revised Code be amended to read as follows:

Sec. 3509.01. (A) The board of elections of each county shall provide absent voter's ballots for use at every primary and general election, or special election to be held on the day specified by division (E) of section 3501.01 of the Revised Code for the holding of a primary election, designated by the general assembly for the purpose of submitting constitutional amendments proposed by the general assembly to the voters of the state. Those ballots shall be the same size, shall be printed on the same kind of paper, and shall be in the same form as has been approved for use at the election for which those ballots are to be voted; except that, in counties using marking devices, ballot cards may be used for absent voter's ballots, and those absent voters shall be instructed to record the vote in the manner provided on the ballot cards. In counties where punch card ballots are used, those absent voters shall be instructed to examine their marked ballot cards and to remove any chads that remain partially attached to them before returning them to election officials.

(B) The rotation of names of candidates and questions and issues shall be substantially complied with on absent voter's ballots, within the limitation of time allotted. Those ballots shall be designated as "Absent Voter's Ballots." Except as otherwise provided in division (D) of this section, those ballots shall be printed and ready for use as follows:

(1) For overseas voters and absent uniformed services voters eligible to vote under the Uniformed and Overseas Citizens Absentee Voting Act,

Pub. L. No. 99–410, 100 Stat. 924, 42 U.S.C. 1973ff, et seq., as amended, ballots shall be printed and ready for use other than in person on the forty-fifth day before the day of the election.

(2) For all voters, other than overseas voters and absent uniformed services voters, who are applying to vote absent voter's ballots other than in person, ballots shall be printed and ready for use on the first day after the close of voter registration before the election.

(3) For all voters who are applying to vote absent voter's ballots in person, ballots shall be printed and ready for use beginning on the first day after the close of voter registration before the election.

If, at the time for the close of in-person absent voting on a particular day, there are voters waiting in line to cast their ballots, the in-person absent voting location shall be kept open until such waiting voters have cast their absent voter's ballots.

(C) Absent voter's ballots provided for use at a general or primary election, or special election to be held on the day specified by division (E) of section 3501.01 of the Revised Code for the holding of a primary election, designated by the general assembly for the purpose of submitting constitutional amendments proposed by the general assembly to the voters of the state, shall include only those questions, issues, and candidacies that have been lawfully ordered submitted to the electors voting at that election.

(D) If the laws governing the holding of a special election on a day other than the day on which a primary or general election is held make it impossible for absent voter's ballots to be printed and ready for use by the deadlines established in division (B) of this section, absent voter's ballots for those special elections shall be ready for use as many days before the day of the election as reasonably possible under the laws governing the holding of that special election.

(E) A copy of the absent voter's ballots shall be forwarded by the director of the board in each county to the secretary of state at least twenty-five days before the election.

(F) As used in this section, "chad" and "punch card ballot" have the same meanings as in section 3506.16 of the Revised Code.

Sec. 3511.10. If, after the first day after the close of voter registration before a general or primary election and before the close of the polls on the day of that election, a valid application for uniformed services or overseas absent voter's ballots is delivered to the director of the board of elections at the office of the board by a person making the application on the person's own behalf, the director shall forthwith deliver to the person all uniformed services or overseas absent voter's ballots then ready for use, together with an identification envelope. The person shall then immediately retire to a voting booth in the office of the board, and mark the ballots. The person shall then fold each ballot separately so as to conceal the person's markings thereon, and deposit all of the ballots in the identification envelope and securely seal it. Thereupon the person shall fill in answers to the questions on the face of the identification envelope, and by writing the person's usual signature in the proper place thereon, the person shall declare under penalty of election falsification that the answers to those questions are true and correct to the best of that person's knowledge and belief. The person shall then deliver the identification envelope to the director. If thereafter, and before the third day preceding such election, the board provides additional separate official issue or special election ballots, as provided for in section 3511.04 of the Revised Code, the director shall promptly, and not later than twelve noon of the third day preceding the day of election, mail such additional ballots to such person at the address specified by that person for that purpose.

In the event any person serving in the armed forces of the United States is discharged after the closing date of registration, and that person or that person's spouse, or both, meets all the other qualifications set forth in section 3511.011 of the Revised Code, the person or spouse shall be permitted to vote prior to the date of the election in the office of the board in the person's or spouse's county, as set forth in this section.

SECTION 2. That existing sections 3509.01 and 3511.10 of the Revised Code are hereby repealed.

SECTION 3. Sections 1 and 2 of this act take effect June 1, 2014.

Texas Senate Bill 14 (2011&2014)

AN ACT relating to requirements to vote, including presenting proof of identification; providing criminal penalties.

BE IT ENACTED BY THE LEGISLATURE OF THE STATE OF TEXAS:

SECTION 1. Section 13.002, Election Code, is amended by adding Subsection (i) to read as follows:

(i) An applicant who wishes to receive an exemption from the requirements of Section 63.001(b) on the basis of disability must include with the person's application:
  (1) written documentation:
    (A) from the United States Social Security Administration evidencing the applicant has been determined to have a disability; or

(B) from the United States Department of Veterans Affairs evidencing the applicant has a disability rating of at least 50 percent; and

(2) a statement in a form prescribed by the secretary of state that the applicant does not have a form of identification acceptable under Section 63.0101.

SECTION 2. Section 15.001, Election Code, is amended by adding Subsection (c) to read as follows:

(c) A certificate issued to a voter who meets the certification requirements of Section 13.002(i) must contain an indication that the voter is exempt from the requirement to present identification other than the registration certificate before being accepted for voting.

SECTION 3. Effective September 1, 2011, Subchapter A, Chapter 15, Election Code, is amended by adding Section 15.005 to read as follows:

Sec. 15.005. NOTICE OF IDENTIFICATION REQUIREMENTS.

(a) The voter registrar of each county shall provide notice of the identification requirements for voting prescribed by Chapter 63 and a detailed description of those requirements with each voter registration certificate issued under Section 13.142 or renewal registration certificate issued under Section 14.001.

(b) The secretary of state shall prescribe the wording of the notice to be included on the certificate under this section.

SECTION 4. Subsection (a), Section 15.022, Election Code, is amended to read as follows:

(a) The registrar shall make the appropriate corrections in the registration records, including, if necessary, deleting a voter's name from the suspense list:

(1) after receipt of a notice of a change in registration information under Section 15.021;

(2) after receipt of a voter's reply to a notice of investigation given under Section 16.033;

(3) after receipt of a registration omissions list and any affidavits executed under Section 63.006 [63.007], following an election;

(4) after receipt of a voter's statement of residence executed under Section 63.0011;

(5) before the effective date of the abolishment of a county election precinct or a change in its boundary;

(6) after receipt of United States Postal Service information indicating an address reclassification;

(7) after receipt of a voter's response under Section 15.053; or

(8) after receipt of a registration application or change of address under Chapter 20.

SECTION 5. Effective September 1, 2011, Subchapter A, Chapter 31, Election Code, is amended by adding Section 31.012 to read as follows:

Sec. 31.012. VOTER IDENTIFICATION EDUCATION.

(a) The secretary of state and the voter registrar of each county that maintains a website shall provide notice of the identification requirements for voting prescribed by Chapter 63 on each entity's respective website in each language in which voter registration materials are available. The secretary of state shall prescribe the wording of the notice to be included on the websites.

(b) The secretary of state shall conduct a statewide effort to educate voters regarding the identification requirements for voting prescribed by Chapter 63.

(c) The county clerk of each county shall post in a prominent location at the clerk's office a physical copy of the notice prescribed under Subsection (a) in each language in which voter registration materials are available.

SECTION 6. Effective September 1, 2011, Section 32.111, Election Code, is amended by adding Subsection (c) to read as follows:

(c) The training standards adopted under Subsection (a) must include provisions on the acceptance and handling of the identification presented by a voter to an election officer under Section 63.001.

SECTION 7. Effective September 1, 2011, Subsection (a), Section 32.114, Election Code, is amended to read as follows:

(a) The county clerk shall provide one or more sessions of training using the standardized training program and materials developed and provided by the secretary of state under Section 32.111 for the election judges and clerks appointed to serve in elections ordered by the governor or a county authority. Each election judge shall complete the training program. Each election clerk shall complete the part of the training program relating to the acceptance and handling of the identification presented by a voter to an election officer under Section 63.001.

SECTION 8. Chapter 62, Election Code, is amended by adding Section 62.016 to read as follows:

Sec. 62.016. NOTICE OF ACCEPTABLE IDENTIFICATION OUTSIDE POLLING PLACES. The presiding judge shall post in a prominent place on the outside of each polling location a list of the acceptable forms of identification. The list must be printed using a font that is at least 24-point. The notice required under this section must be posted separately from any other notice required by state or federal law.

SECTION 9. Section 63.001, Election Code, is amended by amending Subsections (b), (c), (d), and (f) and adding Subsections (g) and (h) to read as follows:

(b) Except as provided by Subsection (h), on offering to vote, a voter must present to an election officer at the polling place one form of identification described by Section 63.0101.

(c) On presentation of the documentation required under Subsection (b) an election officer shall determine whether the voter's name on the documentation is on the list of registered voters for the precinct. If in making a determination under this subsection the election officer determines under standards adopted by the secretary of state that the voter's name on the documentation is substantially similar to but does not match exactly with the name on the list, the voter shall be accepted for voting under Subsection (d) if the voter submits an affidavit stating that the voter is the person on the list of registered voters.

(d) If, as determined under Subsection (c), the voter's name is on the precinct list of registered voters and the voter's identity can be verified from the documentation presented under Subsection (b), the voter shall be accepted for voting.

(f) After determining whether to accept a voter, an election officer shall return the voter's documentation to the voter.

(g) If the requirements for identification prescribed by Subsection (b) are not met, the voter may be accepted for provisional voting only under Section 63.011. For a voter who is not accepted for voting under this section, an election officer shall:

    (1) inform the voter of the voter's right to cast a provisional ballot under Section 63.011; and

    (2) provide the voter with written information, in a form prescribed by the secretary of state, that:

        (A) lists the requirements for identification;

        (B) states the procedure for presenting identification under Section 65.0541;

        (C) includes a map showing the location where identification must be presented; and

        (D) includes notice that if all procedures are followed and the voter is found to be eligible to vote and is voting in the correct precinct, the voter's provisional ballot will be accepted.

(h) The requirements for identification prescribed by Subsection (b) do not apply to a voter who is disabled and presents the voter's voter registration certificate containing the indication described by Section 15.001(c) on offering to vote.

SECTION 10. Subsection (a), Section 63.0011, Election Code, is amended to read as follows:

(a) Before a voter may be accepted for voting, an election officer shall ask the voter if the voter's residence address on the precinct list of registered voters is current and whether the voter has changed residence within the county. If the voter's address is omitted from the precinct list under Section 18.005(c), the officer shall ask the voter if the voter's residence, if listed, on identification presented by the voter under Section 63.001(b) is current and whether the voter has changed residence within the county.

SECTION 11. Effective September 1, 2011, Chapter 63, Election Code, is amended by adding Section 63.0012 to read as follows:
Sec. 63.0012. NOTICE OF IDENTIFICATION REQUIREMENTS TO CERTAIN VOTERS.

(a) An election officer shall distribute written notice of the identification that will be required for voting beginning with elections held after January 1, 2012, and information on obtaining identification without a fee under Chapter 521A, Transportation Code, to each voter who, when offering to vote, presents a form of identification that will not be sufficient for acceptance as a voter under this chapter beginning with those elections.
(b) The secretary of state shall prescribe the wording of the notice and establish guidelines for distributing the notice.
(c) This section expires September 1, 2017.

SECTION 12. Section 63.006, Election Code, is amended to read as follows:
Sec. 63.006. VOTER WITH REQUIRED DOCUMENTATION WHO IS NOT ON LIST.

(a) A voter who, when offering to vote, presents the documentation required under Section 63.001(b) but whose name is not on the precinct list of registered voters shall be accepted for voting if the voter also presents a voter registration certificate indicating that the voter is currently registered:

(1) in the precinct in which the voter is offering to vote; or

(2) in a different precinct in the same county as the precinct in which the voter is offering to vote and the voter executes an affidavit stating that the voter:

    (A) is a resident of the precinct in which the voter is offering to vote or is otherwise entitled by law to vote in that precinct;

    (B) was a resident of the precinct in which the voter is offering to vote at the time the information on the voter's residence address was last provided to the voter registrar;

    (C) did not deliberately provide false information to secure registration in a precinct in which the voter does not reside; and

    (D) is voting only once in the election.

(b) After the voter is accepted, an election officer shall:

(1) indicate BESIDE the voter's name on the poll list that the voter was accepted under this section; and

(2) enter the voter's name on the registration omissions list.

SECTION 13. Section 63.009, Election Code, is amended to read as follows:

Sec. 63.009. VOTER WITHOUT CERTIFICATE WHO IS NOT ON LIST.

A voter who does not present a voter registration certificate when offering to vote, and whose name is not on the list of registered voters for the precinct in which the voter is offering to vote, shall be accepted for provisional voting if the voter executes an affidavit in accordance with Section 63.011.

SECTION 14. Section 63.0101, Election Code, is amended to read as follows:

Sec. 63.0101. DOCUMENTATION OF PROOF OF IDENTIFICATION.

The following documentation is an acceptable form [as proof] of photo identification under this chapter:

(1) a driver's license, election identification certificate, or personal identification card issued to the person by the Department of Public Safety that has not [or a similar document issued to the person by an agency of another state, regardless of whether the license or card has] expired or that expired no earlier than 60 days before the date of presentation;

(2) a United States military identification card that contains the person's photograph that has not expired or that expired no earlier than 60 days before the date of presentation.

(3) United States citizenship certificate issued to the person that contains the person's photograph;

(4) a United States passport issued to the person that has not expired or that expired no earlier than 60 days before the date of presentation; or

(5) a license to carry a concealed handgun issued to the person by the Department of Public Safety that has not expired or that expired no earlier than 60 days before the date of presentation.

SECTION 15. Section 63.011, Election Code, is amended by amending Subsections (a) and (b) and adding Subsection (b-1) to read as follows:

(a) A person to whom Section 63.001(g) or 63.009 applies may cast a provisional ballot if the person executes an affidavit stating that the person:
   (1) is a registered voter in the precinct in which the person seeks to vote; and
   (2) is eligible to vote in the election.

(b) A form for an affidavit required by this section must be printed on an envelope in which the provisional ballot voted by the person may be placed and must include:
   (1) a space for entering the identification number of the provisional ballot voted by the person; and
   (2) a space for an election officer to indicate whether the person presented a form of identification described by Section 63.0101. (b-1) The affidavit form may include space for disclosure of any necessary information to enable the person to register to vote under Chapter 13. The secretary of state shall prescribe the form of the affidavit under this section.

SECTION 16. Subsection (b), Section 64.012, Election Code, is amended to read as follows:

(b) An offense under this section is a felony of the second degree unless the person is convicted of an attempt. In that case, the offense is a state jail felony.

SECTION 17. Subsection (b), Section 65.054, Election Code, is amended to read as follows:

(b) A provisional ballot shall be accepted if the board determines that:
   (1) from the information in the affidavit or contained in public records, the person is eligible to vote in the election and has not previously voted in that election;
   (2) the person:
       (A) meets the identification requirements of Section 63.001(b) at the time the ballot was cast or in the period prescribed under Section 65.0541;

(B) notwithstanding Chapter 110, Civil Practice and Remedies Code, executes an affidavit under penalty of perjury that states the voter has a religious objection to being photographed and the voter has consistently refused to be photographed for any governmental purpose from the time the voter has held this belief; or

(C) executes an affidavit under penalty of perjury that states the voter does not have any identification meeting the requirements of Section 63.001(b) as a result of a natural disaster that was declared by the president of the United States or the governor, occurred not earlier than 45 days before the date the ballot was cast, and caused the destruction of or inability to access the voter's identification; and

(3) the voter has not been challenged and voted a provisional ballot solely because the voter did not meet the requirements for identification prescribed by Section 63.001(b).

SECTION 18. Subchapter B, Chapter 65, Election Code, is amended by adding Section 65.0541 to read as follows:

Sec. 65.0541. PRESENTATION OF IDENTIFICATION FOR CERTAIN PROVISIONAL BALLOTS.

(a) A voter who is accepted for provisional voting under Section 63.011 because the voter does not meet the identification requirements of Section 63.001(b) may, not later than the sixth day after the date of the election:

(1) present a form of identification described by Section 63.0101 to the voter registrar for examination; or

(2) execute an affidavit described by Section 65.054(b)(2)(B) or (C) in the presence of the voter registrar.

(b) The secretary of state shall prescribe procedures as necessary to implement this section.

SECTION 19. Section 66.0241, Election Code, is amended to read as follows:

Sec. 66.0241. CONTENTS OF ENVELOPE NO. 4. Envelope no. 4 must contain:

(1) the precinct list of registered voters;

(2) the registration correction list;

(3) the registration omissions list;

(4) any statements of residence executed under Section 63.0011; and

(5) any affidavits executed under Section 63.006 or 63.011.

SECTION 20. Subtitle B, Title 7, Transportation Code, is amended by adding Chapter 521A to read as follows:

CHAPTER 521A. ELECTION IDENTIFICATION CERTIFICATE Sec. 521A.001. ELECTION IDENTIFICATION CERTIFICATE.

(a) The department shall issue an election identification certificate to a person who states that the person is obtaining the certificate for the purpose of satisfying Section 63.001(b), Election Code, and does not have another form of identification described by Section 63.0101, Election Code, and:

    (1) who is a registered voter in this state and presents a valid voter registration certificate; or

    (2) who is eligible for registration under Section 13.001, Election Code, and submits a registration application to the department.

(b) The department may not collect a fee for an election identification certificate or a duplicate election identification certificate issued under this section.

(c) An election identification certificate may not be used or accepted as a personal identification certificate.

(d) An election officer may not deny the holder of an election identification certificate the ability to vote because the holder has an election identification certificate rather than a driver's license or personal identification certificate issued under this subtitle.

(e) An election identification certificate must be similar in form to, but distinguishable in color from, a driver's license and a personal identification certificate. The department may cooperate with the secretary of state in developing the form and appearance of an election identification certificate.

(f) The department may require each applicant for an original or renewal election identification certificate to furnish to the department the information required by Section 521.142.

(g) The department may cancel and require surrender of an election identification certificate after determining that the holder was not entitled to the certificate or gave incorrect or incomplete information in the application for the certificate.

(h) A certificate expires on a date specified by the department, except that a certificate issued to a person 70 years of age or older does not expire.

SECTION 21. Sections 63.007 and 63.008, Election Code, are repealed.

SECTION 22. Effective September 1, 2011:

(1) as soon as practicable, the secretary of state shall adopt the training standards and develop the training materials required to implement the change in law made by this Act to Section 32.111, Election Code; and

(2) as soon as practicable, the county clerk of each county shall provide a session of training under Section 32.114, Election Code, using the standards

adopted and materials developed to implement the change in law made by this Act to Section 32.111, Election Code.

SECTION 23. The change in law made by this Act in amending Subsection (b), Section 64.012, Election Code, applies only to an offense committed on or after January 1, 2012. An offense committed before January 1, 2012, is covered by the law in effect when the offense was committed, and the former law is continued in effect for that purpose. For purposes of this section, an offense is committed before January 1, 2012, if any element of the offense occurs before that date.

SECTION 24. Effective September 1, 2011, state funds disbursed under Chapter 19, Election Code, for the purpose of defraying expenses of the voter registrar's office in connection with voter registration may also be used for additional expenses related to coordinating voter registration drives or other activities designed to expand voter registration. This section expires January 1, 2013.

SECTION 25. Every provision in this Act and every application of the provisions in this Act are severable from each other. If any application of any provision in this Act to any person or group of persons or circumstances is found by a court to be invalid, the remainder of this Act and the application of the Act's provisions to all other persons and circumstances may not be affected. All constitutionally valid applications of this Act shall be severed from any applications that a court finds to be invalid, leaving the valid applications in force, because it is the legislature's intent and priority that the valid applications be allowed to stand alone. Even if a reviewing court finds a provision of this Act invalid in a large or substantial fraction of relevant cases, the remaining valid applications shall be severed and allowed to remain in force.

Bibliography

Books

Alexander, Michelle. *The New Jim Crow: Mass Incarceration in the Age of Color-blindness*. New York: The New Press, 2010.

Barker, Lucius J., Mack H. Jones, and Katherine Tate. *African Americans and the American Political System*, 4th ed. Upper Saddle, NJ: Prentice Hall, 1999.

Brown, Michael K. *Race, Money and the American Welfare State*. Ithaca, NY: Cornell University Press, 1999.

Connolly, Sean. *The Right to Vote*. North Mankato, MN: Smart Apple Media, 2006.

Danielson, Chris. *The Color of Politics: Racism in the American Political Arena Today*. Santa Barbara, CA: Praeger, 2013.

Elazar, Daniel J. *American Federalism: A View from the States*. New York: Thomas Y. Crowell, 1984.

Elazar, Daniel J. *The American Mosaic: The Impact of the States*. New York: Harper and Row, 1994.

Goldfield, Michael. *The Color of Politics: Race and the Mainsprings of American Politics*. New York: New Press, 1997.

Key, V.O. *Southern Politics in State and Nation*. Knoxville, TN: The University of Tennessee Press, 1984 (1949).

Kousser, J. Morgan. *The Shaping of Southern Politics: Suffrage Restriction and the Establishment of the One-Party South, 1880–1910*. New Haven: Yale University Press, 1974.

Lawson, Stephen F. *Black Ballots: Voting Rights in the South, 1944–1969*. New York: Columbia University Press, 1976.

Manning, Marable, and Leith Mullings, eds. *Let Nobody Turn US Around: Voices of Resistance, Reform, and Renewal*, 2nd ed. New York: Rowman & Littlefield, 2009.

McAdam, Doug. *Political Process and the Development of Black Insurgency, 1930–1970*. Chicago: University of Chicago Press, 1982.

McMillen, Neil R. *Dark Journey: Black Mississippians in the Age of Jim Crow*. Urbana and Chicago: University of Illinois Press, 1989.

Mendelberg, Tali. *The Race Card: Campaign Strategy, Implicit Messages, and the Norm of Equality*. Princeton, NJ: Princeton University Press, 2001.

Quarles, Benjamin. *The Negro in the Making of America*. New York: Macmillan, 1969.

Quadagno, Jill. 1994. *The Color of Welfare*. New York: Oxford University Press.

Valelly, Richard M. *The Two Reconstructions: The Struggle for Black Enfranchisement*. Chicago: University of Chicago Press, 2004.

Walton, Hanes, Jr. *Black Politics: A Theoretical and Structural Analysis*. New York: J.B. Lippincott Company, 1972.

Walton, Hanes, Jr., and Robert C. Smith. *American Politics and the African American Quest for Universal Freedom*, 6th ed. Boston: Longman, 2012.

Walton, Hanes, Jr., and Robert C. Smith. *American Politics and the African American Quest for Universal Freedom*, 7th ed. Boston: Pearson, 2015.

Woodward, C. Vann. *The Strange Career of Jim Crow,* 3rd ed. New York: Oxford, 1955, 2001.

Articles and Chapters

Basehart, Harry, and John Comer. "Partisan and Incumbent Effects in State Legislative Redistricting." *Legislative Studies Quarterly* 16, no. 1 (1991): 63–79.

Behrens, Angela, Christopher Uggen, and Jeff Manza. "Ballot Manipulation and the 'Menace of Negro Domination': Racial Threat and Felon Disenfranchisement in the United States, 1850–2002." *American Journal of Sociology* 109 (2003): 559–605.

Beyerlein, Kraig, and Kenneth T. Andrews. "Black Voting During the Civil Rights Movement: A Micro-Level Analysis." *Social Forces* (University of North Carolina Press) 87, no. 1 (2008).

Davidson, Chandler. "The Historical Context of Voter Photo-ID Laws." *PS: Political Science and Politics* 42, no.1 (2009): 93.

Davidson, Chandler, and Bernard Grofman, *Harvard Law Review* 108 (April 1995).

Dawson-Edwards, Cherie. "Enfranchising Convicted Felons: Current Research on Opinions Towards Felon Voting Rights. *Journal of Offender Rehabilitation* 46, nos. 3 and 4 (2008): 13–29.

Eisenberg, Lynn. "States as Laboratories for Federal Reform: Case Studies in Felon Disenfranchisement Law." *New York University Journal of Legislation & Public Policy* 15, no. 2 (2012): 539–83.

Engstrom, Richard L. "Cumulative and Limited Voting: Minority Electoral Opportunities and More (Voting 45 Years after the Voting Rights Act)." *Saint Louis University Public Law Review* 1 (2010).

Ewald, Alec C. "Civil Death: The Ideological Paradox of Criminal Disenfranchisement Law in the United States." *University of Wisconsin Law Review* (2002): 1045–137.

Ewald, Alec C. "Criminal Disenfranchisement and the Challenge of American Federalism." *Publius: The Journal of Federalism* 39 (2009), no. 3: 534.

Feldman, Stanley, and Leonie Huddy. "Racial Resentment and White Opposition to Race-Conscious Programs: Principles or Prejudice?" *American Political Science Review* 90 (2005): 593–604.

Hill, Rickey. "The Voting Rights Act of 1965: Consequences and Challenges after 30 Years." In *American National and State Government: An African American View of the Return of Redemptionist Politics,* 2nd ed., edited by Claude W. Barnes, Samuel A. Moseley, and James D. Steele, 544–55. Dubuque, IA: Kendall/Hunt Publishing Company, 2007.

Hood, M.V., Quentin Kidd, and Irwin L. Morris. "The Key Issue: Constituency Effects and Southern Senators' Roll-Call Voting On Civil Rights." *Legislative Studies Quarterly* 4 (2001): 599–621.

Itzkowitz, Howard, and Lauren Oldak. 1973. "Restoring the Ex-Offender's Right to Vote: Background and Development." *American Criminal Law Review* 11 (1973): 721–70.

King, James D., and James W. Riddlespeger Jr. "Presidential Leadership of Congressional Civil Rights Voting: The Cases of Eisenhower and Johnson." *Policy Studies Journal* 21, no. 3 (1993): 544–55.

Lewis-Beck, Michael, and Peverill Squire. "The Politics of Institutional Choice: Presidential Ballot Access for Third Parties in the United States." *British Journal of Political Science* 23, no. 3 (1995): 419–27.

Lyles, W. William. "Challenges to Felon Disenfranchisement Laws: Past, Present and Future." *Alabama Law Review* 8, no. 3 (2014): 615–29, http://www.sentencingproject.org/doc/publications/fd_research_liles.pdf (accessed November 21, 2014).

Manza, Jeff, and Christopher Uggen. "Punishment and Democracy: Disenfranchisement of Nonincarcerated Felons in the United States." *Perspectives on Politics* 2, no. 3 (2004): 491–505.

Murphy, Daniel S., Adam J. Newmark, and Phillip J. Ardoin. "Political and Demographic Explanations of Felon Disenfranchisement Policies in the States." *Justice Policy Journal* 3, no. 1 (2006): 14.

Neiman, Donald G. "Equality Deferred, 1870–1900." In *The Civil Rights Movement,* edited by Jeffrey O.G. Ogbar. Boston: Houghton Mifflin Company, 2009.

Pildes, Richard H. "The Politics of Race, review of Quiet Revolution in the South." *Harvard Law Review* 108, no. 6 (1995): 1359–92.

Pinderhughes, Dianne. "Past Patterns and Lessons Learned: Continuing Efforts at Participation in Empowerment Policy." In *Beyond the Color Line: Race, Representation, and Community in the New Century,* edited by Alex Willingham. New York: Brennan Center for Justice at New York University Law School, 2002.

Sperling, Jonathan M. "Equal Protection and Race-conscious Reapportionment: *Shaw v. Reno.*" *Harvard Journal of Law and Public Policy* 17, no. 1 (1994): 283–92.

Tyner, Jarvis Tyner. "Crime-Causes and Cures." In *Let Nobody Turn Us Around: Voices of Resistance, Reform, and Renewal,* edited by Marable Manning and Leith Mullings, 606–15. Lanham, MD: Rowman & Littlefield, 2009.

Yoshinaka, Antoine, and Christian R. Grose. "Partisan Politics and Electoral Design: The Enfranchisement of Felons and Ex-Felons in the United States, 1960–1999." *State and Local Government Review* 37 (2005): 49–60.

Court Cases

Anderson v. Celebrezze, 460 US 780–1983.

Applewhite v Commonwealth of Pennsylvania, 330 M.D. 2012.

Beer v. United States, 425 U.S. 130 (1976).

Burdick v. Takushi, 504 U.S. 428, 433–34, 112 S.Ct. 2059, 119 L.Ed.2d 245 (1992).

Bush v. Vera, 517 U.S. 952 (1996).

Crawford v. Marion County Election Board. Nos. 06–2218, 06–2317.

Dred Scott v. Sanford, 60 U.S. 393 (1857).

Grovey v. Townsend, 295 U.S. 45 (1935).

Harper v. Virginia Board of Elections, 383 U.S. 663.

Indiana Democratic Party v. Todd Rokita. 458 F. Supp. 2d 775; 2006 U.S. District.

League of Women Voters of Indiana v. Rokita.

Lubin v. Panish, 415 U.S. 709 (1974).

McCafferty v. Guyer, 59 Pa. 109 (1868).

Miller v. Johnson, 515 U.S. 900 (1995).

Mobile v. Bolden, 446 U.S. 55 (1980).

Nixon v. Condon, 286 U.S. 73 (1932).

Nixon v. Herndon, 273 U.S. 536 (1927).

Northwest Austin Municipal Utility District No. 1 v. Holder, 557 U.S. 193 (2009).

Patterson v. Barlow, 60 Pa. 54 (1869).

Pennsylvanians against Gambling Expansion Fund, Inc. v. Com., 583 Pa. 275 (2005).

Shaw v. Hunt, 517 U.S. 899 (1996).

Shaw v. Reno, 509U.S. 630 (1993).

Shelby County v. Holder, 570 U.S. ___ (2013).

Smith v. Allwright, 321 U.S. 649 (1944).

South Carolina v. Katzenbach, 383 U.S. 301 (1966).

Texas v. Holder, 1:12-cv-00128.

Thornburgh v. Gingles, 478 U.S. 30 (1986).

United States v. Marcavage, 609 F.3d 264, 273 (3d Cir. 2010).

Winston v. Moore, 244 Pa. 447, 454 (1914).

Newspapers

Barnes, Robert. "Colorado May Have Most Closely Watched Election Official." *Washington Post* (September 21, 2012): A05.

Bartels, Lynn. "Voter Probe Snares Four." *Denver Post* (November 23, 2013): 3A.

Bennett, George. "County Raises Red Flags on 106 Questionable Voter Applications." *Palm Beach Post* (September 26, 2012): 1A.

Chen, David W. "Among Voters in New Jersey, G.O.P. Sees Dead People." *New York Times* (September 16, 2005): B5.

Cleeland, Nancy. "Hermandad Blames INS for Confusing Illegal Voters." *Los Angeles Times* (January 3, 1997): B1.

"Clerk's Office Allows 153 Naturalized Citizens to Vote in Primary." *AP State & Local Wire, Honolulu* (September 27, 2000).

Davis, Jingle. "State Plans to Update Voter Lists." *Atlanta J.-Const.* (February 10, 2001): 4H.

DeAgostino, Martin. "New Senator's Bill Passes Senate; Legislation for Red-Light Cameras Get 31–17 Vote." *South Bend Tribune* (March 2, 2005): B1.

DeAgostino, Martin. "One Compromised Reached; Middle Ground Found on Inspector General Bill, But not Voter ID Measure." *South Bend Tribune* (March 15, 2005): B1.

DeAgostino, Martin. "Senate OK's Voter ID Bill; Governor Likely to Sign Measure." *South Bend Tribune* (April 13, 2005): B1.

Giammarise, Kate. "Corbett Won't Contest Voter ID Ruling; But He Hints at Push for New Legislation." *Pittsburgh Post-Gazette* (May 9, 2014): A1.

Kevin, Dayton. "City Steps Up Search for Illegal Voters." *Honolulu Advertiser* (September 8, 2000): A1.

McBride, Jessica, and Dave Umhoefer. "12 Votes Attributed to Dead People." *Milwaukee Journal Sentinel* (January 22, 2001): 2A.

"No Fraud in Rock the Vote." *Tampa Bay Time* (January 11, 2013): 6B.

Schwartz, John. "Judge in Landmark Case Disavows Support for Voter ID." *New York Times* (October 16, 2013): 16.

Scott, Ishikawa. "Illegal Voters." *Honolulu Advertiser* (September 9, 2000): A1.

Scott, Ishikawa. "Isle Officials Seek Ways to Prevent Illegal Voting." *Honolulu Advertiser* (September 7, 2000): A1.

Shannon, Brad. "Rossi's Case Enters Key Phase." *Olympian* (May 1, 2005): 1C.

"State Uncovers Voter Registration Fraud." *Tampa Bay Times* (March 6, 2013): 8B.

Vogel, Kenneth. "King to Challenge 110 More Votes." *News Tribune* (April 29, 2005): B2.

Wagner, Michael, and Nancy Cleeland. "D.A. Drops Voter Probe After Indictments Rejected." *Los Angeles Times* (December 20, 1997): A1.

Warren, Peter. "Jones: 5,087 Registrants Potential Noncitizens." *Los Angeles Times* (October 14, 1997): B1.

State, Local, and Federal Laws

Election Code, 25 P.S. §3050(a.2).

42 U.S.C. §1973(a).

The House Joint Resolution proposing the Thirteenth Amendment to the Constitution, January 31, 1865; Enrolled Acts and Resolutions of Congress, 1789–1999; General Records of the United States Government; Record Group 11; National Archives.

The House Joint Resolution proposing the Fourteenth Amendment to the Constitution, June 16, 1866; Enrolled Acts and Resolutions of Congress, 1789–1999; General Records of the United States Government; Record Group 11; National Archives.

The House Joint Resolution proposing the Fifteenth Amendment to the Constitution, December 7, 1868; Enrolled Acts and Resolutions of Congress, 1789–1999; General Records of the United States Government; Record Group 11; National Archives.

Indiana Constitution Article 2, Section 2.

Mississippi Constitution of 1890, Article 12, Section 241.

Pennsylvania House Bill 934 (2011).

Pub. Law 107–252 § 301; 42 U.S.C. § 15481.

Public Law 109, 2005.

Public Law 109–246, 109th Congress, 2006.

Texas Senate Bill 14, 2011.

Government Documents

"Breaking New Ground—African American Senators. United States Senate." http://www.senate.gov/pagelayout/history/h_multi_sections_and_teasers/Photo_Exhibit_African_American_Senators.htm (accessed August 18, 2014).

Burton, Cynthia. "No Beyond-the-Grave Balloting Cited." *Philadelphia Inquirer*, November 9, 2005. http://articles.philly.com/2005-11-09/news/25430338_1_ballots-polling-place-democrats-election-day (accessed November 30, 2014).

Cox, Cathy. "The 2000 Election: A Wake-Up Call for Reform and Change." 11, no. 3, January 2001.

Ferro, John. "Deceased Residents on Statewide Voter List." *Poughkeepsie Journal*, October 29, 2006. http://www.poughkeepsiejournal.com/apps/pbcs.dll/article?AID=2006610290381&template=printart (accessed November 30, 2014).

"50th Anniversary of the Civil Rights Act: July 2" *United States Census Bureau.* http://www.census.gov/newsroom/releases/archives/facts_for_features_special_editions/cb14-ff17.html (accessed August 18, 2014).

File, Thom, and Sarah Crissey. Voting and Registration in the Election of November 2008. *Current Population Reports,* July 10, 2012. http://www.census.gov/prod/2010pubs/p20-562.pdf (accessed November 9, 2014).

"Former Governor's Bios." National Governors Association. http://www.nga.org/cms/FormerGovBios?begincac77e09-db17-41cb-9de0-687b843338d0=25&endcac77e09-db17-41cb-9de0-687b843338d0=49&pagesizecac77e09-db17-41cb-9de0-687b843338d0=25&higherOfficesServed=&lastName=&sex=

Any&honors=&submit=Search&college=&state=Any&inOffice=Any&party=&
race=Any&biography=&birthState=Any&religion=&militaryService=&
nbrterms=Any&firstName=&warsServed=& (accessed August 18, 2014).

"Most Children Younger Than Age 1 are Minorities." United States Census Bureau,
May 17, 2012. https://www.census.gov/newsroom/releases/archives/population/
cb12-90.html (accessed November 21, 2014).

Perez, Thomas. "United States Department of Justice, Civil Rights Division."
March 12, 2012. http://s3.amazonaws.com/static.texastribune.org/media/doc
uments/2011-2775_ltr.pdf (accessed July 30, 2014).

United States Department of Commerce, Bureau of the Census. June 1979. The
Social and Economic Status of the Black Population in the United States:
An Historical View, 1790–1978. Current Population Reports, Special Studies
Series P-23, No. 80.

United States Department of Commerce, Bureau of Census. November 13, 2013.
http://www.census.gov/ (accessed August 20, 2014).

Online Publications

Aguilar, Julian. "Feds Reject Texas Voter ID Law." Texas Tribune, March 12, 2012.
http://www.texastribune.org/2012/03/12/feds-reject-texas-voter-id-law
(accessed March 12, 2012).

Allen, Jessie. "Look at the History of Voter ID: A Case Cited to Support Pennsylvania's New Voter ID Law Instead Calls it into Question." Pittsburg Post-Gazette,
September 11, 2012. www.post-gazette.com/Op-Ed/2012/09/11/Look-at-the-
history-of-voter-ID-A-case-cited-to-support-Pennsylvania-s-new-voter-ID-
law-instead-calls-it-i nto-question/stories/201209110190#ixzz26AVgDxOl
(accessed August 2, 2014).

"America Votes 2004." http://www.cnn.com/ELECTION/2004/pages/results/
states/AZ/I/01/epolls.0.html (accessed August 1, 2013).

Berman, Ari. "North Carolina Will Determine the Future of the Voting Rights
Act." The Nation, July 10, 2014. http://www.thenation.com/blog/180608/
north-carolina-will-determine-future-voting-rights-act (accessed November 5, 2014).

Berman, Ari. "Republicans Used to Support Voting Rights—What Happened."
The Nation, April 2014. http://www.thenation.com/blog/179325/democrats-sup
port-voting-rights-republicans-should-too# (accessed August 20, 2014).

Berman, Ari. "The Supreme Court Approves the Country's Worst Voting Restrictions in North Carolina." The Nation, October 8, 2014. http://www.thenation
.com/blog/181925/supreme-court-approves-countrys-worst-voting-restric
tions-north-carolina (accessed November 6, 2014).

Bingham, Amy. "Voter Fraud: Non-Existent Problem or Election-Threatening Epidemic?" http://abcnews.go.com/Politics/OTUS/voter-fraud-real-rare/story?
id=17213376 (accessed August 23, 2014).

Brennan Center for Justice at New York University School of Law. *North Carolina NAACP v. McCrory* (Amicus Brief), October 1 2014. http://www.brennan center.org/legal-work/north-carolina-naacp-v-mccrory-amicus-brief (accessed November 2, 2014).

Carson, E. Ann, and William J. Sabol. "Prisoners in 2011." NCJ 239808. Washington, DC: United States Department of Justice, Office of Justice Programs, Bureau of Justice Statistics, December 2012. http://www.bjs.gov/content/pub/pdf/p11 .pdf (accessed November 28, 2014).

Center for Voting and Democracy. 2009. http://archive.fairvote.org/righttovote/ timeline.htm (accessed October 30, 2014).

Chung, Jean. "Felony Disenfranchisement: A Primer," The Sentencing Project, April 2014. http://www.sentencingproject.org/doc/publications/fd_Felony%20Dis enfranchisement %20Primer.pdf (accessed August 23, 2014).

"Creation and Evolution of the Congressional Black Caucus." History, Art, and Archives, United States House of Representatives. http://history.house.gov/ Exhibitions-and-Publications/BAIC/Historical-Essays/Permanent-Interest/ Congressional-Black-Caucus/ (accessed October 23, 2014).

Evans, Rachel and Joanna E. Cuevas Ingram. "Voting Rights Barriers and Discrimination in Twenty-First Century California: 2000–2013." San Francisco, CA: Lawyers' Committee for Civil Rights of the San Francisco Bay Area, 2004. http://www.lccr.com/wp-content/uploads/Voting-Rights-Barriers-In-21st-Century-Cal-Update.pdf (accessed November 24, 2014).

Everett, Burgess. "Rand Paul Seeks to Expand Voting Rights to Some Ex-Cons." *Politico,* June 22, 2014. http://www.politico.com/story/2014/06/rand-paul-voting-rights-ex-felons-108156.html (accessed August 20, 2014).

Fessler, Pam. "Recent Rulings Alter Voting Laws Ahead of November Election." *It's All Politics: Political News from NPR,* October 16, 2014. http://www.npr.org/ blogs/itsallpolitics/2014/10/16/356710120/recent-rulings-alter-voting-laws-ahead-of-november-election (accessed November 6, 2014).

Friedman, Emily. "Did Joe Wilson's 'You Lie' Outburst Cross the Line on Congressional Courtesy?" *ABC News,* September 10, 2009. http://abcnews.go.com/ Politics/rep-wilsons-liar-shout-violated-congressional-courtesy/story?id= 8537370 (accessed September 22, 2014).

Gomez, Alan. "Kansas, Arizona Win Citizenship Ruling." *USA Today,* March 17, 2014. http://www.usatoday.com/story/news/nation/2014/03/19/immigration-proof-of-citizenship-kansas-arizona/6614245/ (accessed November 6, 2013).

"Governor Corbett Issues Statement on Recent Commonwealth Court Ruling on Voter ID." May 8, 2014. http://www.pa.gov/Pages/NewsDetails.aspx?agency= Governors%20Office&item=15598#.U8f8YZRdXng (accessed July 17, 2014).

Hasen, Richard L. "Dawn patrol." *New York Times,* October 18, 2014. http://www .slate.com/articles/news_and_politics/jurisprudence/2014/10/ginsburg_s_ dissent_in_texas_voter_id_law_supreme_court_order.html (accessed November 5, 2014).

Holley, Joe. "Holder calls Texas voter ID law a poll tax." *Houston Chronicle,* July 10, 2012. http://www.chron.com/news/houston-texas/article/Holder-calls-Texas-voter-ID-law-a-poll-tax-3697707.php#photo-3179975 (accessed July 30, 2014).

Krogstad, Jens and Richard Fry. "Dept. of Ed. Projects public schools will be 'majority-minority' this fall." *Pew Research,* August 18, 2014. http://www.pewresearch.org/fact-tank/2014/08/18/u-s-public-schools-expected-to-be-majority-minority-starting-this-fall/ (accessed November 21, 2014).

Krogstad, Jens and Mark Lopez. "Hispanic Voters in the 2014 Election." *Pew Hispanic Center,* November 7, 2014. http://www.pewhispanic.org/2014/11/07/hispanic-voters-in-the-2014-election/ (accessed November 21, 2014).

Levitt, Justin. "The Truth about Voter Fraud," Brennan Center for Justice, November, 2007. http://www.brennancenter.org/publication/truth-about-voter-fraud (accessed August 23, 2014).

Liptak, Alan. "Supreme Court Allows Texas to Use Strict Voter ID Law in Coming Election." *New York Times,* October 18, 2014. http://www.nytimes.com/2014/10/19/us/supreme-court-upholds-texas-voter-id-law.html?ref=politics&_r=0 (accessed November 5, 2014).

Lopez, Mark, Jens Krogstad, Eileen Patten, and Ana Gonzalez-Barrera. "Latino Voters and the 2014 Midterm Election." *Pew Hispanic Center,* October 16, 2014. http://www.pewhispanic.org/2014/10/16/latino-voters-and-the-2014-mid term-elections/ (accessed November 21, 2014).

Meltzer, Erica. "Boulder County DA Stan Garnett Clears All 17 Suspected Illegal Voters." *Daily Camera,* August 14, 2013. http://www.dailycamera.com/news/boulder/ci_23864751/boulder-da-stan-garnett-clears-illegal-voters-gessler (accessed June 15, 2014).

Murray, Jon. "Video Activist James O'Keefe Targets Colorado's New Mail Voting Law." *Denver Post,* October 22, 2014. http://blogs.denverpost.com/thespot/2014/10/22/video-activist-james-okeefe-targets-colorados-mail-voting/114385/#more-114385 (accessed November 28, 2014).

National Conference of State Legislatures. "Felon Voting Rights." 2014. http://www.ncsl.org/research/elections-and-campaigns/felon-voting-rights.aspx#back ground (accessed October 23, 2014).

No Author. "Ask the Advocate: Is Voter Fraud Really a Problem in Louisiana?" *The Advocate,* November 20, 2014. http://theadvocate.com/news/10719441-123/ask-the-advocate-is (accessed November 28, 2014).

Passel Jeffery, and D'Vera Cohn. "How Many Hispanics? Comparing New Census Counts with the Latest Census Estimates." *Pew Hispanic Center,* March 15, 2011. http://www.pewhispanic.org/files/reports/139.pdf (accessed November 21, 2014).

ProCon.or. "State Felon Voting Laws." July 15, 2014. http://felonvoting.procon.org/view.resource.php?resourceID=000286&print=true (accessed August 20, 2014).

Rau, Alia Beard. "Illegal Immigrant Vote-Fraud Cases Rare in Arizona." *The Republic,* November 18, 2013. http://www.azcentral.com/news/politics/articles/20131105 arizona-immigrant-vote-fraud-rare.html (accessed June 15, 2014).

Richardson, Valerie. "Undercover Video Shows Progressives Condoning Voter Fraud in Colorado." *Washington Times,* October 22, 2014. http://www.wash ingtontimes.com/news/2014/oct/22/undercover-video-progressives-voter-fraud-colorado/ (accessed November 28, 2014).

Ross, Janell. "Where Voting Rights Are Under Attack." *The Root,* August 5, 2013. http://www.theroot.com/articles/politics/2013/08/voting_rights_under_ attack_states_move_to_change_laws.html (accessed August 20, 2014).

Rushton, Bruce. "Dead Man Voting." *Riverfront Times,* April 24, 2002. http://www.riv erfronttimes.com/2002-04-24/news/dead-man-voting/ (accessed June 14, 2014).

The Sentencing Project. "Felony Disenfranchisement." 2014. www.sentencingproject .org/template/page/cfm?id=133 (accessed September 3, 2014).

Slater, Wayne. "Few Texas Voter-Fraud Cases Would Have Been Prevented by Photo ID Law, Review Shows." *Dallas News,* September 8, 2013. http://www.dallas news.com/news/politics/headlines/20130908-few-texas-voter-fraud-cases-would-have-been-prevented-by-photo-id-law-review-shows.ece (accessed July 30, 2014).

Sneed, Tierney. "Voting Rights Battles Rock Lead—Up to Elections." *U.S. News & World Report,* October 17, 2014. http://www.usnews.com/news/articles/2014/ 10/17/voting-law-challenges-in-wisconsin-arkansas-texas-and-elsewhere-roil-election-lead-up (accessed November 2, 2014).

Thernstrom, Abigail. Redistricting, Race, and the Voting Rights Act. *National Affairs,* 1–8, August 20, 2014. http://www.nationalaffairs.com/publications/ detail/print/redistricting-race-and-the-voting-rights-act (accessed August 20, 2014).

Uggen, Christopher, Sarah Shannon, Jeff Manza. "State-level Estimates of Felon Disfranchisement in the United States." Washington, DC: The Sentencing Project, 2010. http://www.sentencingproject.org/doc/publications/fd_State_ Level_Estimates_of_Felon_Disen_2010.pdf (accessed October 24, 2014).

Uggen, Christopher, Sarah Shannon, and Jeff Manza. "State-level Estimates of Felon Disfranchisement in the United States." Washington, DC: The Sentencing Project, 2012. http://www.sentencingproject.org/doc/publications/fd_State_ Level_Estimates_of_Felon_Disen_2010.pdf (accessed November 3, 2014).

Van Sickler, Michael. "Two Voter Fraud Cases Close with Meager Findings." *Tampa Bay Times,* September 4, 2013. http://www.tampabay.com/news/politics/ stateroundup/two-voter-fraud-cases-close-with-meager-findings/2139886 (accessed June 16, 2014).

Von Spakovsky, Hans. "The Threat of Non-Citizen Voting." The Heritage Foundation. http://www.heritage.org/research/reports/2008/07/the-threat-of-non-citizen-voting (accessed July 18, 2014).

Weiser, Wendy R. "How Much of a Difference Did New Voting Restrictions Make in Yesterday's Close Races?" Brennan Center for Justice at New York University School of Law, November 5, 2014. http://www.brennancenter.org/print/12822 (accessed November 5, 2014).

"What Is Same Day Registration? Where Is It Available?" *Demos,* March 1, 2013. http://www.demos.org/publication/what-same-day-registration-where-it-available (accessed November 1, 2014).

Wilson, David C., Michael L. Owens, and Darren W. Davis, "How Racial Attitudes and Ideology Affect Political Rights for Felon." Unpublished paper, 2014. http://www.academia.edu/6255670/How_Racial_Attitudes_and_Ideology_Affect_Political_Rights_for_Felons (accessed November 1, 2014).

Wolf, Richard. "Supreme Court Blacks Wisconsin's Voter ID Law." *USA Today, October* 9, 2014. http://www.usatoday.com/story/news/politics/2014/10/09/supreme-court-wisconsin-voter-id/16985963/ (accessed November 1, 2014).

Zachary, Roth. "After Takeover, Nevada GOPers Ready Voter ID." *MSNBC,* November 12, 2014. *MSNBC,* http://www.msnbc.com/msnbc/after-takeover-nevada-gopers-ready-voter (accessed November 28, 2014).

Index

Abbott, Greg, 119, 143, 160

Absentee ballots: in Georgia, 91; in Indiana, 73, 77, 91, 92, 93; in Michigan, xv; need for proof of identification for, 98; in Pennsylvania, 98, 103; in Texas, 127; voter fraud and, xiii, xx, 77; in West Virginia, 51

ACORN, undercover video of, xix

Advancement Project, 151

African Americans: beliefs on voting, 12; citizenship for, 38; Civil Rights Movement and, 1, 5, 19, 148; commitment to Democratic Party, 11, 12, 120, 123, 156, 160; Congressional Black Caucus and, 156; criminalization of, 43–46; cumulative misery of, 46; discrimination against, 42, 150, 154; disparate impact and, 103, 151; in elected office, 20, 138, 140, 141; electoral power of, 11–12; exclusion from voting, 3, 47; felon disenfranchisement and, 31, 35, 37, 39, 43, 47, 58; by free-slave status, 6t; Great Depression and, 12; impact of voter identification law on, 128, 132, 151; incarceration of, 37, 45, 47; increase in voting, 137; influence of, in politics, 61; life in South, 137, 160; opening up of political arena to, 22; perceptions of, 60; political allegiance of, 11; political empowerment of, 17; political environment of, 3; political parity between whites and, 139; political participation by, 4, 137; political power of, 40, 42; poll tax aimed at, 120; population growth of, 99; public sector and, 22; quality of life for, 2, 23; redrawing of congressional district lines, 20; relative deprivation exhibited in, 2; represssiveness of current policy environment of, 37; Republican Party and, 11, 156; securing political rights for, 1; stack of judicial system against, 39; stereotypes about, 60; struggle for social inclusion, 2; support for Obama, 30, 39–40; voter identification laws and, 82; voter participation and, 21, 22, 27, 29; voter registration by, 15, 16, 137; voter turnout of, 28, 29–30, 138; voting patterns of, 15; voting rights for, 5, 7, 8, 9, 10, 11, 17, 21, 137, 148, 149; voting strength of, 24; young, as most politically engaged, 24; youth vote for Obama, 27

Alabama: black voter registration in, 15; changes in voting rules in, 17–18; federal oversight of voting in, 21; felon disenfranchisement in, 48t, 49t, 51, 52; proof of citizenship laws in, 30; purge of voter rolls in Selma, 141

Alameel, David, 160

Alaska: English-only ballots in, 18; federal oversight of voting in, 21; felon disenfranchisement in, 49t

Alexander, Michelle, 42, 46

Allen, Jessie, 102

All-white primaries in Texas, 121, 123–24, 125

American Civil Liberties Union (ACLU), 150; Advancement Project of, 151

Anderson v. Celebrezze, 87

Annexation, 21

Applewhite v. Commonwealth of Pennsylvania, xxiii, 99–111

Applied challenge, legal distinction between facial challenge and, 101

Arizona: Arizona Taxpayer and Citizen Protection Act in, 70; English-only ballots in, 18; federal oversight of voting in, 21; felon disenfranchisement in, 48, 48t, 50t, 52; proof of citizenship and voting rights in, 152; voter fraud in, xvi, xviii, xix

Arizona Taxpayer and Citizen Protection Act (2004), 70

About the Authors

Donathan L. Brown, PhD, is assistant professor of communication studies at Ithaca College, editor of the *Journal of Race and Policy*, and the lead author of the book *When Race and Policy Collide: Contemporary Immigration Debates* (Praeger, 2014). Dr. Brown conducts research at the intersection of race, rhetoric, and public policy, particularly pertaining to African Americans and Latinos. His work crosses communication studies, law, and political science. Dr. Brown has presented research and delivered addresses around the world in conjunction with many universities and academic organizations. His research has appeared in outlets like the *Harvard Journal of Hispanic Policy*, multiple issues of the *International Journal of Discrimination and the Law, Communication Law Review*, among many others, and has served as guest editor for the *Journal of Latino and Latin American Studies*.

Michael L. Clemons, PhD, is associate professor of political science and internship director at Old Dominion University in Norfolk, Virginia. He is the founding executive director of the Consortium for Research on Race, Diversity and Policy, former director of Old Dominion's Institute for the Study of Race and Ethnicity, and former founding director of its African American and African Studies program. Clemons is also founding editor of *The Journal of Race and Policy*. His research is published in a variety of periodicals including *National Political Science Review, Journal of Latino/ Latin American Studies,* and *Review of Black Political Economy*. Dr. Clemons is editor of the book *African Americans and Global Affairs: Contemporary Perspectives* (Northeastern University Press, 2010). He is completing a manuscript entitled "The Logic of African American Global Participation: A Theoretical and Contextual Approach."